Best wish

Tony Mooney

THE DARK SIDE
OF THE DALE

The grim, gruesome and grisly
history of the Derwent Valley

Tony Kearney

Front cover illustration: Muggleswick Churchyard by Paul Green 2004

Rear cover illustration: England's Grievance Is Discovered In Relation To The Coal Trade, by Ralph Gardner 1655 (courtesy Beamish Museum)

Title page illustration: The Derwent Valley by Brian Clough 2004

Cover design by Paul Green

First edition published in 2004 by:
Dark Dale Publications
27 Summerdale
Shotley Bridge
Co Durham
DH8 0ET

Typeset and printed by:
pro-actif
communications
Tel:01325 488910

ISBN 0-9548242-0-2

AUTHOR'S NOTE

This is a book about history, not a history book. While every effort has been made to ensure that facts and figures, dates and places are historically accurate, it is fair to say that some of the stories recounted here are myths, some are legends and some are simply that - stories.

Beyond the last 150 years, written records of the Derwent Valley's history are few and far between and where they do exist it is virtually impossible to verify the stories they contain. Some of the stories in this book are faithful reproductions of those records which have survived; some are deduced from the scant historical details which do exist and others are legends passed down through the generations.

Readers should remember that, especially in places as remote as the Derwent Valley, the line between fact and fiction can become blurred with age.

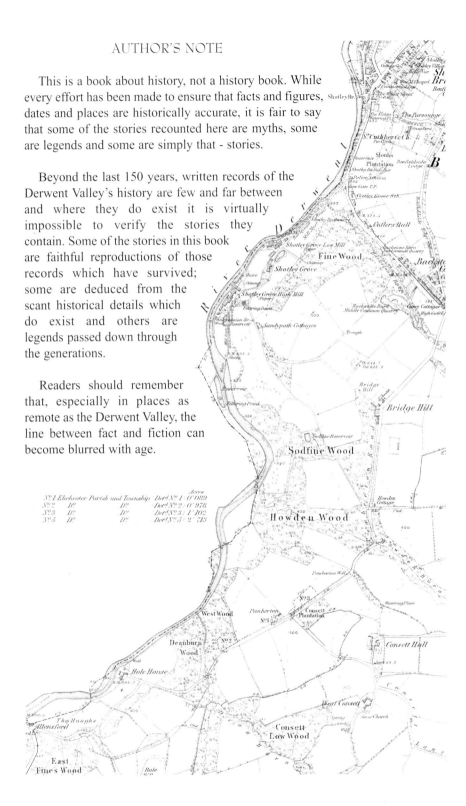

ACKNOWLEDGEMENTS

The publication of this book would not have been possible were it not for the help and encouragement of a number of people.

First and foremost, I would like to thank my family and friends for their constant support over the last five years, not least Libby Kearney-Stemp, Mary Kearney, Paul Green, Eileen Stemp, Mark Shilcock and Brian Clough.

Furthermore, several individuals and organisations have provided invaluable assistance and material in compiling this book: Northern Recording Ltd; The Northern Echo and Durham Advertiser Series newspapers, in particular Peter Barron and Sally Taylor; Syd Neville of Bowes Museum; Durham County Council, in particular County Archivist David Butler and the staff of both the County Records Office and Consett Library; the British Library; Gateshead Library Services; John Uren; Jim Lawson and John Gall of Beamish Museum; the National Portrait Gallery; Durham University Library and the staff of the Fulling Mill Museum; Steve Jones of Wicked Publications and several others.

The Gill Bridge from Muggleswick Churchyard by Brian Clough 2004

MAPS - 1856 Ordnance Survey Map of the Durham banks of the River Derwent (courtesy of Durham County Records Office)

CONTENTS

CHAPTER 1
BRIGANTIA

HIGH among the desolate North Pennines, where the wind blows hard across the open fells, two burns make their journey down to the sea fed by the countless springs and streams which emerge from the moors. Beldon Burn is formed by the streams which cascade from Heatheryhope Moor, Nookton Back Fell, Byerhope Moss and Riddlehamhope Fell. A little further south, Nookton Burn rises up on Nookton Fell and is fed by more than 20 streams which trickle down from Hunstanworth Moor and neighbouring fells. The pair come together at Gibraltar Rock, near the old lead mining village of Hunstanworth, to form the River Derwent.

From its source among the moors, which once formed the lawless borderlands between Durham, Northumberland and Cumberland, the river tumbles 300 metres over 35 miles of steep wooded valley to Derwenthaugh, where it flows into the Tyne. For centuries, that journey towards the sea has produced the force which turned the waterwheels and powered the corn mills, sword grinding mills, iron foundries and paper mills on which the valley's prosperity was built. Before 1966 and the construction of the Derwent Reservoir to regulate its flow, the river ran with even greater force and regularly spilled over its banks in violent floods.

The earliest records of the destructive power of the Derwent come from the Halmote Court records of 1357, which tell of repeated flooding throughout the year, culminating in one great autumn deluge. The storm was so violent that acres of land on the riverside were lost to the floodwaters and the banks were so badly eroded that the river threatened to engulf the corn mill at Swalwell. Down the centuries, floods were commonplace along the Derwent and it was the villages downstream which bore the brunt of the accumulated floodwaters. In 1771, the river, swollen with heavy rains which had almost destroyed the bridges at Blanchland and Allensford, rushed through Swalwell and poured into the streets with such force that villagers were forced to take refuge as best they could as their furniture and meagre possessions were swept away. A boat was sent to rescue an entire family perched on the roof of their home, while an old man and his wife were found clinging to the rafters nearby.

Flooding at Blackhall Mill at the turn of the last century. Before the construction of the Derwent Reservoir, it was commonplace for the river to burst its banks and threaten surrounding villages (Photograph courtesy of Gateshead Libraries Service)

On June 23rd, 1678, a terrible thunderstorm struck Hunstanworth and three villagers were killed by bolts of lightning in a single day, housewife Ann Robinson, an infant named John Ritson and Ann, the daughter of Robert Eggleston. But during the early years of the 19th Century in particular, the valley appeared to be constantly battered by devastating storms. The dam at Blackhall Mill was swept away in one particularly fierce flood of 1834 and in January 1839 it was said that 20,000 trees in Chopwell Woods were uprooted in a single night. But the most destructive of them all came out of nowhere on a summer's day in 1835. On the morning of June 10th it was recorded that the northern counties: "were visited by a violent storm which was attended with loss of life and considerable loss of property. At Shotley Bridge the storm of hail and rain was thoroughly alarming. Pieces of hail fell near four inches in circumference which soon melted and caused the Derwent to overflow which did considerable damage, particularly to the fields near Mr Annandale's paper works. On the following day, a woman named Cawthorn was struck dead in a cottage at Ebchester and another was much burnt." Life on the banks of the Derwent, it would seem, has always been precarious.

7

Precious little evidence exists of the very earliest human settlement in the Derwent Valley - there are no great stone circles or burial complexes to speak of. But men have lived here for thousands of years and they have left their mark. If there is a cradle of civilisation in the Derwent Valley it lies at Knitsley, where a mysterious stone was found which is thought to be one of the earliest signs of life in the area. The cup and ring marked stone, which is of unknown origin, is covered in a series of circular marks, each pecked out with a chisel-like tool. No-one knows exactly why it was created, it may have had some sort of religious significance, it may have been a fertility symbol. A similar stone was found further down the valley at Greenside, near Winlaton. Both the Knitsley stone and Greenside stone had been used as part of a dry stone wall by the time they were discovered in the 20th Century and some experts believe they may once have formed part of a larger, long-since demolished structure. Other such stones have been found next to standing stones or near burial sites around the country, which may have meant that Knitsley and Greenside held some sort of religious importance for the settlers who lived there.

But there are other signs of everyday life scattered up and down the length of the valley. The earliest residents of the Derwent Valley were not farmers, they were hunter gatherers who lived off the forest and probably stuck to the more lowland areas. Simple relics of their time, mainly ancient stone flints, have been found near Blackhall Mill, at Whickham, at Winlaton and at Grey Mare Hill. Many more have been found at Ebchester, close to the riverside, which appears to have been quite a hive of Stone Age industry - worked flints, blades, scrapers and flakes of flint have been uncovered there. More substantial finds of polished Stone Age axes have been made at Winlaton, Gray Mare Hill and again at Ebchester. There are also signs that the settlers were starting to extend their reach further away from the river - perhaps as hunting parties. The discovery of ancient flints suggests the existence of a hunting camp at Edmundbyers and another on Butsfield Fell, implying that the lowland settlers were prepared to travel further up the valley in search of food.

By the Neolithic period - the later Stone Age when the Knitsley Stone may well have been created - the inhabitants of the valley had adopted the practice of leaving more permanent memorials to their dead. A grave barrow dating back to this period was discovered in

The mysterious Knitsley stone, thought to be the oldest surviving manmade object in the Derwent Valley (Photograph courtesy of The Old Fulling Mill Museum of Archaeology, Durham University)

Muggleswick Park and a pot containing what is thought to have been the remains of a cremation was unearthed at The Sneep, above Allensford, in 1910.

The turning point in the valley's earliest history came at some point around 2,000BC when, for the first time, man began to work metal and history entered the Bronze Age. Metal tools meant the inhabitants of the valley could work the land and, as a result, their nomadic lifestyle began to slowly give way to a more settled existence. Quern stones, used to grind flour, have been discovered at Butsfield, which implies that by 2,000BC the settlers of the area were growing their own crops to make their own food. The first farmers also arrived at Edmundbyers, where once only travelling hunting parties made their mark, and left a stone-lined grave covered by an earth mound. Further down the valley, at Summerhill, near Blaydon, a stone coffin was unearthed from a burial mound which contained the crumbling skeletons of a man and woman complete with an intricately decorated urn, thought to have contained food for the journey into the afterlife. Other signs of life from the same period also exist. Buried in the mud at Derwenthaugh was found an ancient dug-out canoe - a hollowed out tree trunk 14ft long - which could be paddled along the navigable stretches of the Tyne and perhaps up the Derwent itself.

But one of the most important archaeological finds in the country dating back to the Bronze Age was found just outside the Derwent Valley, on the windswept moors above Stanhope. In a cave at Heathery Burn, which lies about six miles south of Edmundbyers and two miles north of Stanhope, was found a complete set of household equipment used by a family around 1000BC. During the 19th Century, archaeologists uncovered a fabulous hoard from the site, thought to belong to a Bronze Age aristocrat. The find included a magnificent cache of weapons, each containing a remarkably high lead content which probably meant they were made nearby: eight leaf-shaped spearheads and three leaf-shaped swords along with 19 axes and the moulds to make them. The Heathery Burn hoard also contained parts of a wheeled cart - which the Bronze Age settlers used in battle as well as for domestic travel. There was jewellery: eight bronze rings, bronze bracelets and pins, an armlet and ring made from precious gold and necklaces made of teeth and shells. Perhaps most revealing of all were the domestic bits and pieces found alongside them: a razor, chisels and a big bronze cooking cauldron which still contained bones from beef, mutton and game.

Around the year 400BC, a new people began to arrive on the shores of England - the Celts. They came predominantly from Gaul - present day France and Belgium - and these Celtic colonizers, skilled in the use of iron, settled throughout the British Isles. The Brigantes - a loose federation of families, chieftains and small clans - colonised the North-East from Yorkshire to the borders of Scotland with their great forts centred on South Durham and North Yorkshire. It was this semi-nomadic tribe which became the new owner of the Derwent Valley.

The Brigantian empire was centred behind the vast earthworks of the great hill-fort at Stanwick, near Darlington, although after the Roman conquest a new tribal capital would be set up at Isurium Brigantum, present day Aldborough in North Yorkshire. Although they were chiefly a nomadic people, the classical historian Ptolemy recorded that they inhabited nine towns scattered around the North of England which are thought to include settlements at Catterick, York, Ilkley and modern-day Manchester. The furthest north of these towns was Epiacum - a place which has since been lost to history. Some historians believe that Epiacum was in Northumberland, others say it was at Binchester in South Durham. But in centuries gone by, it was believed that the northernmost outpost of the Brigantes was at Lanchester. This claim was based on the writings of the ancient historian Richard of Cirencester, who claimed the Romans built their fort on the site of the conquered tribes' town.

The Brigantes were a warlike tribe, famed for their skill in battle on horseback and chariot. Severed human heads have been found imbedded in the walls of the earthworks at Stanwick - possibly to provide a ghost army to defend the tribal capital. These Celts lived in a very stratified society, from the king down through the various clan branches. It is thought the newcomers did not drive out the existing population of North Britain, they subjugated them to almost slave status and became a ruling caste of aristocratic overlords and farmers living over their more primitive predecessors. Brigantia was ruled by a royal dynasty under King Volisios followed by his son Dumnoveros who, by the time of the Roman invasion, had been succeeded by his daughter Queen Cartimandua - one of a number of powerful women figures in Celtic society and a contemporary of the most famous of them all, Boudicca.

Again, the Brigantes left few traces of their rule - there were no written records, few artefacts and no permanent dwellings - but there are several clues which suggest the Derwent Valley may have been important to them. There is evidence that the tribe had a significant camp at Medomsley - iron weapons have been found there which date back to the Brigantian period. There are two other important considerations which suggest the Celts may have settled in the valley - lead and wood.

Roman records show that for 200 years before the legionnaires arrived on these shores, Brigantia had traded with Rome, importing luxuries such as pottery and wine and exporting wool and, most importantly, lead. The Celts adopted the Roman custom of using coins as a means of exchange and Brigantian silver coins were certainly in circulation dating back to the time of Volisios. The lead on which this wealth was based was mined in the Pennines, dug from the ground by the Bronze Age tribesmen conquered by the Brigantes.

Although the whereabouts of these lead mines is unknown - and the vast majority were probably in the Yorkshire heart of the Brigantian empire - some may have been in the upper reaches of the Derwent Valley. In the centuries to come, the Romans themselves would mine for lead in the upper Derwent Valley and would build pack roads across the moors to transport the ore - it is possible that these Roman mines and pack roads made use of existing Celtic knowledge.

The other attraction for the Brigantes was timber or, more specifically, oak. The oak was sacred to the Celts and was venerated throughout Brigantia, with worship led by the mysterious and powerful sect - the Druids. The Druids were central to Celtic society - they determined the law, officiated at religious sacrifices, studied science and settled disputes. The Druids held such sway over the Celtic peoples that Rome had carried out a long campaign to exterminate them - firstly in Gaul where their rituals, which included human sacrifice, horrified even Roman sensibilities and then in Britain where the influence of the cult spread from its stronghold on the island of Anglesey.

The Bronze Age Britons who were conquered by the Celtic invaders were still, by and large, primitive hunter-gatherers who found their food in the forest, they did not fell trees, clear farmland or otherwise alter the natural landscape to any great degree. Consequently, when the Celts arrived, the Derwent Valley was still covered by a dense carpet of sacred oak - virgin forest which swept uninterrupted from the banks of the Tyne to the edge of the moors. It seems likely that this would have given the valley an importance to the Celts and indeed the name Derwent and the word Druid both stem from the same source, derw - the ancient Celtic word for oak.

However, a new invader was coming against whom the sacred oak groves, the Druids and the severed heads of Stanwick would provide little defence.

CHAPTER 2 -
BATTLE OF THE GODS

GENERAL Agricola sat on horseback on top of the hill and surveyed the valley before him. The sparkling river ran at the bottom of the steep tree-lined valley, which then sloped upwards towards the moors and onwards to Scotland. High on the wooded hill to his right, out of sight but overshadowing his legions, was the camp of the conquered Brigantes. The captured Celts were already at work moving the huge stones which would pave the latest stretch of his great road which would carry his army northward. Back at their camp, the remaining members of the tribe gave offerings to Brigantia, the High One. They slaughtered a lamb to the goddess, protector of the north, as they did on February 1st every year to pray for the fertility of their beasts and a prosperous spring. This year their prayers were more intense. The old order which had survived for generations was changing. The warriors of the tribe had fought for 30 years to keep the march of the Romans at bay - but the tide of battle had turned decisively against them. Now the enemy was preparing its great stronghold on the banks of the Derwent. Back on the riverbank, an altar was being carved by the stonemasons of the 20th Legion who bore the nickname Valiant and Victorious, under the watchful gaze of centurion Martialis. A new god would rule over the Derwent Valley - Mars, God of War. Satisfied with his decision, General Gnaeus Julius Agricola gave the order to begin building the new fort and turned his horse away to rejoin his legions.

The Roman fort at Ebchester was built in the year 80AD. A myth has grown up that the Roman occupation of Britain was achieved easily, they came, they saw, they conquered and lived in peace for almost 400 years. The reality was far different. Although it was almost 40 years since the Romans had first landed in Britain, progress north had been slow. The Brigantes, the great tribe, or more accurately confederation of tribes which controlled northern England, had eventually offered some resistance to the legions and although there are no records marking the Roman Conquest of the Derwent Valley, it seems highly unlikely their arrival will have been greeted with open arms at the Brigantes' camp near Medomsley.

The Romans invaded Britain in 43AD with an enormous army of 40,000 highly-trained men and were met by fierce, if disorganised resistance from the British. Chief among the British leaders was Caractacus, who waged a relentless guerrilla war on the invaders for almost a decade. But the picture in the north of England was quite different. The Brigantes were led by Queen Cartimandua, who ruled from the tribe's main hill-fort at Stanwick, with her husband Venutius. As soon as the Romans arrived in Britain, Cartimandua - who already had a reputation for cunning - agreed a treaty with the invaders that she be left alone to rule her kingdom. She received lavish gifts from the Romans and continued to rule with minimal interference and, in exchange, the Brigantes were to guard against the Pict tribes to the north in Scotland and remain neutral in the war between the southern British tribes and Rome.

But clearly not everyone in the Brigantian camp was happy about this arrangement. In 47AD, four years after the Romans arrived on these shores, sedition broke out among some of the leading members of the tribe. Some sort of rebellion took place in which a faction of the tribe joined the war being waged by Caractacus. It was sufficiently serious that the Roman legions - who had been poised to mount an all-out assault on the Druid stronghold of Anglesey - were brought back to deal with the rising. The Romans ruthlessly put down the rebellion - although not so ruthlessly as to jeopardize the rule of Queen Cartimandua. According to the Roman historian Tacitus: "The Brigantian rising subsided on the execution of a handful of men, who were beginning hostilities, and the pardon of the rest."

The failure of the rising and the execution of its leaders strengthened the hand of Queen Cartimandua. Shortly afterwards, in 51AD, she made a formal agreement to be a client ruler of Rome, but Cartimandua was to seal her fate when she repaid her debt to the Roman masters who had made her rich and protected her throne. After being crushed in battle in mid-Wales, Caractacus fled north to seek refuge in Brigantia. The queen betrayed Caractacus, who was captured, bound in chains and handed over to the Romans. The symbol of British resistance was then paraded through the streets of Rome in shackles.

The treachery of Cartimandua incensed her people - and the devious queen was about to make matters worse. Her husband

Venutius had himself been the ruler of the Carvetii - an influential sub-tribe of the Brigantes which had its stronghold in Cumbria and the Durham dales. It seems likely that the people of the Derwent Valley owed their loyalty to Venutius who was known as an exceptionally skilful warlord. The marriage was no love-match, it was a dynastic arrangement. Cartimandua wanted the loyalty of the northern parts of the tribe and Venutius hoped to increase his prestige and make Brigantia a bastion against the encroachment of Rome.

But the Brigantian court was about to be rocked by scandal. It emerged that Cartimandua had been having an affair with her husband's friend and armour-bearer - a young man named Vellocatus. When Venutius complained about his wife's indiscretions, she expelled him from the royal capital and put Vellocatus on the throne as her new consort. It was a rash decision and the tensions which had been simmering among the Brigantes for almost 10 years boiled over.

Full scale civil war broke out between, on the one side, the queen and her young lover, backed by the might of Rome, and on the other side her former husband, backed by most of the tribe. Cartimandua had one more trick up her sleeve - she immediately kidnapped Venutius' brother and other members of his family as hostages to prevent an attack.

But it was to no avail. Venutius, described by Tacitus as: "since the capture of Caractacus, the Briton with the best knowledge of the art of war" returned to his stronghold. There he raised an army among the cream of his loyal supporters in Durham and Cumbria, joined by other Celtic chieftains and even a handful of disgruntled Roman auxiliaries. Tacitus wrote: "Incensed at her act and smarting at the ignominious prospect of submitting to the sway of a woman, the enemy - a powerful body of young and picked warriors - invaded her kingdom." At first, the civil war went well for the rebel king, but Rome sent its legions to prop up Cartimandua and although Venutius was able to claim one of Celtic Britain's few victories in battle against Rome, his army was eventually overwhelmed and he once more retreated to his stronghold in the Pennines and Cartimandua was restored to the throne.

Venutius went to ground with his supporters and waited for another chance. It was to be 13 years before he would launch his second rebellion against his former wife and the growing influence of Rome in the still unconquered north of England. Finally, in 69AD Venutius stirred his rebellion and forced Cartimandua out, capturing the great fort of Stanwick and challenging Roman authority in the north. His wife escaped the battle and hid among her former subjects - she was only saved when the Romans staged a dramatic rescue, sending a squadron of cavalrymen deep behind enemy lines to pluck the ageing queen to safety. Finally, after years of struggle, Venutius was proclaimed the new king of the Brigantes and he launched all-out war against Rome. For two years, a series of great battles were fought out across northern England as the Brigantes made their last stand against the invaders and once more they achieved some success in battling the all-conquering Romans to a standstill. But finally they were to be overwhelmed.

Having forced out a client queen, Brigantia was to feel the wrath of the Roman military machine. Governor Petillius Cerealis, fresh from his victories in Germany, was ordered to bring the unruly tribe to heel. In the summer of 71AD, the final movement began. The 9th Legion Hispana, made up of battle-hardened veterans of the German wars and under the personal command of Governor Cerealis, marched out of York and struck northwards against the Brigantes. Meanwhile, the fearsome 20th Legion Valeria Victrix, which 10 years earlier had killed 80,000 of Boudicca's rebels in a single day, also set out from York. Under their banner of the wild boar and the inspired leadership of General Julius Agricola, the 31-year-old rising star of the Roman Army, they headed up the west of the Pennines, through present-day Cumbria and across into Durham. Venutius was caught in a pincer movement and there was nowhere left to run. He made his last stand at Scotch Corner where his men were finally defeated in a great pitched battle against the finest-trained legionnaires Rome could muster.

This time, the Romans were to decisively stamp their authority on the rebellious north. Within two years, the great fort at Stanwick - where the skulls of Brigantian warriors had been embedded in the walls - was abandoned and the Romans began building their own forts nearby. By 79AD, General Agricola, now declared governor of Britain, decided to launch an attack on Scotland from his military headquarters at Corbridge and so complete the conquest of Britain. Beforehand, it would be necessary to deal with any remaining pockets of rebellion in the defeated, but not yet occupied, North. He once more called up his old legion, the 20th Valeria Victrix, for the campaign. Tacitus records: "When summer came he gathered his army and was present everywhere on the march, commending discipline, curbing stragglers: he chose himself the camping-ground: he was first himself to explore estuaries and forests, meanwhile he gave the enemy no peace from sudden raids. By these means, many states which up to that time had been independent were induced to give hostages and abandon their hostility."

In order to speed the legions across the country for the attack on Scotland, and to keep the rebellious Brigantes in check, Agricola ordered the building of several great roads, including Dere Street which ran from York to Scotland. Forts were spaced every 20 miles or so to offer his convoys protection where they were exposed to attack from the hostile natives.

Among these was Ebchester, known to the Romans as Vindomora, which translates as the fort on the edge of the black moor. The name indicates what a forbidding place the Derwent Valley must have been for the legionnaires who first manned it. In the days before the wall, Ebchester stood uncomfortably close to the open frontier, in direct line of attack from the terrifying Pictish tribes to the north. The Brigantes were beaten, but not yet conquered, which left the little outpost exposed in enemy country, a day's march from the nearest reinforcements 19 miles away at Binchester or 14 miles away at Corbridge. Stones uncovered from buildings in the centre of Ebchester fort indicate it was built by men from the 5th Cohort of an unnamed legion, under the command of Centurion Martialis.

The fort commanded the important crossing of the Derwent, built into the hillside in a well-defended position. But just as important as its strategic position was its symbolic position. The fort was built deliberately close to the Brigantes' camp at Medomsley, a humiliating reminder of the Roman victory in Venutius' heartland. The fort was mainly designed as a staging post. Partly, the garrison protected the road and partly the fort offered a safe overnight haven in dangerous country for units of the Roman army marching north to Scotland. There is some evidence that there may have been another fort built at Whittonstall, although it has yet to be excavated, which would have also protected the route to the Tyne.

The first fort was a simple affair. It was built of earth ramparts, each protected with pointed wooden stakes on the top. There were four timber gateways, one on each of the earth walls. Every gateway was flanked by two guard houses and each corner of the earthen walls was protected by a turret. Inside this defensive wall there was room for a cohort, around 500 men, who slept in tents made of animal hide. It was a well defended position, but very basic and of little use as a permanently manned garrison. There is no way of knowing for certain whether the fort at Ebchester ever saw action - but it seems likely that it did. Twice during the early years of the Roman occupation, the British rose against them and overran their forts in the north. In 105AD, the Scots destroyed several Roman outposts in what is now Northumberland, which would have made Ebchester among the last defended outposts of the Empire. Again in 117AD, there was an uprising among the Brigantes which swept right across the north and would have almost certainly brought war to the gates of Ebchester before it was ruthlessly put down.

The first fort lasted for 45 years until it was abandoned during the reign of Emperor Hadrian. Hadrian, who had come to the throne during the Brigantes, rebellion, ordered the building of the Wall which still bears his name today to keep the Scots at bay. But, importantly, many of the forts on the Wall in fact guard against attack from the south - a sign of Hadrian's desire to subdue the Brigantes. Although Dere Street continued to be the main supply road to the north, the building of the Wall changed the focus of Roman military thinking. In 125AD, the legions evacuated Ebchester which had by then been superseded by other bases leading north. Among them was Lanchester, known as Longovicium, which was originally built around 140AD but fell out of use fairly quickly.

But the new strategy did little to quell the local tribes and, after another revolt, the Romans returned to Ebchester, this time building a permanent bastion against the hordes which harried the legions. In 163AD, a great stone wall was built around the earthwork perimeter to keep attackers at bay and the timber turrets and gates were replaced with stone. Inside the compound, six barrack blocks were built in stone. Each barracks contained one great room to act as an open dormitory and living quarters for a century of 80 men, with a separate stone room at the end which was home to the centurion in command of the unit. The largest and most ornate building inside the fort was the headquarters. It was built around a courtyard, which had a hall at one end and a series of rooms leading off it which acted as armouries and store rooms. At the other end of the courtyard stood a statue of the reigning emperor, which could be seen by everyone inside the compound, along with battalion standards and altars to the gods. The most important of these was Jupiter and an altar dedicated to the god of Thunder was created by the men of the legion of the 6th Victrix, who were responsible for the reconstruction of Vindomora. Next to the headquarters was the commandant's house, a large and comfortable building for the commanding officer, his wife and children, and their slaves. The house also featured a typical Roman under-floor heating system and a bath house where the officer and his family could relax in comparative luxury.

Although they were members of the Roman Army, few of the soldiers based at Ebchester and Lanchester would have even seen Rome. The commanding officers may have been natural-born Romans, but most of the soldiers were recruited from among the numerous countries conquered by the empire. Among the earliest inhabitants of Ebchester were the 4th Cohort of Antonine's own Breucorians, a 500-strong infantry regiment recruited from modern day Bosnia, who left their permanent mark in the shape of an altar dedicated to Minerva. Lanchester was even more cosmopolitan. It was occupied primarily by legionnaires recruited in Spain along with a smattering of fellow Europeans. Certainly for a time it was the headquarters of the 1st Cohort of Lingones, recruited from the Bourgogne region of France and beefed up, when the numbers dwindled, with men of the Suevi tribe from Portugal.

The strengthening of the forts at Ebchester and the building of Hadrian's Wall represent the Romans' decision to stamp their rule on north Britain and these impressive fortifications must have been a powerful symbol to the native population. It also marks something of a turning point in the history of the Roman occupation of the north. There were further attacks on the Roman defences, but for the most part these came from Scotland and not the Brigantes. For more than 100 years, the revolts by the northern Britons ceased and they came to live more closely with their conquerors. Certainly by the year 220AD, and possibly earlier, a village, known as a vicus, had grown up outside the gates of the fort at Ebchester - and it was native Britons who lived in it. At Lanchester, there was an even bigger vicus which is thought to have been home to craftsmen, traders and prostitutes earning a living by doing business with the Roman army and the travellers making their way along Dere Street.

As the years progressed, more and more soldiers were recruited to the Roman Army from among the local population. Other soldiers would raise families with local women so the distinction between conquerors and conquered blurred. The constant state of war between Romans and Brigantes faded, particularly around the main settlements. There are some signs that the Romans began to make inroads into the inhospitable hinterland of moor and forest nearby. At Butsfield, there is evidence of some sort of metalworking activity with the remnants of slag from a primitive Roman iron works. Certainly, the Romans began to mine in the upper Derwent Valley and the Wear Valley. The old trail from Stanhope to Ebchester, which passes through Edmundbyers, is Roman and was probably a pack trail to bring coal and lead to Dere Street and the trade routes south. Another road only recently discovered links Ebchester with Hexham. There also seems to have been a mooring of sorts on the Derwent at Ebchester which would have allowed Roman boats to make the journey down river to the Tyne and beyond.

This widening transport network implies that the Romans felt safe enough to venture deeper into what was previously enemy country away from their military strongholds. The Romans returned to Lanchester in 240AD and began reconstructing their previous fort. The stronghold at Lanchester was larger than that at Ebchester and covered six acres - room enough to garrison 1,000 infantry and cavalrymen. The fort formed a parallelogram - 180 yards by 140 yards on the hillside overlooking the great road. It too was an impressive work of defence. It was surrounded by a vellum, or banked ditch, which was 12 feet high and the strong walls of the fort were constructed of stones and mortar. In places, a second ditch protected the approach to the fort. Each of the four outer walls had an entrance, flanked by guard posts and at each of the four corners was a fortified round tower. Little is known about what the fort contained - although there was a commandant's house complete with under-floor heating, a barrack block has been found and a typical communal bath house.

But for all the impressive defensive structures of Longivicium, it does not seem to have been a fort under siege. It was surrounded by a thriving village and a large cemetery stands nearby which is home to at least 12 stone-lined graves and 29 cremation urns - all thought to be civilians from the settlement outside the fort. Fresh water was supplied by wells outside the gates and by that greatest feat of Roman engineering, the aqueduct, which brought a shallow trough of fresh running water straight through the camp from a source two miles away. Here, native British villagers lived side by side with their conquerors and enjoyed the benefits of Roman rule. But the relationship between them went both ways. They traded together and influenced each other. And in the courtyard of the fort, that most potent symbol of Roman domination, they prayed together at an altar built in 244AD. It was an altar not to Jupiter, Mars, Silvanus or any of the other sleek, toned and athletic gods of ancient Rome but to an older, wild-haired figure with staring eyes, Garmangabis - the Brigantian God of the forests.

CHAPTER 3
INTO THE DARKNESS

VERY little is known of Britain in the Dark Ages and even less is known about remote corners of the land such as the Derwent Valley. By the early Fifth Century, the once invincible Roman Empire teetered on the brink of collapse. Crippled by corruption and in-fighting at its heart in Rome, it was also under attack from the tribes it had formerly conquered, particularly the Goth and Visigoth tribes of Germany and Eastern Europe. To protect Rome, the decision was made to withdraw the stretched legions from the most far-flung outposts of Empire.

At some point around about the year 380AD, Emperor Magnus Maximus gave the order to abandon the fort at Ebchester. Within 30 years, the last of the legions left Britain, bringing to an end more than 350 years of Roman rule and leaving the population of the Derwent Valley facing an uncertain future. As the legions marched out of Ebchester and Lanchester, many of the local population would have had very mixed emotions. After more than three centuries in Britain, the Roman garrison had long since ceased to be a conquering and occupying army. The small towns which developed at Ebchester, Lanchester and elsewhere in England were deeply interlinked with the garrisons - the population had largely ceased to be native Britons and had become Romano-Britons who would have been deeply disturbed by the Empire's decision to withdraw.

But there were those who were undoubtedly glad to see the back of the Romans. Away from the Roman towns, the British tribes continued to eke out an existence in the hills, the moors and forests. Periodic rebellion had punctuated Roman rule and unrest became more of a regular feature of life in the years leading up to the withdrawal of the legions. The Derwent Valley, only miles from the last frontier of Roman civilisation, found itself the battleground between a dying Empire and the hordes trying to overthrow it. There are no records which describe the military action which rolled over North Durham in those years, but as Ebchester stood on one of only two routes from Scotland into the heart of Roman England it would have stood directly in the way of the Picts. In 343AD, native scouts of the Roman Army mutinied and overran several military bases in

Tynedale, and the Derwent Valley was a staging post for the Roman attempt to regain control of their lost frontier forts. The area was again under siege in the Barbarian conspiracy of 367AD, when Picts, Irish, Scots and Saxons united in an attack on the North. In both cases, Roman rule was quickly re-established but in 388AD the depleted Romans suffered, for the first time, a series of defeats in battle along the length of the Wall. There is some evidence to suggest that the fort at Lanchester perished in flames - undisturbed red ash has been found on the floor of the basilica and remnants of metals fused together in intense heat have been discovered elsewhere on the site. The fire may have been accidental or it may have occurred long after the Romans had departed - or it may have been lit during one of the increasingly regular incursions by the enemies of Rome. The era of Roman invincibility was drawing to a close. Under attack at home and in Britain, the Romans began to withdraw some of their forces. A further Northern revolt broke out in 408AD and, only two years later, the last of the Roman Army finally left Britain's shores.

The end of the Roman occupation heralded the beginning of the Dark Ages and the Derwent Valley disappeared from recorded history for 500 years. The settlements of Lanchester and Ebchester are not mentioned again until the end of the first Millennium, although it seems reasonable to assume that both were inhabited throughout the intervening centuries. They were extremely troubled years for those who lived through them, exposed to attack from the Celtic tribes on all sides. Local leaders therefore turned to mercenaries for protection, inviting Angle and Saxon warriors from Denmark and present-day Germany to this country in exchange for land.

The Anglo-Saxons - armed gangs who crossed the treacherous North Sea in glorified rowing boats - began to arrive in ever larger numbers, tempted by the prospect of land and the spoils of war. Having originally been brought in as mercenaries, many decided to stay and slowly began to colonize England. By the year 450AD, there were settlements of Anglo-Saxons along the Tyne, the Wear and in Yorkshire. The densely-wooded Derwent Valley was remote, but over the years it too saw an influx of these newcomers, although not in great numbers. One of the earliest known Saxon settlers in the valley is thought to have been named Ceoppa, who built himself a farmstead and well on the north bank of the river in a clearing in the great wood. He died in 685AD and was buried in a site now occupied by Heavy Gate Farm near the town which still bears his name, Chopwell.

A discovery made at Hurbuck, the hamlet between Lanchester and Delves Lane, shows the two sides of these Saxon newcomers. Here a farmer uncovered a hoard of weapons including eight axe-heads and a sword - evidence that the invaders did not come peacefully - but they were found alongside four scythes which the settlers used to cultivate the land. Sometimes by invite, sometimes by stealth and sometimes by conquest, the Anglo-Saxons spread across the country. The war waged against these invaders gave rise to the legend of King Arthur, the British king who resisted the invasion. There are some historians who believe the figure who inspired the Arthurian legend lived and died in the North. He is said to have twice defeated the Anglo-Saxon army led by Ossa The Knife Man in Northumberland and to have eventually died in battle near Hadrian's Wall in 537AD. Many parts of the country claim to be the burial place of King Arthur and one legend names his final resting place as The Sneep, the wooded ravine near Mosswood in the Derwent Valley. Legend apart, the truth was that these were grim times for the population of Northern England and for more than 100 years, intermittent warfare rolled across the country and the people were ravaged by plague and famine.

The turning point in the constant state of war between the Anglo-Saxons and the native Britons came in 547AD. In that year, Ida the Flamebearer - the grandson of Ossa The Knife Man - arrived on the coast of North Yorkshire with 50 ships. It was the biggest Anglo-Saxon fleet to arrive on these shores and each boat was packed with armed men bent on conquest. King Ida wore a ring-mail shirt on his back, a boar's head helmet on his head and a carried jewel-encrusted sword in his hand. The captain of each ship was armed with a sword and wooden shield, his men with simple iron-headed spears - but they made up a formidable force. This small army marched northwards, uniting the pockets of Anglo-Saxon setlers scattered around the North-East and eventually made their way to Bamburgh which Ida proclaimed as the capital of his new Anglo-Saxon Kingdom of Bernicia. For the next three years, Ida The Flamebearer took on the remaining British chieftains one by one until he was established as overking of the North with a vast kingdom stretching across Northumberland, Durham and the Scottish Borders which brought the valley under his command.

On his death, Ida's crown eventually fell to his tyrannical son Ethelfrith - whose cruelty would earn him the nickname The Destroyer. His passion for conquest knew no bounds and he launched into a series of ferocious wars against his neighbours in Scotland, Cumbria and, especially, Yorkshire, where he drove out Prince Edwin, ruler of the Kingdom of Deira and proclaimed himself ruler of the united Kingdom of Northumbria. The Venerable Bede described Ethelfrith as a ravening wolf "devouring the prey in the morning and at night dividing the spoils" and he added: "He ravaged the Britons more cruelly than all the other English leaders." But it was to be in 613AD that Ethelfrith The Destroyer would carve his name in blood into the history books with an act of barbarity unequalled even in that dark time - known as The Slaughter Of The Saints when his men massacred 1,200 defenceless monks outside Chester for praying for a Welsh victory against him.

His reputation now established, Ethelfrith The Destroyer commanded a kingdom from the Firth of Forth to the Humber. But there remained one thorn in his side - the whereabouts of the lost Prince Edwin, the one man who had a legitimate claim on the throne of Northumbria. Eventually Ethelfrith's spies brought news that the prince - now a man of 32 years with children of his own - had taken refuge in East Anglia under the protection of King Redwald. Ethelfrith sent a stark ultimatum to Redwald - murder the prince or face war. Deciding attack was his best form of defence, Redwald gathered his armies and launched a seemingly suicidal attack on Northumbria - the greatest power in England - and the two armies met in Lincolnshire in 616AD. Ethelfrith personally led an attack against the East Anglians, slaughtering dozens by his own hand, before gradually he was surrounded and finally felled by sheer weight of numbers. Ethelfrith The Destroyer lay dead among the mounds of bodies he had slain.

Long-lost Prince Edwin, a man who had spent most of his life hiding in the wild places of England, returned to his homeland a hero and was proclaimed King of Northumbria and overking of England. This time it was Ethelfrith's sons Eanfrid, Oswald and Oswry who were forced to flee to the remote Scottish island of Iona for safety. Northumbria had, through blood, treachery and intrigue, become the most powerful kingdom in the country and under Edwin's 16-year rule enjoyed a short-lived period of stability and peace. That peace was to be shattered in 12 months of savagery the like of which had never been witnessed before - even in the dark days of The Destroyer.

CHAPTER 4
HEAVENFIELD

THE Northumbrians were heathens and worshipped the old gods, chief among them Woden the god of war whose wooden temple stood near Bamburgh. Christianity was coming to the North Country - but its arrival would be soaked in blood on the banks of the River Derwent.

King Edwin, who had moved the capital of Northumbria to his native York, was the first to convert to the new religion after marrying the Christian Queen Ethelburga of Kent. The queen brought with her the missionary Paulinus and the pair finally persuaded Edwin to convert on Easter Sunday, 626AD. On that day, the king survived an assassination attempt when a supposed envoy from the kingdom of Wessex produced a poisoned dagger and thrust it at a startled Edwin. His bodyguard threw himself in the way and took the full force of the blow, but the blade passed completely through his body and managed to wound the king. Miraculously, he survived. Only hours later, the Queen gave birth to a healthy daughter and a grateful Edwin embraced Christianity.

Paulinus built a small chapel on the site of what is now York Minster and there, on Easter Eve 627AD, King Edwin was baptized. The missionary went on to baptize 3,000 of the king's subjects in just 36 days as Christianity began to take a tentative hold among the upper echelons of Northumbrian society - although it would take another generation before it permeated down to his subjects in the remote Derwent Valley who still venerated Woden. But if Edwin believed Christianity would provide permanent protection from the blades of his enemies, he was very much mistaken.

Edwin seemed as much bent on conquest as his predecessors. He brought parts of Wales, including the Isle of Anglesey and the Isle of Man, into Northumbria - but in doing so he sealed his own fate and unleashed on his homeland a terror unprecedented even in those turbulent times. During his long years in exile, Edwin had been taken in by Cadfan, King of Gwynedd, in Wales, and was brought up almost as a brother to the king's son Cadwallon. Yet when he became king, among Edwin's first acts was to wage war against the kingdom of Gwynedd. A petty boyhood rivalry between Cadwallon and Edwin turned into bitter anger over the Northumbrian's treachery.

Cadwallon found willing allies to take on the growing might of Edwin, chief among them being King Penda of the southern kingdom of Mercia. Soon a huge Welsh and Mercian army was assembled - an unholy alliance of Christians and heathens. This alliance made its relentless way northwards, driving the invading Northumbrians out of the south and Wales. Cadwallon proved himself to be one of the greatest generals of his age and was reputed to have won 13 battles and countless lesser engagements. His 14th victory came at the Battle of Hatfield Chase, near Doncaster, in October 633AD where the main Northumbrian army was routed and Edwin and his son were killed.

Edwin's bodyguard recovered his severed head from the battlefield and, amid much public grief, brought it back to York where it was paraded through the streets. But the grim procession was only a foretaste of the horrors to follow. Cadwallon's army entered the city shortly afterwards bringing a reign of unbridled brutality. The empty throne fell to Prince Eanfrith, eldest son of Ethelfrith The Destroyer - who had fled into exile 17 years earlier on the death of his father. Prince Eanfrith decided to attempt to negotiate with Cadwallon and travelled to York with a bodyguard of just 12 hand-picked soldiers. Cadwallon welcomed them into his lair and, once they were trapped behind the city walls, murdered them all in cold blood. Northumbria, leaderless and defenceless, was at his mercy.

Cadwallon, now 34 years old, unleashed an orgy of slaughter on the nation. Village after village was burnt, farm after farm was destroyed, store after store was looted. Everywhere lay the dead and the dying as Northumbria bore the full savagery of Cadwallon's revenge. In less than a year, the greatest kingdom England had yet seen had been reduced to ash. Three kings lay dead, the tattered remnants of the Northumbrian army were scattered among the wild places of the north and the nation was in the hands of a tyrant who appeared to gain pleasure in torture and brutality.

But the hour of deliverance was at hand. Into this mayhem strode Prince Oswald - the lost leader of Northumbria. Oswald was only 12 when his father Ethelfrith died and he too had fled Northumbria.

Now, in its darkest hour after the death of his elder brother Eanfrith, he had assumed the throne and returned to lead his nation into battle. Oswald had been born into a heathen family - but his time in exile had been spent under the tutelage of the monks of Iona and he was now a Christian who was determined to fight at the head of a Christian army. He gathered his men in the North Tyne valley where the remnants of Edwin's great army were brought together to make one last valiant stand against Cadwallon and the massacre of their people.

Word reached Cadwallon behind the battlements of his fortress at York that Oswald had returned. The Welsh general led his all-conquering army northwards - with the intention of completing his work of savage destruction along the way. Cadwallon moved up Dere Street - the old Roman road which brought his armies straight into the Derwent Valley. It is not recorded which towns suffered at his hands - but the route Cadwallon followed would have took him first to Lanchester and then to Ebchester as he closed on his prey. History records that he left a terrible trail of smouldering ruins and mutilated corpses in his wake and that neither women nor children were spared, indeed it was written: "the barbarity of torture too frequently added bitterness to death." There is every reason to suppose that the Derwent Valley suffered the same horrendous fate as the rest of Northumbria and the survivors may well have went north to join Oswald's army - their last hope of vengeance.

Cadwallon's army reached Corbridge then left Dere Street and turned up the Tyne Valley to march on Hexham. Meanwhile, Oswald led his tiny force out to meet the enemy. They were hopelessly outnumbered by the hordes of wild mountain men in Cadwallon's army who camped for the night and, confident of certain victory, indulged in wild revelry and heavy drinking ahead of the battle. Oswald's only hope lay in luring his enemy into some sort of trap - a battlefield which would even the odds, if only a little. He found it at Heavenfield.

Heavenfield lies a couple of miles north of Hexham, in the hills which overlook the town. It is a perfect plateau of land - flat as a table-top - which is crossed by the Wall. In those days, only 200 years after the legions had left, Hadrian's Wall was still intact - a seven-foot high defensive barrier which gave Oswald's army complete protection against an attack from the south. The terrain meant the Welsh could not outflank the Northumbrians, could not surround them and could not bring their overwhelming superiority to bear because of the narrow battleground. There was only one avenue of attack left open to Cadwallon - head on. This would be no battle of tactics, no pitting of rival strategies and generalship - this would be a bloody stand-up fight to the death and victory would go to whichever side could most endure the slaughter.

As the Welsh drank the night away, Oswald gathered his men in the moonlight. He ordered soldiers to go into the nearby woods, fell a tall tree and bring him two straight beams of wood. A hole was dug in the battlefield and his men fashioned a rudimentary cross from the timber. Oswald himself hoisted the cross into position and used his weight to hold it in position while his men secured it into the ground. He ordered his men to kneel in prayer then his words rang out across Heavenfield: "Let us beseech the true and living God Almighty, in His mercy, to defend us from the haughty and fierce enemy. For He knows that we have undertaken a just war for the safety of our nation." That night, Oswald dreamt of St Columba who stood shoulder to shoulder with him, wearing a magnificent robe which glistened and sparkled and reached out to cover every man in his army. "Be of good courage and play the man," the saint told him. "At the break of day, march to the battle. God has promised thee victory over thine enemies and the death of tyrants. Thou shalt conquer and reign."

It is said that Cadwallon laughed openly when he saw the tiny force arranged against him at dawn and unleashed the full fury of his army against them. Screaming battle cries and brandishing axes, the Welsh ran headlong at the Northumbrians and into a hail of spears. Attack after attack broke on the ranks of Oswald's men and the piles of corpses mounted, but the Northumbrians did not buckle. Thousands died that day, slashed by Northumbrian swords, pierced by Northumbrian spears, maimed by Northumbrian axes - and still the Welshmen kept coming. With the symbol of the cross above them, Oswald and his bloodied and battered men held their ground. Finally, the turning point came. As he realised the day would not be his, Cadwallon turned and raced away from the battlefield towards the safety of the south.

As their leader deserted the field, panic swept through the Welsh ranks. The wave of attacks turned into a headlong rush to escape.

Oswald's men, no longer hemmed in, broke into a charge and killed all the enemy they could find. The charge became a slaughter as the Welsh tried to scale the Wall and were cut down in their thousands. Now the hunt was on for Cadwallon, the tyrant responsible for the deaths of countless Northumbrians. In his desperate flight south, the Welsh king crossed the Tyne and its tributary, the Devil's Water with Oswald's men in hot pursuit. Finally, he reached Rowley Burn - the little stream which flows into the Devils Water on the moors between the Tyne and the Derwent. Here, about four miles north of Blanchland and on the edge of the Derwent Valley, the Northumbrians caught up with Cadwallon. He was executed on the spot.

Oswald did not live long after the battle but his legacy did. Heavenfield was the turning point for Northumbria in more ways than one - for the first time the king and his army had fought under the banner of Christianity. In the days that followed, the missionary St Aidan was brought from Iona to set up home on Lindisfarne and made 15,000 converts in a week. A new Christian era was dawning on Northumbria and the Derwent Valley and at this point the first rudimentary churches would have been built. Certainly it is known that several religious hermits lived in the forests around Ebchester throughout this period. According to one local legend, a convent was established at Ebchester at this time by St Ebba, a Saxon princess and daughter of Ethelfrith who died in 670AD. This convent was said to have flourished until 883AD when it was destroyed in a Viking attack, although most historians dispute this. However, it would not be until the Ninth Century that Northumbria would become solely Christian and some pagan rituals such as the worship of wood and water spirits would have continued side-by-side with the new religion.

The Christian era was to bring profound changes and would make Northumbria the most important centre of learning in the western world. Oswald himself died seven years after Heavenfield at the hand of the ageing King Penda - his head and hands cut off and impaled on stakes on the battlefield. St Aidan carried on his work until his own death in 651AD, but he was to be followed by a Christian who would have an even more profound effect on the history of Northumbria.

On the night the great missionary saint died, a 17-year-old shepherd boy saw a vision of Aidan's ascent into heaven and felt called to became a monk himself. The pious St Cuthbert quickly rose through the ranks of the Northumbrian church and by his death in 686AD had become Bishop of Lindisfarne and universally held as a great man of God. The cult of St Cuthbert began even during his own lifetime as he travelled and preached in every corner of the North-East and rejected the prestigious office of Bishop of Hexham to continue a simpler life on Holy Island. Many miracles were ascribed to the humble man of God as he spread the word across the untamed country in which he made his home. The Venerable Bede wrote of St Cuthbert: "He used to visit and preach mainly in the villages that lay far distant, among high and inaccessible mountains which others feared to visit and whose barbarity and squalor daunted other teachers." One of these remote villages may well have been Blanchland. In the village churchyard is a simple cross made of millstone grit. Its age is unknown, but it is certainly very old and it is thought that outdoor services were held in its shadow centuries ago. Whether it was Cuthbert himself or his later followers who preached there is unknown, but the Christian message was spreading into the Derwent Valley.

In 687AD, he died and was carried back to Lindisfarne by his brother monks where he was buried and a shrine was erected to him. When in 698AD, on the anniversary of his death, the bishop's tomb was opened to wash his bones and dress them in silk, as was the cutom of the time, his body was found to be in a perfectly incorrupted state. A cult was beginning to grow around St Cuthbert and the seemingly magical powers ascribed to him by a people still steeped in Pagan beliefs.

At the same time, Cuthbert's home on Lindisfarne was growing in importance as a religious centre. Work began on the now world-renowned Lindisfarne Gospels and The Venerable Bede, who was to become one of England's greatest scholars, was ordained. This was the high-point of Northumbrian power, a centre of religion and learning of unrivalled importance, almost 150 years of peace and prosperity and unchallenged military and economic power.

But for the population of Northumbria, this comparative good life was about to come to an end. The death of Bede in 735AD coincided with the beginning of a 70-year period in which the Golden Age of Northumbria unravelled. Of the 10 kings of Northumbria in this period, three were murdered, five were driven out and two left office to become monks. The country suffered under such turbulent reign - and watching this chaos from across the sea were envious eyes.

The Viking attack on Lindisfarne in 793AD came completely out of the blue and struck terror into the hearts of Northumbria's rulers. On a summer's day in June, a great Viking fleet appeared off the Northumbrian coast and sacked the great monastery which held a unique place in the history of the nation. Many monks were killed, others were taken captive and sold into slavery in the markets of Europe, the treasure houses and religious relics were plundered and the buildings were burned. The Anglo-Saxon Chronicles record: "The ravages of heathen men miserably destroyed God's church on Lindisfarne with plunder and slaughter."

The attack on Lindisfarne was an unprecedented shock to the system. If this, Northumbria's holy of holies, was not safe then nowhere was. That is not to say that the ordinary folk of the North-East spent sleepless nights

St Cuthbert blesses water and cures the servant of a nobleman - one of many miracles ascribed to the holy man. This picture was created in Durham in the closing years of the 12th Century (Picture courtesy of The British Library)

waiting for the long boats of the Norsemen. Contrary to popular belief, the Vikings did not spread rape and pillage indiscriminately along the coast and were not the murderous cutthroats of legend. In fact, most Vikings were farmers and settlers. The Viking raiders carefully targeted the richest pickings, at that time held by the churches and monasteries, and largely left the Anglo-Saxon farmers alone. However, history was written by the monks and the monks certainly did have much to fear from the Norsemen. Consequently, the Vikings developed a fearsome reputation for plunder.

The day the longships arrived out of a clear blue sea off the shore of Lindisfarne marks a watershed in the history of Northumbria and, ultimately, of the Derwent Valley. It set off a train of events which was to determine the course of Durham's history for the next 1,000 years.

Over the next seven years, the Vikings - referred to by one writer as "the hateful plague of Europe" - staged raids at the great monastic centres of the North-East almost with impunity. Jarrow, Whitby, Hartlepool and Tynemouth all felt the rage of the Viking attack and the Northumbrians, weakened through decades of in-fighting, were powerless to stave them off. The monks of Lindisfarne collected their relics, their Gospels and the precious uncorrupted body of St Cuthbert and left for good, settling first at Norham-on-Tweed in the Scottish Borders.

Although the Vikings had a fearsome reputation, the English gave as good as they got during the long years of raids on the coast. Skin cut from the bodies of captured Vikings was nailed to the door of churches across England as a warning to others. Finally, the English achieved a notable success. During a storm, a Viking fleet was shipwrecked on the coast of Yorkshire and all perished bar one - Ragnar Lodbrok, leader of the Viking nation and the most feared fighter from the Orkneys to the Mediterranean. It was a quite a coup for King Aelle of Northumbria - his chief tormentor handed to him on a plate. The king showed no mercy and inflicted a special execution on his prisoner, who was thrown into a pit of venomous snakes. As the poison coursed through his body, the old Viking warrior chanted a death song which promised his sons would avenge his death. Avenge it they did.

In the late summer of 866AD, Ragnar's son Ivar The Boneless returned to England with his two brothers Halfdan and Hubba and an invading army of 10,000 men. They landed in East Anglia and stunned the English by doing what the Norsemen had so far failed to do - they stayed. Having spent the winter encamped in The Fens, the army then launched attacks across England. Abbey after abbey burned and historians recalled that the Viking army were: "nursed in blood and educated in slaughter" and derived pleasure in tearing babies from their mothers and tossing them to each other on the point of a lance, or in tying their victims naked to a tree and carving the symbol of the eagle in their chest.

Eventually, they reached York, captured Aelle and subjected him to the horrific ritual of Blood Eagle. Chained at the wrists, the king was hoisted in the air where his chest was slit open, his rib cage broken and folded backwards out of his body to give the appearance of wings. Salt was poured on the raw flesh and there, still breathing, he was left hanging to die. His death left the North wide open to the Danes. In 875AD, Halfdan sailed his fleet into the Tyne and moored his ships at the mouth of the River Team, where Gateshead now stands. His warriors dug trench defences and waited throughout the winter. It would have been a long winter for the communities of the Derwent Valley, only a few miles away from an encamped Viking army waiting for the spring to release fury on the North. If the fear of the Vikings had not previously touched the ordinary peasants, it did now. Sure enough, come the spring the Vikings moved down the valley and attacked Ebchester, which by this time had an established church worthy of plunder. The invaders also raided the hinterland of Hexham, Gateshead and Finchale, as well as the long-established targets of Jarrow and Tynemouth. The Vikings now began to seize land in what was soon to become County Durham, but mainly settled on the best land in the south and east of the county, leaving the less hospitable north to the Anglo-Saxons. However, several places in the lower reaches of the river such as Winlaton, Axwell and Derwenthaugh may well have been settled by the Vikings and derive their name from Norse sources.

But the increasing Viking incursions forced the community of St Cuthbert on the move again. The monks abandoned Norham after 45 years and moved south once more to Chester-le-Street, carrying their saint with them. Ironically, it was the Danes, who now ruled the northern half of England, who gave the land between the Tyne and the Tees to the community of St Cuthbert as the saint's cult began to influence even the heathens. This point, in 883AD, marks the beginning of County Durham and all the lands of the Derwent Valley were at this time handed over to the religious order which guarded the saint's coffin. But if the monks prayed for peace as they built their new church on the banks of the River Wear and welcomed the first pilgrims who made their way to Cuthbert's tomb, they were to go unheeded.

In 993, the Vikings launched renewed attacks. Under siege from all sides, the community of St Cuthbert decided to abandon Chester-le-Street for a safer haven. Led by Bishop Aldhun and seven monks who carried the sacred coffin of St Cuthbert before them, the procession left on a journey which would take them around the North-east for a full year looking for a new home. According to the historian Symeon of Durham, the monks stayed at least one night on their epic journey in Lanchester and, according to local legend, they also passed through the place now known as Castleside, before finally settling at Durham where they built a chapel to house the sacred relics.

By the close of the first millennium, the Derwent Valley had seen a succession of invaders come and go and had survived bouts of war, famine and disease which would have made life very precarious for the people who lived there. But there were now at least three significant settlements clinging to life, Ebchester, Lanchester and Edmundbyers. Along with these there were perhaps other scattered farms along the densely wooded valley and on the edge of the moors, possibly including Chopwell, Knitsley, Medomsley, Rowley, Muggleswick and Blanchland where there are signs of Anglo-Saxon settlements. The villages would have amounted to perhaps a dozen or so farmsteads clustered around a simple church such as the primitive wooden chapel thought to have existed at Lanchester. And as the Derwent Valley entered the new millennium, they would have prayed there for protection from the sea of troubles which beset them on all sides. In fact, matters were about to get much worse.

CHAPTER 5
THE HARRYING OF THE NORTH

THE snow fell in flurries through the cold morning air and the breath from each of the Normans rose in visible clouds. They were scattered among the narrow city streets of Durham, an army spread thinly between the houses, in ones and twos sheltering beneath the eves of the timber houses or in groups around the stone chapel on the hill.

It was the morning of January 31st, 1069, less than three years after the Normans had defeated King Harold at the Battle of Hastings and claimed control of England. On the previous day, the Norman army, led by the newly-appointed Earl of Northumbria Robert Comine, had marched into the city to seize control of the North's most important political and religious centre and brutally murdered many of the innocent townsfolk. Most of the population of Durham had heard of Comine's imminent arrival and had fled into the forests and hills around the city to wait. Others had not been so sensible. The Normans summarily executed dozens when they entered the city to stamp their will on the North.

The historian Hutchinson wrote: "Comine entered the city with marks of cruelty and tyranny and through the insolence of his own self-sufficiency permitted his troops to give themselves up to rioting and wantonness: they forcibly took possession of the houses, were dispersed through every quarter of the city and committed various enormities against the inhabitants."

The relics of St Cuthbert, which attracted religious fervour and pilgrims' gold, were an important lure to the Normans, keen to establish control of the furthest flung parts of their new country. It was even said that William The Conqueror himself had visited the city to view the miraculously preserved body of the saint and threatened to execute every cleric in the city if the famous body was not uncorrupted. But before the king could gaze inside the coffin, he found himself panic stricken and breathless, with a sudden burning fever. Convinced he was being possessed by a strange force from the saint, William is said to have fled the city and not dismounted from his horse until he had safely crossed the Tees back into Yorkshire, beyond the limits of Cuthbert's mysterious powers.

The skyline of Durham City, showing the castle and cathedral, at the end of the 19th Century (Photograph courtesy of Durham County Record Office)

Whether fact or fiction, it was a powerful story which the soldiers may have pondered as they endured a sleepless night and awaited their first freezing Durham dawn. Some may have also heard the blood-curdling stories of the Durham folk, who in 1006 had defeated the Scottish army led by King Malcolm which was trying to capture the newly-founded city. To celebrate the victory, the city's defenders beheaded several of the best-looking Scottish captives. The heads were washed by four of the city's women, who combed their hair before displaying them on spikes mounted around the city walls. Each of the ghoulish washer-women was presented with the then generous gift of a cow for their troubles.

Whether the French soldiers were still flushed with the success of Hastings, the ease of their entry to the city or an arrogant disregard for these poor unfortunates in the city they now occupied, they let slip their guard with terrible consequences. Despite warnings from Aegelwine, the Bishop of Durham, Comine spread his men through the city, along the maze of single-storey streets, strewn with rubbish, which spilled down the hill to the south of the chapel which stood on the site of the present cathedral. The Normans threw the remaining Anglo-Saxons out of their homes, others slept in the doorways, drunk from the celebrations of their conquest. As Hutchinson wrote: "The Normans, overcome with drunkenness and revelling were totally off their guard."

At dawn, the townsfolk rose. They were joined by a great army of Northumbrians who had been hiding in the hills around Durham and swept into the city. In ones and twos, and by the dozen, the Normans were slaughtered. The Anglo-Saxons cut down their enemy where they found them as the ran through the maze of streets. Carcasses filled the streets and everywhere was the sound of anguished cries in Norman French, muffled by the softly falling snow as a terrible vengeance was meted out.

The surviving invaders, including the terrified Comine and the last of his bodyguard, fled for safety to the Bishop's Palace, pursued by the baying crowd. As they fired volley after volley of arrows into the ranks of their pursuers, the building was set on fire. Those who tried to escape the choking smoke were hacked to pieces with axes as they fled, blinded into the street. The blaze threatened to engulf the tower of the early stone minster and Durham's townsfolk, their hands still dripping with blood from the slaughter, fell to their knees to pray that the minster be saved as Comine and his followers died an horrific death in the dancing flames inside. One account of the massacre said they prayed: "With eyes filled with tears and elevated hands, petitioning Heaven, that by some assistance of the holy saint the structure might be saved from damage."

At the last second, the wind changed direction and the minster was saved. In the blood-soaked streets of Durham, the bodies were beginning to be covered by a layer of snow. Of the 700 heavily-armoured Normans who rode into Durham, flanked by as many foot soldiers, only two escaped to tell the blood-curdling tale. After savouring their victory, an army of Northumbrians was raised and marched south, reaching as far as York before their advance was halted. It was to be the last stand of the Anglo-Saxons.

Infuriated by the audacity of the rebellion, William The Conqueror took personal charge of his armies and marched northwards, raising the siege of York and sending the Northumbrians into retreat. The king, determined to end Anglo-Saxon resistance once and for all, launched a counter-attack into the north. What followed was little more than a bloody slaughter which became known to history as "The Harrying Of The North."

Even to a nation which had known centuries of brutality, the march of the Normans was unprecedented in its ruthlessness. Every village, every hamlet, every homestead was looted and burned. The leaders of the revolt fled into the hills for their safety and, in their absence, the Normans turned on the peasants who were murdered where they were found. The historian Surtees wrote: "The march of the Norman army was traced in blood, the inhabitants were subject to indiscriminate slaughter, the villages were left smoking in ashes and even the convents and monasteries were involved, undistinguished in the common destruction."

William sent his armies through central Durham and through the north of the county towards Hexham. To ensure that he effectively ended all resistance for a generation, not only did William kill everyone in his path, he laid waste to the land as he passed. Every village saw its grain stolen, its livestock butchered, its tools destroyed. Those who survived the massacre died of starvation in the barren fields of north Durham. It was said that for nine years, nothing would grow and the land went untilled. There were reports

Wild animal robbing a tomb to feed on a human corpse - this picture is thought to have been created in Durham at the time of the Harrying of the North (Picture courtesy of British Library)

of the starving peasants eating cats, dogs and even human carcasses to survive. The monk Symeon of Durham wrote of: "Scenes which at every footstep presented traces of destruction - the county lay waste and desolate. The roads of the north were littered with decaying bodies that spread disease. Between York and Durham there was not an inhabited town, only lairs of wild animals and robbers, greatly to terrify travellers."

Although there is no direct evidence of the misery the Normans brought to the Derwent Valley there is little doubt that their progress brought slaughter and famine to this quiet corner of the kingdom. The march of the invaders from Durham to Hexham would have brought them directly through the valley. Although we know there were settlements along the banks of the Derwent and the old Roman road before the Norman Conquest, no buildings from that time survive today and little trace can be found of the Anglo-Saxons who lived in the valley. In 1086, William The Conqueror ordered the publication of the Domesday Book - a ledger chronicling all the lands and property in his new kingdom. While the book records every aspect of life elsewhere in England, it stops at the Tees. North of the river, there was simply nothing to catalogue. So complete was the devastation levied in the Harrying of the North that no buildings or lands worthy of mention survived. It would not be until 1183 and the publication of the north's own version, The Boldon Buke, that Durham would have fully recovered from that terrible spring.

CHAPTER 6
NEW LORDS OF THE MANOR

THE new Norman lords of the Derwent Valley inherited a desolate place. The lands south of the Derwent belonged to the Dean and Chapter of Durham and were therefore closely tied with the church for the coming centuries. The Northumberland bank of the river was divided between a number of Norman barons, the most prominent of whom was Walter de Bolbec, and, in the early days at least, the new lords of the manor must have felt they had a fairly precarious hold on their lands, especially in such a remote place. In the immediate aftermath of the Harrying of the North, the aggrieved Anglo-Saxons lost their lands and their titles to the newcomers and the hand over of power was not exactly peaceful.

In August 1072, William Walcher of Lorraine was appointed Bishop of Durham, the first Norman bishop, and work began on the imposing castle at Durham, a symbol which confirmed the victory of the new power in the land. But the simmering resentment between Anglo-Saxons and Normans was to spill over only eight years later when the bishop's henchmen murdered the popular local leader Liulf of Lumley. Another rebellion threatened and the bishop agreed to meet Lumley's family at Gateshead to make the peace. But when he arrived at the banks of the Tyne on May 13th, 1080, he was met by an Anglo-Saxon lynch mob gathered from around North Durham and his attempts at negotiation were drowned out by cries of "slay ye the bishop". Walcher and his entourage took refuge in a church to escape the baying crowd, but the building was set alight. When they escaped the flames, the mob fell on them and butchered them all. The rebellion then moved to Durham itself where the Anglo-Saxons besieged the castle for four days before being driven off. The uprising was taken so seriously that a second Norman army was sent north under William the Conqueror's brother Odo, the Bishop of Bayeaux. Once the Normans had achieved victory, they set about building a new castle on the northern bank of the Tyne to suppress any further hopes of an Anglo-Saxon uprising and, in August 1093, work began on the most important Norman building of them all, the new cathedral at Durham.

Work on the monumental structure was started by the new bishop, William St Carileph, but would take a generation to complete.

Symbolically, the old Anglo-Saxon minister which stood on the site was demolished and the imposing building we know today began to take shape. Much of the wood which formed the solid beams and rafters and the intricate carvings of the new cathedral was felled in the dense oak forests of the Derwent Valley. The whole area was swathed in trees, a huge impenetrable forest which swept up the valley to the edge of the moors crossed only by the occasional tracks and pack roads. Even these roads remained dangerous for travellers. There are accounts from the early 12th Century of packs of wolves which plagued the inhabitants of neighbouring Weardale and in the 13th Century, the last wild boar in County Durham was reputedly killed in the forests near Durham. It seems likely that both would have thrived in the remote woodlands of the Derwent Valley. Red deer were hunted in the forests of Benfieldside right through until the time of Henry VIII and it appears the whole valley was teaming with wildlife.

As described earlier, the Derwent's name originated in the old Celtic word for oak, and that link survives in the place names of several hamlets scattered near the river, Crooked Oak, where a farm has stood since the 14th Century, Pedom's Oak and Broad Oak. Further down the river, Axwell derives its name from the Norse for sheds made from oaks and Winlaton is derived from the Saxon for twisted oak. In a law suit dating to 1228, the knight Walter de Andre gave evidence in which he claimed it was illegal for monks to take wood from the forest without permission of the bishop and that he had seen monks collecting timber from the Bolbec forest without permission. The deposition implies that the forests on the south bank of the Derwent were a major supply of wood for the Bishop of Durham and there is evidence that much of the timber felled for use in Durham Cathedral came from the area now known as Consett, and also Acton, near Blanchland, including the great oak beams which supported the vaulted roof of the cathedral. Later, the timber from Chopwell would be used to restore the impressive roofs of two of the other great symbols of Norman rule in the north, Bamburgh Castle and Dunstanburgh Castle as well as the first Tyne Bridge.

As the great Christian edifice at Durham began to take shape, it increased the flow of pilgrims to north Durham. The early Norman years saw a great increase in church building in the area and no more so than in Ebchester, which was establishing itself as a small but significant pilgrimage site. The Norman church at Ebchester was built in the year 1100 and probably replaced an earlier existing Anglo-Saxon building. The same reasons which brought the Romans to Ebchester, a safe crossing of the Derwent on the main route from Durham into Northumberland, ensured the village thrived under the Normans. The large cattle market held near Corbridge would have brought farmers and their animals through Ebchester along with other traders and traffic heading north to Scotland. In 1181, Bishop Pudsey founded Sherburn Hospital at Durham, where a master and three priests cared for monks and nuns who had contracted leprosy. The new hospital was given lands on the banks of the Derwent, mainly near Ebchester, to provide an income to pay for its upkeep. Leprosy was the scourge of the time and as well as the 65 lepers cared for at Sherburn, a small hospital existed at Friarside, near Lintzford, and another at Witton Gilbert.

The charter with which the hospital was set up grants Sherburn, "a mill and lands" at Ebchester, implying that a significant part of the village was turned over to the monks "for the pasture of animals for the use of the sick brethren." As well as the importance of the Sherburn lands for the village, Ebchester became an important place of pilgrimage. Travellers came in ever increasing numbers to pray at St Ebba's church before moving on to Blanchland to visit the abbey. Ebchester had long been known as a holy place - hermits, including some women, had made their homes in the forests along the banks of the river and in the remains of the Roman fort. In Bishop Pudsey's time it was known as "the place of the anchorites". In 1292, the Pope granted an indulgence, or special blessing, to anyone who visited the chapel at Ebchester which increased the flow even further and turned the village into a significant religious site.

Further down the river, the religious community at Friarside was said to be founded after the direct intervention of St Godric himself. According to Reginald, in the Life of St Godric, a hermit known as Friar John had for many years searched for a plot of land where he could live in solitude and contemplation, but had repeatedly failed to find somewhere suitable. At some point around 1150, he travelled to Finchale and enlisted the help of Godric, who intervened with the Bishop of Durham and Friar John was given permission to select a site from church lands. The monk eventually found his ideal spot on the banks of the Derwent. When he returned to Godric to tell him he had decided on the area now known as Friarside , the saint described the location in perfect detail although he had never been there. A simple stone building was built at Friarside, 50ft by 20ft with walls more than two feet thick. Friarside hospital comprised of this single building, which was divided between simple living quarters for the friar and a small chapel, dedicated to St Mary The Virgin. Here the friar would tend to the spiritual needs of those living in the forest and

The ruins of Friarside Chapel, which in its day served as a hospital and a place for pilgrims to rest on the journey to Ebchester and Blanchland (Photograph courtesy of Beamish Museum)

the countless pilgrims who passed by this way on the journey from Jarrow to Blanchland. Further down the valley at Stella, a nunnery was established by the sisters of St Bartholomew in 1143 which lasted until the Dissolution when the religious house became Stella Hall.

The Normans were the first to fully conquer the great forest which stood along the banks of the Derwent and many of the settlements which still stand today were founded around this time. Edmundbyers church dates back to 1150, founded on the site of the previous Anglo-Saxon village. Healeyfield, near Castleside, is first mentioned in 1170 when Bishop Hugh Pudsey gave the lands to Alan de Chilton in exchange for property in the Cornforth area, the new lord giving his name to the nearby crossing of the River Derwent at Allensford.

The bishop also granted the manor of Chopwell, known at the time as Ceoppa's weille and comprising 3,800 acres of farmland and forest, to the Abbot of Newminster in 1153. Pudsey was the bishop responsible for the drafting of the Boldon Buke, published in 1183 and containing history's first mention of Consett, then known as Conkesheved and owned by a baker, who identified himself as Arnold, son of Joceline, who lived with his wife Addoc and two sons William and Ralph. By 1264, the township's name was given as Conkysheud, home Sir Jurdan de Eschouland, one of the knights who fought alongside Henry III in the Battle of Lewes. The Boldon Buke also mentions lands at Iveston and refers to the existing townships at Winlaton, Benfieldside, Butsfield, Satley and Rowley among others. At Whickham, a mill, fishery and 35 tenants of the village are mentioned, each villager farming 15 acres and having to do service for the Bishop on three days of every year.

By the 13th Century, many of the villages on the hills which flank the valley were starting to develop. A church was founded at Medomsley to serve the growing village there. The village of Whittonstall dates back to at least 1292, when lord of the manor Guy Darrayos conveyed land and mining rights around Whittonstall and Newlands to Roger Hechan for the sum of one silver obolus a year. A later survey carried out on behalf of Bishop Hatfield in 1437 gives mention to the existence of a timber bridge across the Derwent at Shotley, which the survey said had been built in the 12th Century, and mentions lands there held by Thomas of the Brig. This river crossing also appears to have been the source of several legal disputes, with a succession of court references dating back to 1399 over the ownership of millstones taken from the riverbed at Shotley Bridge.

But the most important church established by the Normans was at All Saints at Lanchester, built using stone taken from the old Roman fort. There is some evidence of an old wooden chapel at Lanchester, dating back to Anglo-Saxon times, and the new solid stone Norman church was a symbol of the change to a new order in the land. The church became one of the most important in the county when the parish was granted collegiate status in 1283 by Bishop Bek. So significant was All Saints that it received a royal visitor in 1306 - King Edward I attended Mass there while passing through Lanchester and made an offering of three shillings to the church in honour of St Lawrence. Collegiate churches were set up by the

Bishop from the late 12th Century - each staffed by a college of canons, who lived together in a monastic manor and each administered a share of the church assets, known as a prebend. At Lanchester, there were seven prebends and a dean, who oversaw the 40 farms on the church estates throughout the valley. According to the Boldon Buke, there were 500 acres of cultivated land at Lanchester in 1183, as well as the meadows and pasture owned by the Bishop. The leading farmer held six acres of land for which he paid a rent of 40 hens and 300 eggs a year. Another 20 villains owned 28 acres between them and four cotmen, or cottagers, held another eight acres between them. As well as paying rent to the church, the villains and the cotmen also had duties of mowing the meadow and making the hay, bringing the swine up from the pasture as required and also bringing greyhounds to the great hunt held every year by the Bishop in the forest of Weardale.

The monastic community at Lanchester was governed by a series of strict rules known as the Articles of Regulation, designed to govern every aspect of life. According to these statutes, the choir monks were required to: "read and sing aloud, distinctly, with full voice and without over skipping or cutting the words, making a good pause in the midst of every verse, beginning and ending altogether, not protracting or drawing the last syllable too long; not hastily running it over, much less intermingling any strange, variable, profane or dishonest speeches." The articles also commanded that they should not: "brawl or chide in the quier or without, but let them keep silent; not murmuring, gainsaying or contending with one another, neyther yet laughing, fleering, staring nor casting vagabond eyes towards the people remayning in the same churche, nor should they go into any common taverne nor tayre in the same; neither exercise wrastlinge, dauncinge or any other hurtful gaymes."

But in the 12th Century, the focus of attention in the Derwent Valley switched from the old Roman settlements of Ebchester and Lanchester to Muggleswick. For several centuries, the village had been a tiny Anglo-Saxon settlement which derived its name from the farmstead, or wick, belonging to the chieftain Moola. At the end of the 12th Century, Bishop Pudsey granted the village to the Prior and Convent of Durham in exchange for the Manor of Hardwick and at some point before 1229 a new church was built in the village. But somewhere around the year 1260 it took on a new lease of life when Prior Hugh de Darlington ordered the building of Muggleswick

The remains of Muggleswick Priory, once the most important building in the Derwent Valley (Photograph courtesy of Beamish Museum)

Manor as a country house or summer retreat for the priors of Durham. Prior Hugh himself lived there for 10 years from 1275 onwards and was remembered for his charity, throwing handfuls of coins from his horse or carriage to the poor as he passed. During his residence, Hugh also opened up his kitchens to the local folk who provided entertainment in exchange for food. The manor was the largest and most important building in the Derwent Valley for several centuries. It was three storeys tall, topped with battlements and protected by walls eight feet thick. The lowest level was an open room which acted as a store for cattle if it had to be defended against marauding Scots or Border raiders. Above was a Medieval hall, with a huge fireplace and a chapel, as well as further rooms for the visiting monks. The manor was surrounded by estates which provided food for the priors and any surplus was taken to Durham to be sold at market. Bishop Walter Kirkham had given Hugh permission to enclose a park at Muggleswick some three miles long by two miles wide, which gave the manor extensive lands to farm and some of the best timber forests in the region to exploit. The monks also enjoyed wide-ranging hunting grounds for deer and boar in the forests and moors at nearby Hunstanworth, from which the village got its name. There were a succession of fishponds adjacent to the manor which were in daily use.

By 1464, Muggleswick Manor had fallen from prominence and was in a state of disrepair, but it still recorded a dairy of 179 cattle and 188 sheep, although the survey reports it was surrounded by the earthworks of previous buildings which were no longer in use. It survived another 150 years and was occupied until 1603, when the then prebend Dr Barnes, removed all the lead from the windows and roof and sold it off in Newcastle. Bad management appears to have been the major contributory factor in the demise of the manor. One contemporary complaint recorded was: "The goodliest wood in the North of England is wasted by the prebendaries and utterly consumed." By the mid 17th Century, the manor buildings were decayed ruins.

But in the daily lives of the villagers who lived up and down the valley, it was the halmote courts and not the great manor houses which played the most important role. These courts met twice a year to elect a bailiff and jury, settle small-scale disputes and pass local laws for the governing of the immediate area and so combined the role of today's magistrates courts and councils.

For example, on November 4th, 1364, the halmote court meeting at Edmundbyers, which was the seat of the local manor house, elected Robert Souter as bailiff for the area. At the meeting on November 30th, 1367, it was reported that a cottage held by John Huker had burnt down. But as the cottage belonged to the Priory of Durham, bailiff Souter was ordered to confiscate all of Huker's goods and take them to Muggleswick to be stored until he could raise 30 shillings to repair the cottage. In July 1368, John Huker was again before the court. He had sold three sheep to Richard de Heswell for six shillings but had never been paid. Bailiff Souter was ordered to seize the money and use it to pay off part of the debt for the cottage. And in 1373, the court issued proclamations to the people of Edmundbyers to root out any poisonous ragwort growing on their lands and also to take it in turns to supply Communion bread.

The laws passed by the halmote courts regulated almost every aspect of life in the parish, although some of the decrees passed appear Draconian today. Tenants were not allowed to buy or sell land without permission from the lord of the manor and no-one was allowed to trespass, cut trees or go poaching on the lord's land. Other laws were passed to ensure that trade and life in the village was protected against neighbouring villages. Villagers were not allowed to sell manure, a highly prized commodity for fertilizer and fuel, to anyone from outside the village or to pay labourers higher wages than their neighbours, to prevent competition and disputes. It was also forbidden to buy ale or other goods outside the village and then sell them to your neighbours. Home-baking was outlawed to protect the rights of the common bake house. Brewers were compelled not to charge more than a penny for a pot of beer, particularly important because ale was the most common drink in the villages where the purity of milk and water could not be trusted and therefore the supply of beer was carefully regulated. In 1354, residents of Benfieldside were given special permission from the court to buy their beer from elsewhere because there were no suitable alehouses in the manor. But there was also protection for the consumer within this system and in one court judgement against an allegation the local brewer had been selling short measures, the punishment was spelled out: "Thin is the drink and slender the measure. If it not be fully paid, may he get a black eye."

Movement or people was also restricted. In 1351, the halmote court in Lanchester fined Juliana del Lone, chaplain John of Brancepath and Richard Wilch for being absent from their land, that is owning land in the village but living elsewhere and therefore not discharging their duties to the landlord.

There was a whole raft of rules and petty regulations governing every detail of life to prevent disputes arising between villagers. Tenants were forbidden to call each other rustic, considered to be a serious term of abuse. It was against the law for pigs to be allowed out without a nose ring. Tenants were not allowed to play ball and were charged with preventing their wives from quarrelling with neighbours. Women were, by law, to restrain their tongues and refrain from using bad or irritating language, or face a fine of 12 pence. The stocks were also considered a suitable punishment for such scolds. Public incontinence by a woman was considered a crime, as was marrying without licence from the lord of the manor. Fines were levied against anyone who drew a knife or raised a staff for evil purpose, while anyone actually striking a blow with staff, knife or sword faced a fine of half a mark.

But for all their attempts at regulation, life for the villagers of the Derwent Valley remained extremely precarious - which the halmote court records demonstrate forcibly. In the middle of the 14th Century, the Black Death struck in Durham. The plague swept through the country like a tidal wave and thousands succumbed to it. There was no protection from it, despite the dozens of folk remedies and prayers which villagers put their faith in and it devastated town and country alike. In the cities there are stories of entire families being boarded up in their homes because one person showed symptoms and of cartmen collecting the bodies from the streets to dump in the plague pits outside the city walls. In the country, the effects were just as devastating but less well recorded. In 1350, the plague struck North Durham. In the village of Rowley, it killed everyone save for one old woman who was the only inhabitant to survive. In Lanchester, the halmote courts imposed no fines that year because the villagers, afflicted by the plague, were too poor to pay and the corn mill produced only half the value it had 40 years earlier. During Medieval times, several villages simply disappeared from the records altogether and, although there is no proof either way, it is thought that some may have been deserted after losing their entire population to the plague. At least three Medieval villages in

Medical knowledge at the time of the Black Death was very basic, as this illustration of a Medieval eye operation, thought to have been created in Durham around the year 1190, shows (Picture courtesy of The British Library)

the vicinity of Lanchester are thought to have been deserted at this time - Greencroft Park, Colepike Hall and Newbiggen - and Black Death may have been responsible.

The plague spread throughout the entire length of the valley. At Edmundbyers, Adam Barbour died of the Black Death and the halmote court of 1368 was left to sort out his financial affairs - it does not record how many of his neighbours also succumbed. Such was the spread of the plague at Whickham that in 1373, John de Belgrave and Nicholas Cooke were given authorisation to seize workmen and coal-bearers within the liberty of Durham because so many miners had died and the pits were standing idle. The countryside probably fared better than the overcrowded, stinking cities where the disease, brought by travellers, could spread like wildfire. But the effect of the plague can best be summed up by the report of attendance at the halmote court in the village of West Thickley, near Shildon in south Durham for 1350: "None from the township, for they are all dead."

CHAPTER 7
FOR WHOM THE BELL TOLLS

THE ravens reached the bodies long before any human dared return. They scattered noisily into the air when the first villagers came back. Strewn around the abbey grounds lay the bodies of dozens of monks, their distinctive white habits stained crimson red where they had been cut down. The irony was, the monks of Blanchland had summoned their own slaughter. Lost in the mist which had descended on the valley, the Scottish invaders had passed by the abbey and reached the bleak Dead Friar's Hill, 1,600 ft above sea level on the Durham side of the river and named after one of the monks' brethren who was lost in a blizzard on the road from Bay Bridge to Stanhope. The monks, thankful that their enemies had passed by, praised the Lord for their deliverance by ringing the abbey bells. But the joyous peal carried over the valley to the Scots, who turned and followed the bells back to Blanchland to butcher the monks, burn the abbey and ransack the storehouses and fields. The corpses lay where they fell for several days before the neighbours dared return to give the monks a Christian burial.

The Barony of Bolbec was created early in the 12th Century by Henry I, who handed over estates formerly belonging to the Earl of Northumberland to Walter de Bolbec III. Bolbec, whose father had fought alongside William The Conqueror at the Battle of Hastings, now assumed the ownership of extensive lands on the north bank of the Derwent. The Bolbec family originated in the Picardy area of France which was home to the Premonstratensian order, nicknamed the White Canons after the colour of their robes, who lived a strict but simple life. In 1165, de Bolbec founded a Premonstratensian abbey at Blanchland in honour of the Virgin Mary, home to 12 canons. The order quickly grew in importance and wealth and became one of the most significant religious orders in the north. In 1215, King John granted all the lands around Blanchland to the abbey - something in the region of 5,000 acres of sparsely populated farmland, fell and moor - and from 1295 onwards, the abbot of Blanchland was allowed a seat in the House of Lords. A church was built in 1225 and at its height the religious community was home to around 40 monks.

But life on the edge of the Derwent Valley was difficult. Regular incursions by the Scots left the valley in an almost permanent state of siege. One of the earliest mentions of such forays comes from 1138, when King David of Scotland overran the whole of Northumberland and the Derwent became a safe haven for those fleeing his advance. The Prior of Hexham recorded: "He received reinforcements for his army from Normans, Germans and English, from Northumbria, Cumberland and Teviotdale, the Lothians and Picts and Scots. No-one knew their number, for others uncalled for allied themselves to this army for love of plunder. They destroyed churches and monasteries. Many of the inhabitants of Northumberland fled into the Bishopric of Durham and concealed themselves in the waste and desolate country which surrounded the village of Tanfield. But, even there, they were traced and butchered by the invaders, who returned with immense booty which the fugitives had vainly endeavoured to conceal."

From 1296 to 1314, there were a succession of armed raids by the Scots into northern England, plundering the monasteries and castles, raiding livestock and causing carnage throughout Northumberland. The inhabitants were forced to take extraordinary measures to protect themselves and their property. During the 1950s, a fabulous hoard of coins was unearthed at Whittonstall, which is thought to have been buried at some point around 1311. The hoard included more than 1,200 silver coins, hidden in a metal casket sealed with wax, which were minted during the reign of Edward I and Edward II as well as Scottish and Irish coins. One third of the coins had been minted in the North of England. Why the owner did not return for his hidden treasure will never be known.

In 1314, Edward II led his army north to meet the Scots at Bannockburn, staying the night in Lanchester on the way. The battle was a disaster for the English and a momentous victory for the Scots. From that point onwards, the Scots raided almost with impunity. The religious sites of Hexham and Blanchland were a primary target for the rampaging Scots and also had to provide food and shelter for the pursuing English army. There are rumours that a secret passage ran from Blanchland abbey towards the river to aid the monks escape and, although this has never been verified, secret rooms and hiding places were discovered in the chimney flue of the old abbey. But if they were in danger from the Scots, the monks themselves were not averse to raiding their own neighbours during hard times.

In 1327, the abbey faced its biggest threat yet. In January of that year, Edward II - a man almost universally recognised as one of the worst leaders England has ever had - was removed from the throne in a palace coup staged by his scheming wife, Queen Isabella, and her lover, Sir Roger Mortimer. His son Edward III, then aged just 14, was placed on the throne as a puppet king. Weakened by intrigue and ruled by a novice king, England appeared to be at the mercy of the Scots. On the very night of Edward's coronation, an army of more than 20,000 Scots under the leadership of Earl Douglas and Earl Moray crossed the border and ran rampage over the whole of the north, capturing livestock and destroying entire towns, including Blanchland where they burned down the abbey.

But if it was a moment of danger for England, it was also the opportunity the young king needed to assert his leadership with victory over the invaders. Edward summoned his army and led 40,000 men north to Durham, where they camped for five days awaiting news of the enemy. Finally, word reached him that the Scots were a mere 10 miles away. So great was the enthusiasm to do battle that the English formed up as soon as the news reached the city. At midnight, fanfares sounded and the great army left the gates of Durham with a teenage boy at the head of 500 mounted knights and rank after rank of men-at-arms under the flowing banners of the king.

It was to prove a fiasco. The Scottish army was made up of 4,000 knights and 20,000 men, "bold and hardy, armed after the manner of their country". The Scots had developed a formidable reputation for

King Edward III who, as a teenage boy, led his armies through the Derwent Valley to humiliating defeat at Stanhope. He would have his revenge in later life at the Battle of Neville's Cross (Picture courtesy of the National Portrait Gallery, London)

their ability to conduct lightning attacks in war - they travelled light, with provisions strapped to their horses, and could survive on basic rations for weeks on end. The pursuing English were cumbersome in comparison, comprising of heavy horse, lengthy supply trains and extended ranks of men.

By day break, the English were scattered across the trackless moors of North Durham. The contemporary historian Frossart described the progress of Edward's proud army: "Day began to appear as the battalions were assembled at different posts, the banner bearers then hastened over heaths, mountains, valleys, rocks and many dangerous places without meeting any level country. On the summits of the mountains and in the valleys were large mosses and bogs and of such extent that it was a miracle that many were not lost in them, for each galloped forwards without waiting for either commander or companion, those who fell into them found difficulty in getting any help to them. Many banners reclined there and several baggage and sumpter horses never came out again. In the course of the day there were frequent cries of alarm, as if the foremost ranks were engaged with the enemy, which those behind believing to be true, they hurried forward as fast as possible over rocks and mountains, sword in hand, with their helmets and shields prepared for fighting, without waiting for father, brother or friend. False alarms were occasionally raised of the enemy being at hand, which was caused by the stags that startled at the tumult of men on the heaths ran about distractedly in large herds among the troops."

On the evening of the second day, when an exasperated Edward had yet to lay eyes on the wily Scots, he ordered the slow wagons loaded full of provisions be sent back to Durham and each man was issued with a single loaf of bread to carry or strap to his saddle. For days, the English army stumbled around the moors and dales of North Durham and South Northumberland. Eventually, Edward reached Haydon Bridge and there the English: "remained for three days without bread, wine, candles, oats or other forage." A matter of days after setting out from Durham in such high spirits, the English army was at a low. The weather was dreadful, the loaves of bread had run out and the soldiers were hungry, the ranks murmured and the officers talked of treason. To stave off the threat of mutiny, Edward announced that a knighthood and a pension of £100 a year for life would be granted to anyone who would bring him definite news of the whereabouts of the Scots.

Edward re-crossed the Tyne and reached Ebchester, then marched his bedraggled army along the north bank of the Derwent. In mid-afternoon on the fourth day since they left Haydon Bridge, the nobleman Thomas de Rokeby caught up with Edward's army bearing the news the king had been desperately waiting for - the Scots were camped at Stanhope and had been there for the last week, awaiting Edward. Frossart wrote: "As soon as the king heard this news, he ordered his army to be prepared and turned his horses to feed in a field near a monastery of white monks which had been burnt, and which was called in King Arthur's time Blanche Lande. The king was received by the abbot and confessed himself, ordering masses to be said for housel as were devoutly inclined."

Edward's army stayed at Blanchland for several days in late July and early August to recuperate before moving off to Stanhope, where the Scots had built a small town of wooden huts on the south bank of the Wear. Both sides formed up for battle on opposite sides of the river, which was in torrent and dangerous to cross because of the rocks and stones. Under the curious rules of warfare which then existed, English heralds were sent across to ask either for permission to cross to the Scots' side for battle or to invite them over to the north bank to fight there. The Scots, however, were going nowhere. They sent back the reply: "that the king and his barons saw that they were in his kingdom and had burnt and pillaged wherever they had passed and that, if it displeased the king, he might come and amend it for they would tarry as long as it pleased them."

Then, leaving a division of men to guard the crossing, the bulk of the Scots returned to their huts for the night. The English therefore, "lay that night very uncomfortably upon the hard ground, among rocks and stones, with their armour on; not could they get any stakes for the purpose of tying their horses; or procure either litter or forage, or any bushes to make a fire." As the English suffered in the open air, the Scots lived it up in their huts: "where they made marvellously great fires and, about midnight, such a blasting and noise with their horns that is seemed as if all the great devils from hell had been come there."

The stalemate continued for almost four weeks, despite a sneak Scottish attack in the dead of night by a hand-picked raiding party who came within a whisker of killing the king of England. Frossart wrote: "The Lord James Douglas took with him about 200 men at arms and at midnight crossed the river at such distance from the camp that he was not noticed, and fell upon the English army most valiantly shouting 'Douglas for ever! Ye shall die ye thieves of England!' And he and his companions killed more than 300 and he galloped up to the king's tent and cut two or three of its cords, crying at the same time 'Douglas, Douglas for ever!' And in his retreat he lost some of his followers but not many."

Finally, after 26 days, a Scottish knight was captured who revealed under torture that an order had been sent out in the camp for the entire Scottish army to be ready to follow Douglas' banner by vespers that evening. An emergency council of war was called by the English generals, led by their teenage king, which concluded that an all-out attack on their hunger-ravaged men could be expected that night and "from their sufferings by famine, which they could endure no longer, make it a very bloody and doubtful combat". Edward prepared to make his last stand. The English lit enormous bonfires to illuminate the riverbank so they could see the attack coming and lined up in battle formation in the darkness. They waited all night long. Daybreak revealed the Scottish camp to be empty and a patrol captured two Scottish trumpeters who revealed that their countrymen had left at midnight and were now five leagues away, heading back to Scotland.

Frossart wrote: "Some of the English however mounted their horses, passed the river, and went to the mountain which the Scots had quitted and found more than 500 large cattle, which the enemy had killed, as they were too heavy to carry with them and they wished not to let them fall into the hands of the English alive. They found there also more than 300 cauldrons made of leather with the hair on the outside, which were hung on the fires, full of water and meat, for boiling. There were also upwards of 1,000 spits with meat on them prepared for roasting and more than 10,000 pairs of old worn-out shoes made of undressed leather which the Scots had left there. There were found five poor English prisoners whom the Scots had bounden naked to the trees, and some of them had their legs broken."

The Scots returned home but the whole month-long affair had turned into an expensive disaster for the boy king. So costly was the invasion and the stand-off at Stanhope Park that Edward was forced into the extraordinary step of having to pawn the crown jewels to pay for it. The damage done by the Scots and the occupation by Edward's army cost the Blanchland estates dearly. The abbey claimed compensation from the royal stores at Newcastle for its losses during the summer campaigns of the two armies. The monks claimed to have lost 40 acres of wheat and rye, 100 acres of oats, 100 acres of hay and 500 sheep. The claim was settled by a donation of 20 marks from the royal treasury.

The abbey was ransacked again in 1347 by the Scottish army of King David II, although on that occasion Edward would have his revenge at the Battle of Neville's Cross. But when the abbey was finally destroyed, it was not by Scots, but by the English. It faded in importance over the following centuries and its true death knell was finally sounded in the reign of King Henry VIII and the dissolution of the monasteries. In 1536, the king sent his commissioners to Blanchland and they found a monastery on its last legs. There were only nine monks left and it had just £40 to its name, not enough to bribe its way out of trouble as other religious houses managed to do. The monastery was broken up and in 1546, the lands were distributed by Henry to John Bellow and John Bloxham. Eventually, the estates passed into the hands of the Radcliffe family and then, through marriage to Sir John Forster of Bamburgh, whose family held them through the turbulent years of the 18th Century.

But the abbey decayed, its stones used for house-building, its chapel overgrown, its cloisters crumbled with only the old Celtic cross of St Cuthbert remaining. In 1730, an unknown author wrote of Blanchland: "The old church is in ruins, the walls decayed, the bell gone, the graveyard a lost God's acre, but an old stone cross, the symbol of Christianity, remains to tell us that this is consecrated ground and, if uncared for, is still a place of the hallowed dead."

But, it seemed, the hallowed dead remained. For generations, it was said that the ghosts of the slaughtered monks haunted the grounds of the abbey, wandering the ruined chapel where their anguished moans and groans of despair could be heard. And at midnight, a funeral knell rang from the bell tower, though the bells had long been missing. The apparitions were seen so regularly and were so terrifying, that no-one from the village would ever venture out at night. Sir Walter Basant spent time in Blanchland with Mr Hilyard, the young Oxford scholar brought to the Derwent Valley as a tutor for the young Tom Forster. In 1710 Basant wrote: "Brush and bramble grow around the chapel and cover the old graves, whose very mounds have now disappeared and are level with the turf. Among them rises an old stone cross, put up no-one knows when. It is truly a venerable and ghostly place. In the twilight or moonlight, one may see or think he sees the ghosts of the murdered friars among the ruins. In the dark winter evenings the people said they could be heard when the wind was high, chanting in the chapel and every year on that day when they rang the fatal bell and so called the Scots, may be heard at midnight the ringing of a knell. Many are those who can testify to this miracle and at night the venerable ghost of the abbot himself may be met sometimes upon the bridge.

View of Blanchland village in 1905
(Photograph courtesy of Beamish Museum)

"But this may be rumour, for the people of the place are rude, having no learning at all, little religion, but certainly great credulity and prone to believe all they hear. Certainly I have never met the abbot's ghost, though I have often stood upon the bridge after midnight alone or with Mr Hilyard. On the other hand I have heard on wintry nights the chanting of the dead monks very plainly. While we were there I heard so many ghost stories that I began to suspect something wrong and presently was not astonished that the number and dreadful, fearful aspects of the ghosts had greatly increased since we came to the place, inasmuch that for years after (and no doubt until now) the simple people of the village were frightened out of their lives if they had but to cross the quadrangle or fetch water after midnight."

Blanchland was said to be cursed by the ghosts of the dead monks for centuries. But, thanks to one of the most remarkable churchmen ever to have taken holy orders, they ceased in the mid 18th Century and returned to their graves. Nathaniel Lord Crewe was born in Northampton in 1633. He was extraordinarily handsome, gifted and took a great interest in style and fashion. After choosing a career in the church, he eventually made his way through the ranks to be appointed Bishop of Durham at the age of 40. Lord Crewe lived in Durham Castle and appeared in public dressed in his finest clothes. He also insisted on travelling in style, in a coach pulled by six black horses or on the Wear, rowed in a decorated boat by liveried oarsmen. In 1699, then aged 67, the bishop married his second wife, Dorothy Forster, who was 24 years old and the heiress to all the lands around Blanchland.

When Lord Crewe died in 1722, at the age of 89, he had no heir and the church and monastery site were little more than rubble. In 1747, the father of Methodism John Wesley visited Blanchland and wrote: "This place is little more than a heap of ruins." But Lord Crewe's will bequeathed that a charity be established to restore the church and in 1752, the trustees began rebuilding the church and the model village which now surrounds it. Once the church was restored, the haunting ceased as if the monks slept more soundly.

CHAPTER 8
THE BUTCHER RACE

THE young king woke in a cold sweat, beads of perspiration forming on his brow and his nightshirt sticking to his frame. He rose, still trembling and confused in the half light of dawn and stumbled from his tent into the open. The cold air hit him, taking his breath away. The river mist was silently drifting through the camp where his armies slept. And despite the attention of his bodyguard, suddenly alarmed at their king's distress, he felt alone. Before him, the remnants of the camp fires were reflected in the waters of the river and the village of Ryton stood deserted in the face of the advancing army. He caught his breath and wrapped his arms around himself to protect against the chill of the autumn morning. The dream was still vivid - St Cuthbert himself had come to him and warned the king not to cross into Durham and set foot in the saint's own lands, or face disaster. He shuddered and became conscious of the men-at-arms nearby watching their leader with growing concern. It shook him from his nightmare and he grew angry at his own childish doubts. Here he stood, King David II of Scotland, at the head of the greatest army that country had ever sent forth to do battle. The blood of his father, Robert The Bruce, his nation's greatest leader, coursed through his veins.

He was taught in the cosmopolitan courts of France and knew more of the world than the ill-educated Scottish nobles and rag-tag of foot soldiers which followed them. He would not be seen to cower from a visitation by a long-dead saint - even if by legend Cuthbert did protect Durham from harm. He was only 22 years old and he knew many of the nobles thought him a pale imitation of his illustrious father, but David was determined to prove himself in one glorious campaign against the old enemy, the English. Thinly-stretched, with many of its best men away fighting in France, England lay at his mercy. He had a chance to gain for himself a place in history to surpass even his father. Now, with the cream of Scotland encamped on the north bank of the river awaiting his order to march, nothing would stop him from his date with detiny - not even a warning from St Cuthbert. As the mists began to clear, King David II gave the order to break camp and cross the river to do battle.

The tide of war between England and Scotland was turned by Robert The Bruce. For a century, the English had enjoyed the upper hand over their northern neighbours, who were divided among themselves. The state of affairs lasted until Robert gained control of Scotland in 1306 and waged war on the English, sometimes in great battles such as Bannockburn in 1314 and sometimes in raids into England, bringing terror to those living in the northern counties. By 1328, Robert had won his war of independence and a peace treaty was concluded with the English. Unfortunately, Robert The Bruce died the following year while his son David was only five years old. The boy was sent to Normandy for his own safety as the sporadic war between the two old enemies flared up again, leaving Scotland to its feuding chieftains. King David returned home in 1341 at the age of just 17 to claim his throne and reunite Scotland.

Events hundreds of miles away were then to have a profound effect on the north of England. In 1337, war broke out between England and France, Scotland's ally, in a conflict which became known as the Hundred Years' War. The early stages of the war were fairly low key as the two armies jockeyed for position on the Continent but in 1346, the English invaded Normandy, sacked the city of Caen and crossed the River Seine near Paris. In August, the 30,000 strong English army, one of the largest ever assembled at that time, defeated the French at Crecy and went on to lay siege to Calais. The French now called on their Scottish allies for help against their common enemy, England.

It was an opportunity the young king could barely turn down. As the son of the great Robert The Bruce, he needed a victory in war to make certain his place as leader of Scotland and subdue those nobles who had controlled the country during his absence in France. To the Scots it represented too good of an opportunity to strike the old enemy. With such a massive military force currently fighting in France, it was widely assumed that England had been emptied of soldiers and was there for the taking. It was now autumn, the defenceless barns were full and the animals fattened for winter. Northern England lay at his mercy.

On October 7th, 1346, the Scottish invaded England. They attacked through Cumbria rather than the usual eastern routes over the border and laid siege to Liddell Castle for four days before they finally breached its walls. It was here that the Scottish invaders developed their reputation for barbarity. The castle's commander, Walter Selby, was beheaded by the invaders without being allowed to make his final confession, because he was thought by the Scots to be a traitor. David then wheeled his armies around and advanced down Tynedale, where they captured Hexham and sacked the famous abbey during an occupation lasting for three days. They advanced through Blanchland, where once more the beleaguered monks found themselves in the way of a plundering army. After raiding Blanchland, they moved on to Ryton, where David crossed the Tyne and moved south to the Derwent and Ebchester.

There are few records as to what happened to Ebchester during the Scottish invasion, but some reasonable deductions can be made. Almost certainly, the village would have been deserted by the time the Scottish army arrived. In March, the king had ordered that proclamations be made in Durham, Northumberland and Yorkshire that all men between the ages of 16 and 60 who were capable of bearing arms be arrayed for the defence of the north. Those who were too feeble were to provide substitutes. For the campaign, Yorkshire provided 15 men-at-arms, 29 cavalrymen and 3,000 archers. The likelihood is that Durham would have provided something of a similar order, which meant that most of the able-bodied men of the Derwent Valley would have been away with the army when the invasion came. Similarly, those left at home would probably have melted away into the hills and forests before the invading army. Before the invasion, King David issued orders that the towns of Hexham, Corbridge, Durham and Darlington were not to be burned during the attack because he intended to use the stores there for his campaign. The implication is that the burning of all the other towns and villages they found on the way was fair game. As the Scots advanced they brought bloody mayhem with them, looting and burning along their path. The accounts of the march of the Scots refer to extreme cruelty by the invaders, of towns pillaged and many killed, neither the young nor women being spared. The contemporary Anonimalle Chronicle said: "Then the King of the Scots and his people came from Hexham to the town of Ebchester, destroying and robbing all the surrounding countryside."

It appears the Derwent Valley fared worse than most. Ebchester may well have gone up in flames when the Scottish army crossed the Derwent on or around October 15th, 1346. Those who watched helplessly, hidden in the trees on the hills overlooking their burning homes, would have seen the huge force of 2,000 knights and another 12,000 foot soldiers cross the river and make their way uphill towards the Browney Valley. Lanchester may well have suffered a similar fate as the Scots marched towards Durham and made camp at Bear Park where the Browney meets the Wear.

Meanwhile the English were gathering for battle. The armies were mustered at Richmond in North Yorkshire and moved north. As King David was crossing the Tyne at Ryton, the English moved forward to Barnard Castle and on October 16th, as the Scots reached Bear Park, the English were camped at Bishop Auckland. The English were outnumbered, possibly with as few as 5,000 men, mainly bowmen from the northern counties. The army was divided into three units, one under the command of Henry Percy of Northumberland, the Durham men under the command of William Zouche, the archbis hop of York and the Yorkshiremen under Thomas Rokeby, the sheriff of Yorkshire. The two great armies spent the night of October 16th resting only a few miles apart and preparing for battle.

The bloodiest day in Durham's history dawned wet and cold. The Scottish earl William Douglas led a raiding party out of Bear Park south, possibly trying to reach Darlington. They reached Merrington, near Ferryhill, when disaster overtook them. In a blanket of thick fog, they ran into a detachment of English cavalry which was moving forward looking for the invaders. According to the Chronicle of Lanercost: "While the Scots were plundering the town of Merrington, suddenly the weather became inclement, with thick fog. And it came to pass that when they heard the trampling of horses and the shock of armoured men, there fell upon them such a spasm of panic that William and all those with him were utterly at a loss to know which way to turn. Wherefore, as God willed, they unexpectedly stumbled, to their astonishment, upon columns of my lord the archbishop of York and Sir Thomas de Rokeby, by whom many of them were killed, but William and two hundred with him who were on armoured horses escaped for the time but not without wounds."

What followed became known as the Butcher Race. In a blind panic, the Scots turned and fled. Many of those on horses escaped - but the foot soldiers stood little chance against the English cavalry. The Scots made a desperate flight over the two miles from Thinford back towards their main army waiting beyond the safety of

*Engraving showing the south-west prospect of Durham City
in 1745 by Samuel and Nathaniel Buck - one of the earliest
surviving pictures of the city
(Photograph courtesy of Durham University Library)*

Sunderland Bridge as the English cavalry cut them to pieces as they
fled. They were skewered on English lances, felled by English
swords and trampled under foot as the sounds of the dying mixed
with the thunder of heavy hooves. A handful of exhausted survivors
reached the bridge - and may have looked back to see 500
Highlanders lying dead along the track of the Butcher Race.

The battlelines were now drawn along the line of the current road
from Dryburn to Darlington. The battle effectively took place on a
narrow ledge on a slope of open moorland. Steep slopes on the
Durham side of the battlefield and a series of ditches and fences on
the other side hemmed the battle in and hampered the movement of
the armies. The Scots formed up just to the south of the current
Dryburn roundabout in three units, the centre commanded by King
David II himself, with William Douglas' army to his right and the left
under Robert Stewart. Ahead of them were the English, pennants
fluttering in the breeze. They formed up on a ridge at Crossgate
Moor - the Durham men in the centre under the archbishop of York
facing King David's men. To the English right was Lord Percy of
Northumberland, to the left Rokeby of Yorkshire. At that moment,
two Benedictine monks from Durham Cathedral made their way to
the Scottish ranks to call a truce before the battle began. Suspecting
a trick, King David had them held and ordered they be executed,
although in the ensuing confusion, the order was never carried out.

The Battle of Neville's Cross
(Picture courtesy of La Biblioteque Nationale, Paris)

The Scots attack began at lunch-time, but found it hard going because of the ditches and fences which hampered their way. The slow moving Scots were in perfect range for the English archers high on the ridge who cut them to pieces with withering fire from their longbows. Bitter hand-to-hand fighting now ensued and the English line was pushed back, but held. At several points during the battle, fighting stopped by mutual agreement to allow the armies to pause and regroup.

Finally, the English called up their reserves, waiting near Neville's Cross. They attacked on the flanks, forcing the Scots back and back. Thousands now lay dead and the survivors retreated in a shambles. All that was left of the Scottish army was King David's men in the centre which felt the full force of the English charge. Surrounded now by all three divisions of the English army, the king's position was hopeless. The Scots fought a bloody and courageous last stand until just 80 men were left protecting the king from the battle around him.

The wounded king was found cowering beneath a bridge, the shafts of two arrows sticking out from his bleeding body, protected by the last eight of his noble bodyguard. He had been tracked down by Northumbrian squire John Copeland to his hiding place beneath Aldin Grange Bridge over the River Browney. Only hours earlier he had been at the head of a great army - now he was almost alone. In the ensuing scuffle, the king's sword was knocked from his grasp by Copeland. Whether it was his frustration at his change in fortunes, a defiant last stand or a fit of royal temper, King David threw a final punch with his metal gauntlet, knocking out two of Copeland's teeth. Or perhaps it was the knowledge that a warning had gone unheeded and had led to this disastrous day and more than 10,000 dead scattered across the battlefield.

From the ramparts of Durham Cathedral, the monks began an ominous plain chant of Te Deum, which carried over the battlefield as the Scots retreated in disarray pursued by the English who cut them down as they caught them. Some reached Findoun Hill near Sacriston where they made a last disorganised stand before they were massacred. Others fled for Scotland and home. No-one knows how many died that night on the lonely tracks through the forests of the ravished Tyne and Derwent valleys as the English finally caught up with their quarry, but it was to be a long time before a Scottish army was sent south into St Cuthbert's lands again.

CHAPTER 9
THE ONE TRUE FAITH

BY 1536, Henry VIII was at war with the Catholic Church over his divorce from Catherine of Aragon. The king and his closest advisor Thomas Cromwell - then the most hated figure in England - turned their attention to the religious houses of England, sending commissioners, Dr Richard Layton and Thomas Legh, to tour the country and assess the wealth of the monasteries, which were then to be closed down and their assets transferred to the Crown.

Over the next few years, the abbey at Blanchland was closed and fell into ruins as its lands were divided by the Crown. The small priory at Muggleswick was closed down, as was the Abbey of Newminster, which owned all the lands around Chopwell. For 400 years, the nuns of the convent of St Bartholomew of Newcastle had held Stella - they too were thrown out. The last inhabitant of Friarside Hospital was removed from his seclusion, the friar was given a £5 annual pension for life and the bell which had tolled for four centuries was taken away. The Crown confiscated the land and sold it on, eventually becoming the property of the Tempest family before becoming part of the Gibside estate. Across the valley - and across the country - the lands owned by the Church were taken away and sold off.

When Henry died in 1547 he left three children, Edward, Mary and Elizabeth, and a bitter legacy of religious division which was to last for generations. England lurched from Protestant Edward to Catholic Mary to Protestant Elizabeth.

Meanwhile, there were some who secretly plotted to restore the Catholic faith and replace Elizabeth with her cousin, Mary Queen of Scots. A shadowy conspiracy was uncovered to release Mary from Tutbury Castle in Staffordshire and marry her off to the Duke of Norfolk - a leading Catholic nobleman - who would seize the throne with the help of foreign troops.

Norfolk was arrested in the autumn of 1569, and taken to the Tower but Elizabeth suspected there were others involved in the plot, chief among the suspects being Charles Neville, the 6th earl of

Westmoreland. The earl had inherited his father's title and family seat at Brancepeth Castle when he was just 21. Now aged 27, Westmoreland was not a military man - he was passionate about field sports and little else - but he was the brother-in-law of the admitted traitor Norfolk and he was also opposed to Elizabeth's rule. Charles Neville held genuine religious grievances against Elizabeth but also resented the declining power of his ancient family in the new Protestant state. The same could be said of Thomas Percy, the 7th earl of Northumberland - whose father had died on the scaffold after the failure of the Pilgrimage of Grace and who, as a child, had been placed into the guardianship of Sir Thomas Tempest.

Shortly after Norfolk's arrest, Elizabeth issued the first of three summonses to the earls of Westmoreland and Northumberland to attend court and explain themselves. Fearing, probably with some justification, they were to be arrested, they declined the invitation. It may never be known whether the pair were involved in the Riddoplhi plot all along or whether they were simply propelled into their course of action by the fear of arrest. Northumberland would later deny any knowledge of the plot, but Westmoreland certainly appeared to be preparing for the rebellion - months beforehand he had secretly sold the manor of Winlaton to a group of Newcastle gentlemen for £3,000, money which would have provided funds to finance the revolt. Regardless of their original intentions, the pair were now set on a deadly course.

On November 13th, 1569, Northumberland, Westmoreland and a number of their retinue held court at Raby Castle. With the Queen's suspicions aroused and little in the way of arms or men, it seemed that any form of rising would be futile and lead straight to the scaffold. It is said the plotters dithered and had almost decided on abandoning the plan when Westmoreland's wife Jane, sister of the imprisoned Norfolk, called on all those assembled to strike against the Queen for the sake of the one true faith and their illustrious lineage. The persuasive countess carried the day and the rebels declared themselves for the Rising. The meeting broke up and the participants went home. At around midnight, Thomas Percy was woken from his sleep at Prudhoe Castle by his servants with news, later found to be false, that the Queen's soldiers were near and were to arrest him. Percy rose from his bed, gathered all his available men and sped to Brancepeth Castle to meet Westmoreland. The Rising Of The North was underway.

Into this uprising strode the remarkable figure of John Swinburne, a farmer from Chopwell who was to have a dramatic impact on the history of the North. The lands around present day Chopwell had, for several centuries, been owned by the Abbot of Newminster, who at the beginning of the 16th Century, leased Chopwell Hall to Thomas Swinburne. In 1527, the abbot granted a 51-year lease on the estate, which then included five farms, to John Swinburne, son of Thomas. Three years later, the Bishop of Durham issued the estate a licence to dig for coal on the estate - the first records of coal mining in the Chopwell area. When the Dissolution of the Monasteries took place in 1536, ownership of the lands leased by the Swinburne family passed from the Church to the state and, although the family's lease continued, it was the Crown which became their new landlord.

When John Swinburne died in 1545, the estate fell to his son, also named John. It appears that the young John Swinburne, described by the great historian Robert Smith Surtees as "a man of daring and active character", was a zealous supporter of the old religion. Many in the North still adhered to Catholicism and others were aggrieved by their treatment at the hands of the new Protestant establishment - in order to have the financial clout to assert its authority the church was raising rents and enforcing Protestant ways. Nine years before the rising, Swinburne had been involved in a financial dispute with the Bishopric of Durham which escalated into violence. Swinburne was trying to claim mining rights over the neighbouring coal-rich district of Kyo, then part of the bishop's manor of Ryton. In 1562, the dispute came to blows with two of the bishop's servants Robert Saunders and Robert Hedworth being: "sore bett and hurt" The case was settled in the bishop's favour, Kyo was to remain part of Ryton manor and Swinburne was to pay compensation of 40 shillings to Saunders and 20 shillings to Hedworth. He was also told that he could transport coal across the bishop's land - but only if he paid rent to do so.

So by 1569, a disgruntled and alienated mass of the population was ready to join a rising - and Swinburne was ready to lead it. Contemporary accounts suggest the Rising of the North had three leaders, Northumberland, Westmoreland and Swinburne. However, it has been suggested that undue attention was focused on the two earls because of their elevated rank and the real driving force behind the entire enterprise was the common farmer from Chopwell. Among his closest lieutenants were Robert Tempest and his son Michael, of

Holmeside Hall near Lanchester. The Tempests were one of the oldest and most influential Catholic families in the North and Robert was the nephew of Sir Thomas Tempest, who had served with distinction in the last great Catholic rising against the Tudor dynasty - the Pilgrimage of Grace. So it was that Swinburne, the Tempests and dozens of their friends and tenants from the Derwent Valley and Lanchester left their farms, raised the banner of the Catholic faith and marched to Brancepeth to join the rebellion.

On the afternoon of November 14th, the rebels entered the great city of Durham. According to contemporary reports they were up to 1,500 strong. The earls took a body of men up to the cathedral and set about removing all traces of Protestantism - the communion table was smashed, the English prayer books were burned and trampled underfoot and new altars were erected. George Bowes, the Queen's loyal man in the North, wrote: "At iii of the clocke in the afternoone, the said erles with others to the number three score horsemen armed with spears and daggers, entered the minster at Durham… and theyr toke all the books, but one, and theyme and the comunyon table defaced, rentt and brok in peces".

The earls then issued a proclamation to the people, declaring that the rebellion was not against the person of Elizabeth, but in favour of the old religion and against the noblemen and advisors she had surrounded herself with. If they genuinely believed that Elizabeth would come to no harm in the rebellion, they were naïve. The accession of Mary as Catholic queen would require the death of the existing monarch - even exile would pose a constant threat to the stability of the realm. It was a point not lost on Elizabeth. When news reached her of the rebellion, she is reported to have replied: "I will ordain them such a breakfast as never was seen in the north before." The Earl of Sussex, Lord President of the Council of the North, was ordered to halt the rising in its tracks.

The Bishop of Durham and his entourage fled before the rebels and Catholic Mass was heard once more in Durham Cathedral. Elsewhere across the county, Roman Catholics came out of hiding - Mass was heard at the church in Witton Gilbert and elsewhere. In the whole of Durham, only George Bowes, constable of Barnard Castle, held out for the Queen.

Bowes did not have enough men to take to the field against the rebels and instead retreated inside his stronghold for the duration of the rising from where he sent the Queen intelligence on the progress of the rebels.

On November 15th, the rebels heeded Thomas Percy's cry "To arms without delay - to York and then to London" and set out from Durham to head south. The following day they reached Darlington, then known as Darnton, led by Swinburne. According to Bowes, when the army entered the town they amounted to 400 horsemen and 900 foot soldiers, although most, Bowes reckoned, were unarmed. Once more, the Catholic Mass was heard, although, according to Bowes, Swinburne used a stick to beat a reluctant population until they attended. He wrote to the Earl of Sussex: "Masse was yesterday at Darnton and John Swinburn, with a staffe, drove before him the poor folks to hasten them to hear the same."

King Henry VIII, whose war with the church spelled the end of religious houses such as Blanchland Abbey and Friarside Hospital (Picture courtesy of the National Portrait Gallery, London)

Queen Elizabeth I who ordered rebels be hanged before their families in villages across the Derwent Valley (Picture courtesy of the National Portrait Gallery, London)

At Darlington, the rebels issued a further proclamation which, significantly, was more strongly-worded than that heard on the steps of Durham Cathedral. It accused the Queen of "heresy" - a grave charge with grave consequences - and said Elizabeth's intransigence in matters of religion threatened the country with a foreign invasion, which was somewhat ironic given that Norfolk had already asked for the help of French and Spanish troops. The Darlington proclamation ended with a call on all Elizabeth's subjects to join the rebellion.

The rebels continued their march south but, on November 19, it was the Queen's turn to issue a proclamation of her own - and it left the rebels with no doubt that the outcome of their enterprise could only be in victory or death. The Queen named Westmoreland, Northumberland, Swinburne and Tempest as the instigators of the plot, saying they had: "committed, perpetrated, made and done dyverse unlawful offences contrary to their natural dewties of allegiance and have levied and gatherd to theym great nombres of hir Majesties subjects as well as horsemen and footmen." The proclamation declared the leaders of the rising to be "rebels and disturbers". The Queen then issued an order to the common foot soldiers: they were to return to their homes and stay there and, in exchange, they would be pardoned once the enterprise was over. The proclamation made it clear that no such pardon would be extended to the ringleaders she had already named.

For the earls, Swinburne and the Tempests, there could be no going back. They pressed on, through Richmond and Ripon. Ten days after the rising started, the rebel army arrived at Wetherby - by now made up of 4,000 foot soldiers and 600 horse - although other sources say they were treble that number. But it was to prove the high point of the rising.

News reached the rebels that, during the night, soldiers loyal to the Queen had arrived at Tutbury Castle and spirited away Mary Queen of Scots south to the heavily fortified town of Coventry. Meanwhile, the earl of Sussex with 3,000 well-trained and heavily armed men had left York while the earl of Warwick was hurrying north with reinforcements thought to number more than 7,000. The game was up. The rebels considered the possibility of trying to capture Hartlepool, then defended by only 300 men, where they could wait for help from abroad, but the idea was dismissed. They also considered the possibility of doing battle with Sussex in the hope they could raise Catholic reinforcements in Yorkshire before the arrival of Warwick's army. Instead, they returned north to besiege George Bowes' garrison in Barnard Castle, which fell after 10 days.

Despite having held County Durham for a month, the rebel army was disheartened by the failure to recruit help and in no real condition to fight. When news reached them that the Queen's army had reached Northallerton, they panicked and fled, first to Auckland and then to Hexham. Warwick's men were now in hot pursuit, at one stage occupying Winlaton where they burnt the Catholic chapel of St Anne's to the ground. The rebels' men were deserting in droves and heading back to their farms. On December 13th, with Warwick's men closing in, the army was disbanded and the Rising of the North was over without a single battle having been fought. All that remained now was for those that were left to flee for their lives.

The leaders took to the forests and moors of Northumberland and Cumbria, splitting up into smaller groups to evade capture and try to find passage into the safety of Scotland. Lying low in the wastes of northern England during that bitterly cold December, the former lords of the realm slept rough in the forest and dressed like peasants and outlaws to avoid capture. The dwindling band took refuge with the ageing but still notorious outlaw John Armstrong, known as John of the Syde. In a letter to Lord Cecil, dated December 22nd, Sussex said the remaining rebels had been driven off and had lost all their horses, so miserable was the fugitives' plight that Westmoreland had taken to dressing as a thief. He added that they were now thought to be staying at the home of John of the Syde: "a cottage not to be compared to any doge kennel in England. Such is their present mysery they were not 50 horse and my Lord of Westmoreland changed his cote of plate and sword with John of the Syde to be more unknowen." On Christmas Eve, Lord Hundson wrote: "The erles rebells and their principall confederates do lurke and hide themselfes in the woodes and desertes. The erles have changed their names and apparell and have made themselffes lyke to the outlawes of Liddersdale."

Most managed to evade their pursuers and crossed the border, reaching Farnihurst Castle, near Jedburgh, home of the sympathetic Sir Thomas Ker. Northumberland, however, was not so lucky. The outlaw Hector of Harelaw, having promised to take the earl to people who could help him cross the border, led Northumberland into an ambush where he was captured. Hector received £20 for his treachery and the earl was taken in chains to York where he confessed his role in the enterprise. Despite personal pleas for clemency from The Pope and the King of Spain, he was beheaded on The Pavement in York in August 1572. His head was mounted on a spike at Micklegate, the main entrance to the city, as a warning to deter other traitors. Several years later, sympathisers removed the earl's head and buried it in a nearby churchyard, giving rise to one of York's most enduring ghost stories in which the earl's decapitated body walks the city streets searching for its missing head.

By January 7th, most of the principal rebels had reached Farnihurst, Westmoreland in the uppermost tower and Lady Northumberland in the lower chamber, along with Swinburne, Robert and Michael Tempest. Sussex engaged one of his many spies - Robert Constable of Flamborough - and ordered him to Farnihurst in order to "work sum feate to betrap some of them". Constable, a distant kinsman of Westmoreland, was concerned about his mission to trick the rebels into returning to English soil on the promise they would not be harmed, while the reality was they would almost certainly be executed. However, the promise of a hefty payment and lands was enough to persuade Constable to betray his cousin and the other fugitives.

Constable reached Farnihurst on January 9th and found Westmoreland, Swinburne and the Tempests along with Lancelot and William Hodgson of Lanchester and Lancelot's son John Hodgson of Greencroft hiding out. They had dinner together and, as Constable later told the countess of Westmoreland, talked of Hector of Harelaw, the man who had betrayed the earl of Northumberland into the hands of the Queen, who they "wished his head to have been eaten amongst us at supper." With his feet now literally under the table, Constable tried to gain Westmoreland's confidence and, as the fire flickered in the great hall of the castle, spoke of the shame that he had been brought on the ancient house of Neville. As he spoke to his treacherous cousin, the earl's tears flowed abundantly. The earl passed Constable a ring which he asked him to take to his wife at Brancepath with the message: "to take no care nor thought for him, for all his care was for her and her children." He added that one day he hoped to recover the Queen's favour and restore the family's fortunes. Constable told him that once the furore had died down, the earl should visit him at his house in England and he would smooth things out. Constable would later claim that this devious invitation was to allow the Queen a chance to spare Westmoreland's life, although it seems more likely that he would have been handed over to the tender mercies of Sussex.

Westmoreland told the spy to visit Lady Jane at Brancepath and ask her for a gem and a fine horse to give to Sir Thomas Ker in payment for his hospitality in harbouring the fugitives. Constable reported the request to his spymasters and was told to meet the countess and continue the intrigue. When he eventually met her and recounted the miseries Westmoreland had suffered, it was reported: "the tears overhayled his cheeks abundantly." He then begged her to keep their conversation secret and handed over the earl's ring and message. Overjoyed at hearing news of her husband, Lady Jane prayed to God for the deliverance of Westmoreland, his colleagues and Constable and handed over the jewellery as requested, which promptly found its way to the royal coffers.

Constable paid several visits to Brancepeth Castle, but his devious plan was in vain. The fugitives eventually escaped into exile. Swinburne left for Dumbarton and was spirited across the sea to Flanders before eventually pitching up in Madrid where he saw out the rest of his life on a pension from the King of Spain. Robert and Michael Tempest stayed in Scotland until August 1570 when they escaped to France from Aberdeen. Both ended up in Spain where they met up with Swinburne. Michael is thought to have stayed with his comrade in arms and saw service with the Spanish army in the Low Countries. His father Robert is known to have been in Rome in 1586, but all three died in exile.

But back home, the terror was just beginning. Those who had taken part in the rising were rounded up - and the chance was taken to settle old scores. Under Bowes, the newly appointed provost mar-shal, 917 men from County Durham were convicted of taking part in the rising and another 1,500 bought themselves a pardon, many more than ever took up arms. At least 100 rebels were imprisoned in Durham Castle awaiting judgement and, when it came, it was savage. The Queen demanded an example be made of the rebels. She told Sussex that all the commoners who had taken part were to be executed in their own villages as a warning. She issued him with the order: "You are to proceed, thereunto, for the terror of others, with expedition. Spare no offender. Let the bodies fall to pieces where they hang."

Stunned by the savagery of the orders, Sussex dithered, expecting a show of royal clemency, but it was not forthcoming. Shortly afterwards, the Queen wrote to him again, saying that she: "Somewhat marvelled that we have hithertto harde nothing from you of any execution don by martiall law as was appointed to be don upon those of the meaner sorte." This time Sussex got the message and the hangings began.

Over the next few weeks, 28 men were hanged in Durham City, 14 in Billingham, nine in Kirk Merrington, five in Bishop Auckland and four in Aycliffe. It was the proud boast of Sir George Bowes that: "For 60 miles in length and 20 in breadth between Newcastle and Wetherby there was hardly a town or village where we had not executed at least one of the inhabitants." By the time the killings were done, Bowes claimed to have hanged 230 men in County Durham - each in front of his friends and family and each left, in accordance with Her Majesty's instructions, until they rotted from the branches. No corner of the county escaped the retribution - one rebel was hanged at Benfieldside, one at Medomsley, two at Whickham and one at Broomshields, near Satley. Those who had marched out of the Derwent Valley in the late autumn to defend what they saw as the one true faith returned in the spring to hang from its trees.

Anger was mounting among the common people over the savagery of the retribution. The severest punishment was meted out to the poorest: 19 of the principal leaders of the rising in Durham were named by Act of Parliament, but not one was executed. Eleven of them, including Swinburne and the Tempests, went into exile and the remaining eight bought themselves pardons. The Queen issued orders that no-one with estates of substance or freehold land was to be put to death - execution was to be reserved for the poor. As Sir Thomas Gargrave wrote to William Cecil on April 8th, 1570: "The common people say the pore ar bothe spoylyd and executyd and the gentlemen and ryche escepyth."

The Crown immediately seized lands belonging to the principal rebels. Westmoreland's lands at Cornsay and Hedleyhope were taken, as were the earl of Northumberland's lands at Tanfield,

Tanfield Lea and Beamish. The Greencroft estates of Robert Claxton were taken and Swinburne's lands at Chopwell were confiscated, including his plot at Derwentcote where the infant steel industry would later be born. Among much land awarded to Bowes for his service to the Queen during the rising was a 120-acre plot at Collierley, present day Dipton. Eventually, Elizabeth granted Swinburne's lands at Chopwell to Robert Constable for his services as a spy.

This estate was to have something of a chequered history ending in gruesome murder. On his death, it was discovered that Robert Constable had been embezzling government funds and, as a posthumous punishment, the lands were taken back into the ownership of the Crown. Robert's son and heir, Sir William Constable, eventually persuaded King James I to return the bulk of the lands to the family but the woodlands were to remain Crown property, under the day-to-day running of a bailiff, John Rutherford of nearby Black Hall. Timber from the manor of Chopwell was a prized commodity and when the defences of Berwick needed repair, the town turned to Chopwell to supply the wood.

However, it became apparent that all was not well on the estate and twice, in 1595 and 1597, the authorities in Berwick were forced to write to Lord Burghley complaining of financial irregularities in their dealings with Chopwell. A further complaint was levied locally in 1598 against John Rutherford, alleging that he had felled 100 oaks belonging to the Queen for his own profit. The Constable family sold the land at the end of the Elizabethan era and in 1613 it was became the property of Ambrose Dudley, alderman of Newcastle. Almost immediately, Dudley had Rutherford removed as bailiff and the management of Chopwell Woods was given to Henry Sanderson, the sheriff of Brancepath. If Dudley thought that removing Rutherford, who had already come under suspicion at least once for lining his own pockets, would put an end to the matter he was very much mistaken. The former bailiff held Dudley personally responsible for his downfall and the loss of his livelihood. Matters came to a head in 1615 when Rutherford, backed by an armed gang of his relatives and friends, launched a raid on Chopwell manor and ambushed Dudley and a group of his friends at Westwood. The indictment which was later issued declared John Rutherford, his relatives Charles, Hugh and Gawen Rutherford and their confederate William Shafto outlaws: "for forcibly entering into the manor of Chopwell with intention to kill and slay Ambrose Dudley esq, George Gifford and others at a place called Westwood, in which affray William Shafto struck the said George Gifford a mortal wound in the thigh, of which he soon died, with an iron lance".

The Rutherford gang were outlawed and the family's property, Black Hall, was forfeited to the Crown, although it does appear that in later years, after the furore had subsided, Charles Rutherford returned there and lived out the rest of his days unmolested by the law.

CHAPTER 10
OUTLAWS

SCATTERED across the upper Derwent Valley are dozens of pele towers, fortified farmsteads built around a well-defended centre. The towers are made with thickened stone walls to withstand attack and inside there is enough room for a farmer to gather his flock together for protection. Many now lie ruined, some are still there and others are just place names on a map. But for hundreds of years they were an essential means of defence for the farmers of the Derwent Valley faced with the nightly onslaught of the mosstroopers.

Mosstroopers and border reivers haunted the nightmares of Derwent Valley farmers for 500 years. They were little more than common cattle thieves, but their way of life became the stuff of myth and legend. In a land where it was often virtually impossible to eke out an existence, theft became an all too common means of survival. For centuries, the lawless border lands had been subject to periodic raids by the Scots and the theft of a neighbour's stock was so attractive an option in hard times that even the monks of Blanchland were known to join in. In Medieval times, such foraging for stock on neighbouring lands became a way of life. The border reivers were themselves farming families who owned lands and defended their own pele towers against theft from neighbours. But at night they would venture forth to steal, herding together those animals they could find and driving them back to their own farmsteads. The most famous reiver families lived in the wilds of Tynedale and targeted the Derwent Valley for attack, stealing animals at the point of a sword or later a pistol. But, as well as fighting off attack from the north, the Derwent Valley produced its own home-grown reivers, the ravines which criss-crossed the upper valley and countless moorland hideaways providing shelter for their midnight raids. At a time when life hung by a thread, losing a herd to the mosstroopers could have devastating consequences for a family and defences against their raids became ever more elaborate. By the 19th Century, the rule of law had driven the mosstroopers from memory - but not before they had etched themselves a permanent place in the history of the Derwent Valley.

The first recorded mosstrooper in the Derwent Valley was named Pedom, although it is difficult to say how much of his story is myth and how much is legend. He gave his name to the hamlet of Pedom's Oak, which has borne that name since at least 1380. He was said to raid at night into the Tyne and Wear valleys, driving the cattle back to his farmstead on the banks of the Derwent. For years he escaped undetected, but was eventually named in court and outlawed, which meant the bailiff could arrest him on sight. Pedom was forced to flee his farm to evade capture and took to the fells above the valley for some time, eventually taking refuge in a dense wood where the hamlet now stands. At the centre was a monstrous, decayed old oak tree. Pedom hollowed out the deadwood of the trunk and cleared a space inside which could hold him and up to 20 lambs at once.

From his new secret hideaway in the forest, Pedom was able to carry on his raids, living in the oak tree during the day and venturing out at night to carry off his neighbour's stock. The number of raids increased as Pedom, without his farm to support him, turned to theft as his only means of survival. The farmers of the Derwent Valley suspected the culprit, but Pedom always managed to elude them and make it safely back to his secret lair. He was never caught, but was eventually found lying dead next to his oak tree and his hideaway was discovered. The tree was felled by villagers and Pedom was buried beneath a cairn of stones on the spot where he was found.

With the oldest stories of the reivers, it is difficult to tell where legends based in truth end and straight-forward storytelling begins. Among the most popular stories dating back to this time is the legend of Stirling of Stirling's Bridge. On the banks of Hyselope Burn, near Healeyfield, are several mounds of stones - all that remains of a once significant village many centuries ago. According to legend, this village was once defended by a lone man named Stirling against the advances of a strong band of mosstroopers. The only bridge leading to the village was made up of two roughly hewn tree trunks, cut to the same length and stretched across the river to provide a simple crossing. As the outlaws approached the village, Stirling is said to have held off the entire gang despite repeated attempts to storm the bridge over the flooded river. Repulsing attack after attack, Stirling hacked at the bridge until finally he managed to dislodge the trunks which fell into the swollen river and left the reivers stranded on the far bank. However, as he made his one-man stand, a smaller group of the outlaws had moved further down the valley and managed to cross at Allensford, coming up behind him and cutting off his retreat. Outnumbered and surrounded, the valiant Stirling leapt for the far bank of the river rather than face being cut to pieces, but failed to reach safety and was swept away to his death in the fast-flowing current. The reivers, now safely across, turned their attention to the undefended village, murdering everyone they could find, looting the stock and finally burning the houses.

If some of the stories of the reivers may be a little fanciful, there are others which are well-documented and show how dangerous a profession it was, with many ending their days on the gallows. On January 21st, 1528, a band of Tynedale reivers led by William Charlton, alias Willie O'Shotlynton, the foremost raider of his day, entered County Durham at the head of a large gang which included the notorious outlaws Harry Noble, Archibald Dodd and Roger Armstrong. In one of the most daring raids carried out, the gang struck as far south as Wolsingham and drove off a large herd of cattle. As they returned, O'Shotlynton took his gang through Muggleswick where they stopped outside the house of the Reverend Father Forrest, priest to the scattered and lawless parish. Halting outside his home, O'Shotlynton called out loudly to the priest to come forth, for he had more useful work for him to do back in Northumberland. For good measure, he warned the priest that if he delayed he would perish in the flames of his own home. Father Forrest, believing O'Shotlynton was earnest and wanted him to be chaplain to his men back in Bedlington, came out. In fact, Father Forrest was wanted to act as an informer to provide details on where the reivers could raid in Muggleswick. The unsuspecting priest was seized and thrown on the back of a horse, where his feet were tied to prevent his escape. The procession of outlaws, cattle and kidnapped man of God then continued on their way north.

But, unknown to O'Shotlynton, while his men had been raiding and burning in Durham, the Bailiff of Hexham had assembled a band of men who awaited their return. When they reached the Tyne crossing at Hexham, O'Shotlynton found his way barred by a small army of men and turned to find another route home. The Tyne was in full mid-winter flood and he knew his chances were slim, but tried his last hope - a race to the crossing at Haydon Bridge. On arrival, his last hopes were dashed. A posse of men raised by the bailiff was already in place and the gates to the bridge were found to be "barred, chained and locked fast".

In the ensuing battle, O'Shotlynton and his friend Noble were killed and most of their men were captured. Two of them, Dodd and Armstrong, were executed. The bodies of the dead reivers were hung in chains, Dodd at Newcastle, Armstrong at Alnwick, O'Shotlynton at Hexham and Noble at Haydon Bridge as a warning to others. Meanwhile, Father Forrest was released and returned to Muggleswick, where he tended to the spiritual needs of his lawless flock until his death in 1550.

But by far the bloodiest recorded encounter in the wars between the reivers and farmers of north Durham came during the raid which became known as the Rookhope Ryde. Behind Whiteleas Farm on the road between Blanchland and Edmundbyers, the moor rises towards a ridge known as Knookton Edge. On this moor, the Rookhope Ryde came to an end with a bloody battle fought on December 8th, 1569. A band of reivers from Tynedale decided to take advantage of the ongoing Rising Of The North, when the northern earls, their supporters and their men-at-arms were distracted by the revolt against the rule of Queen Elizabeth I. The reivers, led by Henry Corbyl, Symon Fell and Martin Ridley were able to raise a force of 100 men and planned a hit-and-run raid into defenceless Weardale.

They moved undetected across the border into Durham, over the wide open expanse of Knookton Fell and entered Weardale Forest at Rookhope Head. In just four hours, the raiders gathered together 600 sheep and cattle from the unguarded forest pastures and began to drive them north towards their Tynedale homes. But by now the alarm had been raised. Word reached George Emmerson, the bailiff of Weardale Forest, and he set off to Eastgate where he raised a posse of 50 men to pursue the raiders. The Weardale men knew the land well and were able to move quickly, while the Tynedale reivers had to drive 600 animals across foreign country. The Weardale posse were able to overtake their quarry and chose to attack at Knookton Cleugh, a steep ravine surrounded by a bog passable only by a narrow track of dry ground.

By now the Tynedale reivers were strung out through the ravine, the leaders having almost reached the far side while the shepherds driving the animals were towards the rear. The Weardale men then charged down the sides of the ravine, firing their muskets and pistols. Panic spread through the reivers ranks. The sheep and cattle bolted, some charged up the narrow path, others hurtled headlong into the bog. The Tynedale men at the front tried to turn and come to help those at the rear, but their path was blocked and the terrified animals added to the confusion of the congested battle. For an hour, the two sides fired at each other. The battle finally ended when Henry Corbyl was killed. Three more of his men lay dead in the ravine and 11 of the reivers were captured while the others escaped to their Tynedale homes. Of the dalesmen, George Carrick was killed and several more were wounded.

The reivers' raids kept the Derwent Valley poor, despite having enough good farmland for the valley to prosper. The extent of the problem can be gauged from a survey carried out in 1569, the very year of the Rookhope Ryde. The survey of the Barony of Bolbec showed that it consisted at that time of Bromehaugh, Rydding, Helye, Shotley, Slaley and Mynstreacreas. It went on: "These places are very well inhabited with men of good service and have very good farms, able to keep many cattle and get plenty of corn and hay and were it not for the continued robberies and incursions of the thieves of Tynedale which so continually assault them in the night as they can keep no more cattle than they can house safely at night." Accurate as that picture may be, it neglects to mention the Derwent Valley's own home-grown mosstroopers.

In Muggleswick church there is a memorial stone dedicated to possibly the most infamous mosstrooper of them all. Rowland Harrison, known throughout the Derwent Valley as Rowley, died on September 24th, 1712 following a long and adventurous life of crime. Undoubtedly, Harrison was indeed a mosstrooper who operated in the Derwent Valley for many years, but several stories have grown up around his life which have added to his legend.

Throughout the late 17th Century, Harrison lived at The Shield, a small pele tower near Muggleswick where he farmed and regularly carried out raids on neighbouring dales in tough times. Harrison lived constantly in the shadow of the noose but always managed to escape undetected through the dale and was never brought before a court of law. The poet Barrass refers to one night in which Harrison stole eight cows and a bull from his neighbours, a feat he would repeat again and again over his career. Harrison lived with his wife, a member of the notorious Graeme clan of Cumberland, probably the most well-known reiver family in the North, and she had a reputation as fearsome as that of her husband. It was said that when her larder ran low, instead of serving meat to feed the family she would place his riding spur, known locally as a hough, in his dish as a sign that if the family were to eat, Harrison would first have to steal food for the table. According to the legend, when she did so she would utter the words: "Ride, Rowley, ride. The hough is in the pot." Although Harrison managed to avoid the clutches of the magistrates throughout his life, he was brought before an Ecclesiastical Court for his alleged sins against his neighbours and was ex-communicated - the gravest punishment which the church reserved. Consequently, when he died he was buried outside of the church walls on unhallowed ground. But in 1728, Muggleswick Church was rebuilt and extended to cover his grave - finally bringing Rowley Harrison back within the fold 16 years after his death.

According to local legend, witness after witness reported seeing Harrison's ghost riding across the moors above Muggleswick in the months after his death - carrying on his midnight raids from beyond the grave. The figure riding his black horse and brandishing his pistol was seen thundering down the moorland tracks near his old home at The Shield and farmers still reported their stock going missing overnight. The apparition which haunted Muggleswick overshadowed the approach of Christmas and children were kept behind locked doors at night. On Christmas Eve, 1712, a heavy snowstorm set in as midnight approached. Many villagers had gathered at the Black Bull Inn at Edmundbyers to celebrate, including four men from Muggleswick. As the snow fell harder, the landlord advised them to head for home and to keep their eyes open for Rowley Harrison as they crossed the moor. They left, heads bent against the wind as they trudged through the falling snow towards their own village. On the road, they were overtaken by a horseman, who headed down the track to The Shield - the home where Harrison had died more than three months earlier. Nervously, they followed and peered into the farmyard. Suddenly, the cloaked figure of Rowley Harrison emerged from the shadows, pistol in hand, and the four villagers backed away terrified into the empty barn behind them. It was two hours before they were found. Mounted militiamen, scouring the moors for mosstroopers, followed the tracks down to The Shield and found the four men cowering in the barn, which had been bolted from the outside. They were promptly arrested for being on the premises without a lawful reason, bound and were questioned.

Suddenly, as the lawmen listened to their implausible tale, out of the darkness rode a horseman at breakneck speed, swinging his sword above his head as a woman's voice cried: "Ride, Rowley, ride. Away out o'er the moors - they'll never get you," and the horseman thundered out of the farmyard and into the night. The bewildered militiamen took to their heels and fled themselves, leaving the four terrified villagers still bound in the barn. It was Christmas morning before the detachment returned and they were finally freed.

No-one knew what had become of Rowley Harrison's wife, who was thought to have called to her husband once more that night and no-one dared return to The Shield to find out. The apparition was seen regularly throughout the winter and spring, although less and less frequently and by the summer it appeared that the ghost had ceased his midnight rides. During the late summer, a farmer named George Proud bought land in Muggleswick and moved into the village, where the newcomer heard the ghostly tales of Rowley Harrison. Proud, however, dismissed the story as nonsense and boasted he would be willing to visit The Shield at midnight on Christmas Eve, alone, to prove his point. He even joked that he would bring along a plum pudding, mince pies and bottle of wine for Harrison should he meet him there.

Proud was good to his word, although he must have had a feeling of dread as he approached the darkened homestead with a lantern held high above his head. The flickering light cast a red glow on the darkened corners of the farmyard and as he pushed open the creaking door into the deserted farmhouse, the rats scurried away from its glare. His feet left impressions in the dust as he crept into the empty living room as his lantern lit the shadowy corners of the room. But he froze in terror when from the top of the unlit stairs he heard a woman's voice croak: "Ride, Rowley, ride, the hough is in the pot," which even the stranger knew was the cry which preceded the ride of the Rowley Harrison's ghost. Trembling, he climbed the stairs and pushed open the door at the top. Inside was a pitiful sight. Lying on a bed of rags was Rowley Harrison's widow, an old woman who seemed to be at death's door. Her eyes were wild and staring, but she was emaciated and weak with hunger.

The farmer sat on the edge of the filthy bed and gave the woman food, which she ate morsel by morsel. As she ate, she told Proud her story. Her father had been an honest farmer, who turned to thieving cattle when the family were threatened with starvation in hard times and had been joined in his battle for survival by his brothers. Eventually, she met and married Rowley and he too had become a mosstrooper to provide for her. But with her husband gone and no friends among her neighbours nor means of supporting herself, she had turned to the family trade herself, borrowing her dead husband's clothes and fearsome reputation. She raided her neighbours at night to steal enough food to live on. But as she grew ill and too weak to ride, she had been unable to feed herself and slipped ever closer to death in her filthy hovel.

According to Proud, she told him: "I am a Graeme. I am the last of the Graemes and I must be worthy of my name," and asked the visitor to return the following day. But as he made his way from the house, he was startled to see the stables fly open and the widow ride out on Rowley's black mare. She was once more dressed in his cloak and wearing his sword at her side. The widow Harrison called across the farmyard to him: "See, I go to Rowley and all the Graemes who have gone before. Goodbye." With that, she turned her horse and thundered off over the moors into the blackness. She was never seen again. The following day, several people living at Eddy's Bridge reported hearing a rider approach the swollen Derwent late at night, followed by a wild cry and the sound of something splashing into the river. And, according to the legend, the cry can still be heard on Christmas Eve when the snow lies thick - the cry of the last of the Graemes.

The outlaw way of life was coming to an end. At the same time as Rowley Harrison plied his midnight trade near Muggleswick, further down the valley lived Thomas Raw - the last of the mosstroopers. Between Castleside and Allensford, on the old road north to Scotland, lies Wharnley Burn Farm. The farm is one of the oldest inhabited buildings in the valley and was mentioned in the Boldon Buke. The Raw family farmed at Wharnley Burn for generations, when they were not fighting for the Crown in countless Border battles. Like his forefathers, Thomas Raw was also a mosstrooper, with a reputation as the wildest of them all. Historian Fred Wade wrote: "Raw had the reputation for being a bold, fearless man, plying his lawless trade where others dare not venture. He was a good horseman and his knowledge of the hills and dales of his native valley brought him safely home to Wharnley Burn after many a fruitless chase on the part of the border warden and his men."

Raw, like several of his contemporaries, was excommunicated by the church because of his sins which meant that on his death his corpse could not be buried in consecrated ground. Raw's name was called out in every church from Hunstanworth to Medomsley and in the market places of Hexham, Slaley, Stanhope and Wolsingham as an outlaw who was not to be admitted to church and who was not to be offered any assistance by his Christian neighbours. Despite the order, Raw carried on with his nightly work, stealing cattle and robbing his neighbours store houses before retreating to Wharnley Burn. The house was a thatched pele tower with three ground floor rooms. The middle room was Raw's bedroom which contained his great oak-carved bed and had a door which led directly to the stables so he could make his escape if ever the forces of law took him by surprise. It was, however, unlikely that the warden's men would be able to reach him. On a hill above the farm stood a great oak tree from where Raw could see for miles. The hill acted as his look-out point to allow him to make good his escape, not returning until the chase had died down.

Raw died peacefully in his bed on January 30[th.] 1714 and, in accordance with his wishes, was buried beneath the oak tree on his look-out hill, where his grave still lies. Scorched into the fireplace of Wharnley Burn farm were his initials, TR, where he practiced with his branding iron before he set out to capture cattle and claim them as his own. Here, as elsewhere between Allensford and Blanchland, the mark of the mosstroopers is still stamped on the Derwent Valley.

CHAPTER 11
THE TIMBER AND THE AXE

THE smallest and most unlikely of things can change the course of human history and, in part at least, the timber of the Derwent Valley would play a role in one of the defining moments of English history, a bloody civil war, the death of a king and the birth of Parliamentary democracy.

The great forest of the Derwent Valley had already provided timber for the building of Durham Cathedral, Bamburgh Castle, Dunstanburgh Castle and the bridge over the River Tyne. But in 1294, King Edward I found a new use for the valley's wood - warships. The king ordered the building of 20 galley ships to protect the coast of England, one of which was to be built at Newcastle and the shipwrights of the Tyne turned to Chopwell to provide the necessary wood.

More than 300 years later, his successor Charles I also turned his attention to the construction of a new warship. In 1635, the king ordered the building of a new flagship for his fleet - the mightiest warship ever to sail the seas. Phineas Pett, the greatest naval architect of his day, began work on the vessel, to be named The Sovereign Of The Seas. She was to be the first three-decked warship in history and the pride of the English fleet. Pett and his son Peter headed north, to the Crown estates at Chopwell to begin work. In June 1635, Pett's diary records that he arrived at Chopple Woods, and set his son to work. A small army of lumberjacks were soon at work in the wood, felling the thousands of great oaks needed for construction and the quiet forest began ringing to the sound of hundreds of axes hacking through the trunks. More foresters were sent to Brancepeth, while on the Tyne a great collier barge was prepared to take the timber south. In all, 2,500 trees were felled at Chopwell, a quarter of the enormous wood, along with 1,400 from Brancepeth. Heavy horses dragged the timber miles across country to the staithes at the Tyne where it was hauled aboard the barge and taken south on the tortuously slow journey to the naval dockyards at Woolwich on the Thames. The majestic ship Pett built, with decks, gunwales and cabins born on the banks of the Derwent, was like no other ever seen. She was 232 feet long and 48 feet wide, beautifully carved and guilded, while her three decks were armed with an array of 100 canon. The Sovereign Of The Seas was finally launched two years later, a marvel of her age. During a distinguished career, she saw repeated action in the wars with the Dutch and survived countless naval battles before she was finally destroyed in 1696 while in dry dock at Chatham after a lighted candle started a fire in a cook's cabin.

But the great warship was built at a heavy price. The bill for construction arrived at £41,000, plus another £25,000 for her canons and to meet the cost the king levied a new tax - Ship Money. Since the days of the Viking raids, the ports of England had been taxed to pay for the upkeep of the navy because they had most to gain from protection on the seas. But with his treasury empty and a great naval building programme underway, Charles ordered that the tax be paid by every town in the country, coastal or otherwise. This extra tax was met with anger across the country and became one of the prime causes of the coming civil war.

The relationship between king and commoners, as represented by Parliament, had been in decline throughout the reign of James I but matters would, quite literally, come to a head when his son Charles took the throne in 1625. The new king was arrogant, conceited and a firm believer in the divine right of kings - the theory which held that God had placed the monarch on the throne and that as God could not be wrong, neither could his choice of ruler. It left Charles on a collision course with a Parliament intent on asserting the rights of the people, or at least that section of the people which it represented.

The obstinate king and Parliament argued endlessly - particularly over taxation and religion. Finally, in 1629, Charles had the doors of Parliament padlocked to prevent the MPs from meeting. For 11 years, he ruled without allowing Parliament to sit and raised money through fines, the sale of titles and taxes imposed without consultation. The introduction of Ship Money in 1635 to pay for The Sovereign Of The Seas was the final straw and one MP, John Hampden, refused to pay the new tax. He was brought to court and convicted - but opposition to the monarch grew around him and his stand against the king.

The growing hostility to Charles escalated into open rebellion when the king made a disastrous foray north of the border which brought war to the Derwent Valley. The king, fired by his belief in

The earliest surviving map of County Durham, created by John Speed in 1610, shows the development of the Derwent Valley (Picture courtesy of Durham County Council Cultural Services)

The ford at Ebchester where the Scots crossed the Derwent on the way to capture Durham (Photograph courtesy of Beamish Museum)

his divine right to rule, attempted to impose a new prayer book on Scotland which would have forced the Scottish bishops to adopt Anglican practices. The decision provoked fury in Scotland, where Charles' Catholic wife and Popish ways were viewed with deep suspicion. There were riots and the leaders of the Presbyterian Church met in Edinburgh to sign The Covenant of the Scottish Presbyterians - some in their own blood - to resist the changes. Preparations for war got underway and when word reached an incensed Charles that the Scots were again plotting an alliance with the French, he determined to send an army against them to impose his will. However, Charles' coffers were bare and - much to his frustration - the king was forced to recall Parliament to raise the money he needed for his war.

When Parliament finally met in 1640, not only were the majority opposed to any sort of military expedition against Scotland, they used the opportunity to air all the pent-up grievances which had festered for the last 11 years. A furious Charles immediately closed Parliament down again and launched his war against Scotland without the backing of his MPs.

It was a disaster. In August, a Scottish army made up of 20,000 foot soldiers and 2,500 cavalrymen under the brilliant general Alexander Leslie, the earl of Leven, marched into England and within five days had reached the Tyne. Facing him were an English army stationed at Newcastle under Lord Conway - a large enough body of men but made up of dispirited troops far from their London home. Leslie ruled out a frontal attack on the well-defended city and decided to cross the Tyne into Durham where he could attack Newcastle from the Gateshead bank. The bulk of the Scottish army was sent to find a way across the Tyne and arrived at the village of Newburn, opposite Stella Haugh, close to the mouth of the Derwent. Here the steep gorse-lined banks which flanked the Tyne gave way to flat meadows where the river could be forded in four separate places between the reed beds. Conway ordered a detachment of the English army out of Newcastle to halt the enemy and 3,000 infantrymen and 1,500 horse dashed along the southern bank with orders to defend the crossing at all costs. To keep Leslie's men at bay, the English hastily constructed two great earthwork forts by the river and placed 400 sharpshooters armed with muskets and four pieces of canon in each. But the Scots already had the higher ground on the north bank of the river, placing their own canon overlooking the battlefield and soldiers in positions in the houses, lanes, hedgerows and church tower of Newburn. One English soldier's letter home summed up the gloomy mood among the English infantry: "Their army appeared marching on the hills above the ford when we were drawing into our miserable works in the valley where we lay so exposed". As his men spent the night in the forts awaiting the morning's battle, Lord Conway set up his headquarters in Stella Hall.

At about 1pm on August 28th, 1640, a Scottish cavalry officer wearing a black feather in his hat rode down to the Tyne to allow his horse to drink and was felled by a single shot from an English sniper. It proved the signal for battle to start. As the English guns fired at the ranks of Scottish cavalry waiting to cross the river, Leslie's artillery pulverised the English defences and snipers on both sides picked off the enemy. For three hours, the canon blazed until the largest of the two forts received a direct hit, killing 20 English soldiers. The breastworks were breached and the defenders, having watched their comrades cut to pieces by the explosions with no word of reinforcements, fled. At low water, the first detachments of Scots cavalry forded the Tyne and were met by their English counterparts in a fierce battle among the narrow lanes in which the English initially got the upper hand. But now, all the artillery fire the Scots could muster was poured into the second fort and its defences crumbled. With both forts pounded to dust, thousands of Scottish infantry waded across the Tyne and the remnants of the English army ran. Around 60 of their comrades lay dead, mostly in the forts which had been blasted apart by canon fire, and as many as 200 Scots lay on the battlefield alongside them. One contemporary observer described it as: "an infamous and irreparable rout. Never had so many ran from so few with less ado."

That night Leslie's army camped at Ryton and celebrated their great victory. There is a story that, as the Scots crossed the Tyne, a large portion of the king's men were encamped at Whickham and the arrival of the enemy caused panic among the soldiers and the general population alike. One account recalled: "The parsons of Ryton and of Whickham first rifled their own houses and then fled, leaving nothing but a few prayer books and pamphlets, and one old cloake, with an old woman being the only living Christian in the towne, the rest being fled." Indeed, so great was the soldiers' hurry to escape the advancing Scots that they didn't have time to decamp and instead set fire to their tents to prevent them falling into enemy hands. This blaze is said to have spread to an outcrop of an underground coal seam which burnt for 30 years afterwards - and at night flames and smoke issued from underground at various places around the valley much to the consternation of the residents.

The Scots marched into Newcastle and, three days later, walked unopposed into Durham City. The remnants of Charles' army had fled before them, stripping the city of weapons and supplies on the way south. Rushworth wrote: "As far as the City of Durham, it became a most depopulated place; not one shop for four days after the fight open; not one house in ten that had either man, woman, or child in it; not one bit of bread to be got for money for the King's army had eat and drank all in their march to Yorkshire; the country people durst not come to market, which made the city in a sad condition for want of food."

The Scots occupied Durham for a year and demanded tax of £350 per day be paid by the citizens to feed the occupying army. When it was slow in coming, the invaders smashed their way into the great cathedral and desecrated some of the artefacts they found there. When the army finally left in 1641, they had sown the bitter seeds of hatred which their kinsmen would reap less than 10 years later.

Humiliated, Charles was forced to recall Parliament in November 1640 where the MPs flexed their muscles and demanded a series of concessions from the king. But with king and Parliament now implacable enemies, the final showdown was merely postponed. It came little more than a year later on January 4th, 1642, when the king sent troops to Parliament to arrest five of his bitterest critics. Word reached Parliament and the men were spirited away, but it was the spark which lit the flame.

Charles left London and began to recruit troops to impose his will on the rebellious MPs while the Parliament also began to stockpile weapons and raise an army. In August 1642, Charles raised his standard at Nottingham and the civil war was underway.

As the nation embarked on this fratricidal war between Royalist cavaliers and Parliamentary roundheads, every corner of the country was forced to choose sides. By and large, the North-East supported the king with Newcastle in particular a Royalist stronghold. But there were those who held out for Parliament, including many among the Puritan communities of the upper Derwent Valley. The civil war tore apart villages and even families.

In the North-East there was the added complication of the ever-present threat from Scotland. There was a requirement already in place that tenants must be prepared to provide men, equipment and horses if necessary for border service and during this period Muggleswick and Edmundbyers provided 32 men and horses for duty. So the defence of the Derwent Valley fell not just on regular soldiers but on every able-bodied man who lived there.

Initially, things went well for the king, although he was unable to force a decisive victory. After a year of successive defeats, Parliament was forced into drastic action and, during the winter of 1643, drew up an alliance with the Scots - the Solemn League and Covenant - which promised the Scots the religious reforms they demanded in exchange for military help. It was to prove one of the turning points in the war and put the Derwent Valley once more in the frontline of the fighting.

In January 1644, an invasion force poured south into England. Alexander Leslie, returned once more with a Scottish army of 15,000 foot soldiers, 3,000 horse, 500 dragoons and 120 artillery guns.

Many Scottish incursions had taken place over the centuries but none as big as this and none with the support of at least some of the English. Facing the Scots was a tiny Royalist army under Sir Thomas Glemham, only half of them armed. Pitifully outnumbered and outgunned, they had no option but to retreat behind Newcastle's city walls, where they were joined by a local militia raised by the mayor. The Scots raced towards Newcastle, but English reinforcements reached the city just one day before Leslie arrived. The Scots stormed the outpost at Shieldfield but stopped short of an all out attack on the city and instead opted for a siege.

Leslie's Scots then wheeled around and turned to the south and found themselves encamped on the north bank of the flooded Derwent at Ebchester. To carry the massive army across the river, the Scots began cutting down trees to build a massive bridge. It took three whole days to construct and was as impressive a feat of engineering as ever graced the banks of the River Derwent. Across it now rolled the largest army ever to invade County Durham which would turn the course of the civil war in the North. Half the might of the Scottish army crossed the river during the last night of February, the remainder making the journey on March 1st, watched by the bewildered villagers and on through Medomsley to Chester-le-Street. After victories there and at Hylton Castle, they captured Sunderland and tightened the noose on Newcastle. The city finally fell on October 19th and the whole area was to be under Scottish occupation for more than two years.

The intervention of the Scots and the capture of the North helped Parliament turn the course of the war. Over the next two years, the Roundheads won battle after battle until Charles was eventually captured in 1646 and held prisoner while Parliament debated what to do with him. However, the king escaped and launched a second brief war in an attempt to win back his throne, but it proved futile and instead simply hardened hearts among the Parliamentarians. Finally, Charles was put on trial for treason and, though defiant to the last, was convicted. On January 30th, 1649, King Charles I was taken to the scaffold and beheaded.

The execution of the king did not put an end to the wars. His heir was proclaimed King Charles II by the Royalists - a move supported by some of the Parliamentarians, many of whom were not republicans opposed to the monarchy itself, merely to the excesses of Charles I. In fact, most were appalled at his execution. Only when the army marched on Parliament, arrested 45 MPs and prevented another 146 from entering the building did the remaining 75 members charge the king with treason - and few of those were prepared to sign his death warrant. Showing a great deal more political skill than his late father, Charles II agreed a deal which persuaded the Scots to change sides - and it fell to Oliver Cromwell himself to lead a force north to take on the renewed Scottish threat.

Today, Clockburn Lonnen is little more than an overgrown track which leads from Durham City to the Derwent at old Winlaton Mill, then on to Winlaton and Newburn on the Tyne. In the mid 17th Century however, it was the main highway to the north and it was down this road that Cromwell led his army of 16,000 men, eight regiments of cavalry and eight regiments of foot, including the newly-formed Coldstream Guards. Cromwell encamped at Whickham, where the parish church records the overnight death of one of his soldiers, although the cause is not clear. Cromwell's army was well-fed, they were reportedly loaded down with bread, cheese and biscuits, but what they lacked were tents. Cromwell himself slept in one of the village's cottages and there were 100 small tents provided for the officers, but the rest of the men had to fend for themselves in the barns they found or else sleep in the fields.

On the morning of July 15th, 1650, Cromwell's army headed north along Clockburn Lonnen to Winlaton and on to battle. Seven days later they crossed into Scotland and marched on Edinburgh. Facing Cromwell was the brilliant Leslie, who six years earlier had brought his troops into England via Ebchester and had fought alongside Cromwell at Marston Moor. Now the two were implacable enemies. Leslie chose to fight a guerrilla war and harried and harassed the English at every turn. The frustrated Roundheads walked into ambush after ambush and the number of dead mounted with every skirmish. The English were also running out of supplies and, as the weather turned for the worse, thousands fell sick from exposure.

By the time the English reached Edinburgh, 4,000 of Cromwell's men - a quarter of his army - were too ill to fight. After a brief siege they decided to cut their losses and head home, Leslie was now closing in to destroy what was left of the English army, bottled up on a narrow strip of land outside the town of Dunbar. One English officer wrote home that he commanded: "a poor, shattered, hungry, discouraged army." Surrounded, exhausted and facing annihilation, Cromwell was staring disaster in the face but for a remarkable turn of events. Although Leslie was in day-to-day command of his troops, the supreme commanders were the committee of the Covenanters - the group of senior Presbyterian churchmen who had signed the Covenant and who insisted in meddling in the battle plans and upholding public morals. Around 3,000 of Leslie's best men were sent home for swearing, the general was denied permission to fight on a Sunday when the English were unprepared and, finally, the ministers insisted he abandon his impregnable defences and fight in open country to prove the righteousness of their cause. Cromwell launched an audacious attack before dawn and in ferocious combat routed the Scots. His army, which by now numbered only 11,000 men, took 10,000 Scottish prisoners that day. The English had little choice but to release the wounded and the dying, to fend for themselves. The remaining 5,000 prisoners were to become part of one of the most shameful episodes of British history, known in Scotland as The Durham Death March.

The Scots were to be brought back to England to prevent them from re-enlisting in Leslie's army. Once south of the border, they were to be transported to the colonies to act as slave labour on the plantations. At the crack of dawn on September 4th, the march began. The prisoners covered the 28 miles to Berwick in one day, arriving well after dark that night. Along the way, dozens tried to escape and every one was executed on the spot. The English soldiers ate from Scottish supplies captured at the battle - but there was nothing for the prisoners. Civilians tossed them a little bread as they passed, but it amounted to very little. They quenched their thirst in puddles on the roadside and from rancid pools in the ditches as they passed. Within a matter of hours, the first started falling sick.

Dysentery and typhoid began to set in among the bedraggled Scots - and they began to fall. When they arrived at Morpeth, the prisoners were held in a walled cabbage field, where they stuffed themselves with the raw vegetables, leaves and roots. It poisoned their bodies and more and more fell by the wayside. Dozens now lay dead in the Northumbrian countryside, the ditches filling with their corpses. They died of their wounds, they died of exhaustion, they died of disease and they lay where they fell. When they arrived at Newcastle, the Scots were held in St Nicholas' Cathedral for the night. In the morning, 500 could not get up from the pews. The last stretch was the worst. The contorted faces of the prisoners as they made their painful progress along Clockburn Lonnen told their own story. Late in the afternoon of September 11th - a week after setting off from Dunbar - the march finally staggered into Durham. Only 3,000 of the Scots made it, more than 2,000 lay dead by the roadside. For the survivors, their sorrow was only just beginning.

When the Scots occupied Durham from 1640 to 1642, they had exacted a heavy price from the citizens and it had not been forgotten. Now the Scots were imprisoned in the same great cathedral and were given no fuel and little food. Sir Arthur Haselrigge, Cromwell's man in Newcastle, was nominally in charge of the prisoners and ordered the mayor of Durham to ensure they receive whatever provisions were necessary. He told Parliament that the prisoners were sent a daily supply of bread, ate pottage made of oatmeal, beef and cabbage and that the sick were treated in a hospital in the castle where they ate mutton broth and veal broth.

The reality was very different. Tons of supplies sent from Newcastle and relief from the villages of Durham was siphoned off by the guards. Those prisoners who had money or jewellery could buy food, but most of the supplies were sold on in the markets of Durham. Weakened by disease and exhaustion and now starved by their captors, 30 men a day were dying in the splendour of the great cathedral. Haselrigge, ensconced in his headquarters in Newcastle, was at a loss to explain the continuing deaths despite the constant flow of supplies. He wrote: "Notwithstanding all this, many of them died - and few of any other disease than the flux (dysentery). Some were killed by themselves, for they were exceedingly cruel one towards the other. If any man was perceived to have any money, it was two to one he was killed before morning and robbed. If any had good clothes that a prisoner wanted, he would strangle the other and put on his clothes. They were so unruly, sluttish and nasty that it is not to be believed. They acted like beasts rather than men."

As September turned into October, the cold began to bite. The supplies of coal sent to the prisoners went the same way as the food and the Scots resorted to tearing the cathedral apart for firewood. Every sliver of wood was taken and burnt, regardless of its religious significance. The pews, the altar and great carvings, all made from oak felled on the banks of the Derwent, went into the fire. The tombs were ripped open and destroyed in the hunt for firewood and jewellery to buy food. The graves of the Neville family in particular were desecrated and the bones of the skeletons scattered around the church. And all the while the death rate crept up until be the end of the month 100 men a day died in Durham - their remains tossed into a mass burial pit in the sacred grounds of the cathedral.

By the end of October, 1,600 prisoners had died in Durham Cathedral - sometimes slowly by starvation, sometimes quickly by murder, sometimes agonisingly by disease. Of the 5,100 men who began the march from Dunbar, just 1,400 were left alive two months later. Of the survivors, 900 were transported to the American colonies to work as slaves on the plantations of New England and Barbados, the rest were drafted into the army.

Amid the wild enthusiasm for Cromwell's vital victory at Dunbar, the stain of what followed in Durham's lanes and great cathedral was all but forgotten. Cromwell was proclaimed Lord Protector of England at the head of The Commonwealth - the culmination of a decade of bloodshed. It was to last for just 11 brief years.

In the final days of the Commonwealth, it became increasingly obvious that the monarchy was to be restored. Cromwell himself had been offered the Crown but refused - having spent a decade trying to overturn the authority of kings he was not to become one himself. There were those who argued vehemently for the establishment of a permanent Republic - among them John Hall of Shotley Bridge who became a leading writer on the subject. But the nation, tired of warfare and turning against the austerity of the Puritans, seemed overwhelmingly in favour of the return of the Stuart dynasty. At this time, in spring 1660, a mysterious stranger named Selby came to live in the Derwent Valley at Winlaton. For several months he kept himself to himself save for one thing - he craved news of the national political situation. In an age before mass communication, when information travelled slowly from one corner of the kingdom to another, such detail was hard to come by but Selby distinguished himself by inquiring over the state of the nation and whether the monarchy was to be restored. Finally, on May 8th, Charles Stuart returned from exile and was proclaimed King Charles II. The new king, anxious to put and end to the fratricide which had plagued England for a generation immediately passed an Act of

Indemnity - which pardoned all those involved in the previous government from accusations of treachery - except for one group, those who had signed the death warrant of his father Charles I. Within hours of the news reaching the Derwent Valley, Selby walked off into Winlaton Woods and hanged himself. Rumours soon spread that Selby was in fact one of the regicides who had signed away the life of the old king. As a suicide, Selby was denied a Christian burial in consecrated ground. Instead his body was removed and, at midnight, was taken to a crossroads half a mile north of Winlaton. There a stake was driven through his heart to exorcise his ghost and, in a token show of abhorrence for what he had done, each villager paraded passed his grave and threw three stones until a small pile of rocks grew up on his final resting place.

Muggleswick Churchyard (Photograph by Brian Clough)

CHAPTER 12
PLOT

FOLLOWING the Parliamentarian victory in the civil war, many Royalist sympathisers found there was a price to be paid for supporting the losing side. The Royalists were often Anglicans, Cromwell's Parliamentary roundheads were a stronghold of Puritanism, the strict Protestant sect. So the civil war was not just a political struggle, it also had fairly well-defined religious tones which regularly came to the surface. Priests, then cornerstones of every community, were forcibly removed from their parishes if they found themselves in opposition to the new rulers.

One such priest was John Duery, who in 1629 was appointed to the parish of Edmundbyers where he preached for 20 years. But in 1649, the victorious Parliamentary forces sent commissioners to the Derwent Valley to survey their newly-won domain and Duery was expelled from his office for protesting loyalty to the Crown from his pulpit. Along with the loss of his job and his living, expulsion meant the loss of his home and he was forced to leave the village. But in 1660, Duery returned to his parish, re-appointed as village priest by the newly-restored King Charles II.

In neighbouring Muggleswick, the transition was even more turbulent. In November 1641, the Rev Richard Bradley was appointed priest of the parish where he found himself at odds with his new flock, a Royalist cleric among a congregation of Puritans. Within a year of his arrival, civil war had broken out and he found himself increasingly isolated among a community which refused to worship with him or to take the sacraments. Eventually, Bradley reported dozens of his flock to the law for absenting themselves from Communion - then a punishable offence. This bitter stand off between priest and congregation continued for several years until eventually, in the later stages of the war, Bradley, along with many other Durham priests, fled the invading Scottish army. The newly-liberated Puritans of Muggleswick appointed their own priest to take charge of matters spiritual - Thomas Roger, a man whose views echoed their own.

However, on the restoration of the monarchy, Puritan preachers were removed from office across the country. Thomas Roger, like his brethren elsewhere, was thrown out of the parish he had ministered to for 15 years, much to the disgust of his flock. For a year and more, the parish of Muggleswick was left without a priest until finally their patience was exhausted and a delegation of worshippers approached the minister of Ryton, who was also prebend of Durham, to ask for a replacement. What they were told infuriated them even more. Durham had decided to make John Duery, the priest of Edmundbyers and as far removed from Puritan sympathies as was possible, the new minister for Muggleswick.

In 1661, the rebellious Puritans of Muggleswick drew up a petition, signed by 62 of them, including women and children, insisting Duery was an unsuitable candidate. All the signatories had previously been indicted by Bradley for absenting themselves from Communion. The petition presented to the House of Commons on their behalf by George Lilburne MP, complained they had been without a suitable preacher: "yea, ever since any of us that are now breathing were borne, to our soul's great griefe and dreadful hazard of destruction." They went further, refusing to accept Duery as their new priest in the harshest of language: "because we knew him to be no preacher and his life and conversation scandalous ... a simple, yea we dare say, sinful minister who is ignorant of the very principles of religion."

The recalcitrant flock made life so difficult for the church's new appointment that he left within a year and Muggleswick was once more without a priest. Eventually, they appointed their own, an unnamed minister who was more sympathetic to their views. But when senior churchmen at Durham got wind of the new appointment, they sent their own priest, by the name of Braidley, to take over at Muggleswick. Farcical scenes followed. When Braidley arrived in Muggleswick, he refused to take services for his rebellious worshippers - and refused to allow anyone else to do so. Within weeks the Puritans were locked out of the church, forcing them to hold outdoor services. The situation then degenerated further, as the rivals tried to out-shout each other as both preached sermons at the same time, even using the church bells to drown out the other's words. The petition signed by the Muggleswick men goes on to describe Braidley as: "one of the most deboist amongst the sonnes of men for hee will neither preach himself, nor yet permit others; but upon the Sabbath day he took the locke from the church doore and fastened on one of his owne so that the parishioners were forced to stand in the church yard to discharge their divine duties with their minister in cold, frost and snow to the infinite dishonour of the Almightie, the great griefe of their minds and the dreadful indangering of themselves in that stormy time of the yeare; other times before, he came into the church whilst our minister was in his exhortation and stood up beside him reading with a loud voyce in a book to overtop the sound of his words; afterwards pulled him by the coate while hee was in the pulpit; but when neither of these would cause him to desist from duty, he goes and rings the bell all aloud."

It was against this backdrop that the mysterious events of the Muggleswick Plot unfolded - a fiercely independent Puritan population fresh from civil war which suddenly found itself back under a restored monarchy and an established church trying to impose its will on its rebellious parishioners. In 1662, at the height of the zealous battle between Braidley and his rival minister, the first murmured rumours began to spread of a conspiracy centred on Muggleswick - a conspiracy which had no less an aim than the overthrow of the Royalist government and a return to the Puritan Commonwealth. To this day, the plot remains shrouded in mystery and there are those who maintain that there was in fact no conspiracy - merely an overreaction by jittery authorities terrified at a return to the bloodshed of the civil war. But there does seem to be some evidence that dark forces were at work on the moors of Muggleswick Park that spring and summer - secretly meeting at the dead of night among the secluded ravines and gullies to plot their next move.

The newly-formed Baptist church was suspected of playing a central role in the conspiracy. John Ward, a lead mining agent from Muggleswick, was born in 1630 and became a member of the first Baptist church in the Derwent Valley. He was baptized on October 13th, 1652 by preacher Thomas Tillam and within three years had been elected an elder of the church, joined in the new faith by his wife Eleanor. Thomas Tillam left the north in 1656 to preach elsewhere, leaving John Ward as the founding father of the fledgling church in the Derwent Valley with fellow members John Jopling of Foxholes, Anthony and Elizabeth Hunter of Edmundbyers and other locals John Redshaw and Joseph Hopper. The Baptist church at Rowley, which opened in 1652 - the year Tillam baptised John Ward

- is reputedly the oldest in England but if today the religion is respected, in the 17th Century it was greeted with a mixture if suspicion and ridicule. All new members of the church were baptized in the River Derwent at Eddy's Bridge and the ceremonies drew a large crowd of spectators from the curious locals.

The strict Baptists were closely associated with the Puritan movement whose leaders favoured the abolition of the monarchy and the restoration of the Commonwealth which had flourished under Oliver Cromwell. Some northern Puritans were known to favour the armed overthrow of King Charles II and the authorities, over whelmingly backed by the local gentry, were on edge for their opponents to make a move. Religious tension was in the air and it became known that several seditious meetings had been held in Muggleswick Park, the huge tract of open land on the border of the valley. The plotters took advantage of the area's reputation as a hotbed of witchcraft to keep the curious at bay as horsemen rode in to meet at the ruins of the old priory. The fear among the authorities was that someone would emerge "to lead the psalm-singing rascals on the banks of the Derwent."

In March 1662, the spark was lit when John Ellerington of Blanchland approached the local justices of the peace to say that he had been present at some of the seditious meetings and he wished to inform on his co-conspirators. Before the justices of the peace, he swore an oath implicating the Baptists of Muggleswick in a bloody plot to overthrow the king and church. His statement read: "That he hath known divers seditious meetings in Muggleswick Park within the last six months, sometimes in the house of one John Ward, who is one of their chief preachers, sometimes at the house of John Readshaw, Robert Blenkinsopp and Rowland Harrison who were met together."

Ellerington then went on to name a succession of plotters who he had heard making plans for the rising, including many residents of the Derwent Valley. These people, he claimed, had come together to secretly swear allegiance to this plot and gave details of their murderous intentions. They met, he said on Muggleswick Common: "where they did mutually take an oath of secrecy not to discover their design, which was to rise in rebellion against the present government and to destroy the present Parliament which had made a law against liberty of conscience, and to murder all bishops, deans

107

and chapters, and all ministers of the church and to break all organs in pieces and to destroy the common prayer books and to pull down all churches; and farther, to kill the gentry that should either oppose them or not join with them in their design. That they intended first to fall upon Durham, to seize any magazine that might be there, or money in any treasurer's hands, and the plunder of the town."

His statement went on: "That they did boast of many thousands of Annabaptists and Independents that were to join with them in the nation, with whom they had daily correspondence by letters and messengers, upon which employment the said informant had been divers times sent to divers persons; and he heard them lately say that some Papists were lately come to their party."

The rising, he said, had been set to take place on March 25th, three days after he approached the magistrates, but at the last moment the plotters had agreed to postpone it for a month to see whether Parliament would make any concessions to their cause. A small number of Catholics, claimed Ellerington, had lately agreed to join the revolt and the plotters felt that their numbers would swell with every day they delayed thereby increasing their chances of success. He added that plotter Lewis Frost of South Shields, had undertaken to use the delay to provide arms and ammunition.

Ellerington's statement caused panic in high places. Alarm spread through the cloisters of Durham Cathedral among the bishop and his closest advisors who, if Ellerington's evidence was to be believed, were themselves in imminent mortal danger. The plot, he told them, was part of a national uprising planned for October 12th, 1663 when they would seize Newcastle, Durham and York and await their brethren around the country taking control of other cities. Having just emerged from the Commonwealth and the dark days of the civil war, the fledgling monarchy and its agents in the provinces took such reports seriously. Some of the allegations had a ring of truth about them. There was a significant opposition to the restoration across the country, the new Baptists were viewed with widespread suspicion and anger was fermenting over the new Bartholomew Act, which amended the Book of Common Prayer along High Church lines.

The Bishop of Durham turned out his militia who rushed to Muggleswick looking for an armed insurrection. They found only the hapless John Hopper of Black Hedley, who was travelling home on horseback from Ireland and, although armed, he played no part in the alleged plot. The Puritan armies, if ever they existed, had vanished into the moorland mist. But the militiamen, under the command of Sir Thomas Davison, stayed in Muggleswick and declared a form of martial law. Every household in the lawless district was ordered to light up a candle and hang it in the window all night to prove the inhabitants were home. The meetings, however, are thought to have continued under cover of night. Over the coming months, dozens of suspected plotters were arrested and the net spread wider to capture alleged leaders of the movement around the country. As the list of arrested men grew ever longer, the local gentry armed their retinue for protection against the rebels.

Meanwhile, back in Durham, Ellerington was warming to his task. Whether he was persuaded to do so, or whether he welcomed the attention his allegations received, his claims grew ever more outlandish. So far, the list of plotters covered only the yeomen farmers and members of suspect religious sects. But in his second statement, Ellerington turned to members of the gentry. He implicated the Presbyterian Timothy Whittingham of Holmside and the Sunderland MP George Lilburne, who had earlier presented the petition to Parliament on behalf of the Muggleswick faithful. Despite both being of high rank, they were immediately arrested and detained for three months before being released when no evidence could be found against them. Ellerington also named Sir Henry Witherington of Northumberland, a former MP and High Sheriff of the county, and Edward Fenwick of Stanton. These latter two were believed to be Catholics and were left alone by the authorities who, despite their nerves, could see how preposterous was Ellerington's claim that two leading papists would join an enterprise to depose Charles II and replace him with a new Cromwell.

Although evidence for the existence of a plot was looking increasingly shaky, tensions remained high for a year. Troops of horse were stationed at Durham throughout 1663 and loyal addresses flowed into the palace from every corner of the country, while armed associations were formed for the defence of the realm. An investigation into the alleged plot took place and, eventually, in December 1663, justices Henry Widdrington, James Ogle and Ralph Jennison were brought together to examine witnesses.

On December 1st, 1663, George Proud of Ebchester gave evidence that he had heard that two troops of horse were gathered at The Hollins, opposite Ebchester. He also gave evidence that he had witnessed two heavily armed scouts, each carrying a glittering broadsword, ford the river at Ebchester. Neighbour Thomas Richardson gave evidence to the inquiry that he had heard armies of men with swords had been seen riding between Ebchester and Shotley Bridge under the command of John Hopper. The evidence for a plot was subsiding - only second hand accounts emerged before the justices, no-one had actually seen the armies of cutthroat Puritans for themselves. When John Hopper was called to give evidence, in which he told that he had returned from Ireland after staying with friends for five or six weeks and had been spotted armed and on horseback on the banks of the Derwent, it appeared the entire plot had hinged on a case of mistaken identity.

But, if there was no armed insurrection, there was still evidence that secret oaths of sedition had been sworn on Muggleswick's bleak moors. The leader was alleged to be John Jopling, the Baptist. Jopling had been the gaoler of Durham before he lost his job on the restoration of the monarchy. Ironically, he now found himself behind the bars of his own prison. John Ward, the Baptist minister and the plotters' own preacher, was also taken. John Redshaw, a third member of the Baptist congregation was arrested, along with Lieutenant Colonel Paul Hobson. Rowland Harrison, who would later become infamous throughout the Derwent Valley as a mosstrooper, was thrown into prison along with brothers John and Mark Taylor of Eddy's Bridge, John March of Eddy's Bridge, George Readshaw, John Oliver and Ralph Isley of Edmundbyers and Michael Ward of Shotleyfields.

In all, 12 men from Muggleswick parish and dozens more from elsewhere in the north: Sunderland, South Shields, Crawcrook and elsewhere were arrested and gaoled for their part in the conspiracy, although their sentences appear to have been lenient. The heaviest sentences were reserved for Jopling, who spent many years in prison, and Hobson, who was sentenced to be transported to Jamaica and spent the remainder of his days as far removed from the wild moors of Muggleswick as could be imagined.

CHAPTER 13
THE DEVIL IN THE DALE

THE men in the fields saw them first. The hoes fell silent, the digging came to a halt as they watched, in ominous silence, the procession moved up the rutted track, kicking up dust. They came up the road from Newcastle, slowly trundling their way along the twisted pack road. As the labourers dropped their tools and made their way back to the village, one by one their neighbours came from their homes, women clutching the children close, and gathered together, staring into the early summer sun. At the head of the mounted procession came the learned justices, Sir James Clavering and Sir Richard Stote, sombre in their judicial regalia. Behind them rode a small posse of militia flanking the simple cart, which was rocked by the deep ruts left by the hundreds of cartwheels which had passed this way before. In the back sat the poor, bewildered servant girl Ann Armstrong - self-confessed witch.

The villagers of Edmundbyers assembled in hushed fear, craning their necks to get a view of the witch who had afflicted them for months, but also fearful of catching her gaze less the evil eye fall upon them. This servant of Satan had come to reveal her accomplice, the witch who hid among them as their neighbour yet rode at night to her coven to plot mischief against the village. Armstrong's eyes passed along the line, examining each face in turn before her gaze finally settled on the old woman and she raised a trembling arm to point at Dorothy Green. Amid the disbelief of the villagers and her frantic protestations of innocence, militiamen roughly bundled the widow woman into the back of the cart along with her accuser and the procession turned. The last time Dorothy Green ever saw her Edmundbyers home was from the back of the cart as they led her away up the rutted road to Newcastle.

Throughout the spring and early summer of 1673, terror spread up and down the Derwent Valley. Ann Armstrong, a simple teenage servant girl from nearby Birkenside Nook, had confessed to witchcraft and a full investigation was launched. Rumours of satanic worship and covens spread, neighbours came under suspicion and more and more outlandish stories spread. The bounty for denouncing a witch could be as high as £2, a then tidy sum, which

The fear of witches was so great that in one day in August 1650, 16 supposed servants of Satan were hanged in one day on Newcastle's Town Moor, as this contemporary illustration from Ralph Gardner's England's Grievance Discovered In Relation To The Coal Trade shows (Photograph courtesy of Beamish Museum)

provided a further incentive to root out the evil in their midst. Belief in the occult was almost universal and every 17th Century village had its suspected witch, but the Derwent Valley had more than most.

Evidence of witchcraft appears to be as old as Satan himself, but in years gone by the punishments had not necessarily been as severe as might be suspected. In 1582, for instance, a "notorious enchanter and sorcerer" had been sentenced to do penance in the centre of Durham wearing a paper bag over her head and then do the same at two other local parish churches. Humiliating it may have been, but it could hardly be described as brutal. Things changed with the emergence of the Puritans - religious zealots who saw the Devil's work everywhere and were fired with righteous fervour to do battle with the forces of evil. During the late 1640s, the notorious witch-finder general Matthew Hopkins brought more than 100 men and women to the gallows in East Anglia as he sought to rid England of the curse of witchcraft. Three years later, the great witch trials came to the North-East.

In 1649, a witch-hunt swept across Newcastle. The city had supported the losing Royalist cause during the civil war and the local magistrates, anxious to prove their Puritan credentials with their new rulers, let loose a witch panic. It began in March when a series of minor incidents and everyday mishaps across the city were said to be the work of witches. Within weeks, the terrified citizens saw the Devil's hand everywhere, accusations flew and the common council of the town sent two constables north to Scotland to hunt for an infamous witch-finder, whose name is not recorded, to search out the servants of Satan in the city. That year, the witch-finder had been in Berwick where he brought 30 alleged witches to justice and was paid 20 shillings for each. He agreed to rid Newcastle of its witches for the same price - and he ensured he was paid handsomely.

Over the coming months, 30 poor women were accused of sorcery by their terrified neighbours and were arrested. Each was brought to Newcastle Town Hall and stripped to the waist. The witch-finder would push a pin beneath their clothes to see if they bled - those who did not were proven witches. Despite their desperate pleas of innocence, 27 of the suspects were found guilty. In one August day in 1650, 15 witches, one wizard and nine moss-troopers were dragged to the Town Moor and, before a baying crowd of thousands, were strung up and hanged. Another two were executed in Durham City on the witch-finder's evidence. His work done, the witch-pricker left the city and headed north, finding even more lucrative work in Northumberland where he was paid up to £3 for each witch brought to justice. There were those who dismissed the business as dangerous nonsense, including the eminent Northumberland landowner Henry Ogle who had the Scotsman arrested. Under questioning, he was exposed as a charlatan: when he thrust the pin through the suspect's clothes, he admitted, he deliberately ensured it followed the folds of the poor woman's skirts and did not pierce the skin. He was thrown out of England and returned to his native Scotland where he was eventually convicted of his crimes. On the gallows, he claimed responsibility for the execution of more than 220 witches during his long career.

So the residents of the Derwent Valley were well aware of the evils of witchcraft. Theirs was a precarious existence and many and varied were the misfortunes which befell the residents of the valley. Crops on occasion failed, the animals on which the villagers entire life depended would, sometimes, go lame and there were times in which their very future seemed threatened. In July 1610, the plague returned. Whickham Parish Register records that in that month: "The plage began at Storye's in the South Field, whereof died Storye and his three children." The Black Death made regular reappearances over coming years. The Whickham register records: "In August 1626, George Watson's three children died of the plaig this month" and again, in February 1645, "Ann Harrison died of the plauge and a considerable number died of the plauge in lodges on the fell." In an age of ignorance, such natural calamities were often blamed on supernatural sources.

The first accusations against Ann Armstrong are thought to have been made by John March, the miller. March lived at Eddy's Bridge and had leased the corn mill at Muggleswick since 1639. Twice a year he paid rent to the Dean and Chapter of Durham, 35 shillings a year which he paid in two instalments due on Whit Sunday and Michaelmas. March was a yeoman farmer, which made him a respectable figure in the area and, as well as his lease on the corn mill, he had land where he farmed livestock and a croft nearby. During the subsequent witch-trial, March gave evidence that his horse had been bewitched and one of his oxen had also fallen under a spell. During a visit to Birkenside Nook, the servant girl Ann Armstrong had heard his name mentioned and began to talk to him. She asked if one of his oxen had lost the use of its limbs. Surprised, he replied that it had and asked how she knew. He was shaken by her answer. Armstrong told him she had heard Mary Hunter and "another woman at a meeting of divers witches confess to the divvil that they had taken the power of that beast, and she not knowing her name." Asked by the justices what became of his beast, March told them: "The ox continues lame and has no use for his hinder leg, but pines away likely to die."

The arrests began. Ann Armstrong was taken into custody and between February and April of 1673 began to confess she was a witch, naming the villagers who had conspired with her to do the Devil's work in the Derwent Valley. Next to be questioned was Mary Hunter, a widow who lived at Birkenside Nook with her farmer son Anthony. Both were arrested. Mary Hunter told the justices that she had seen John March and his wife at Eddy's Bridge as they rode home from Bywell and admitted that she had transformed herself into the likeness of a swallow and flew under the mare's belly several times until she gained power over it. Armstrong was taken to

Edmundbyers to pick out the woman she had seen with Mary Hunter and there Dorothy Green was arrested.

What made Ann Armstrong and Mary Hunter confess to witchcraft we may never know, but confess they did and with terrible consequences.

Armstrong revealed to her inquisitors how she had first fallen into the clutches of the Devil during a visit to Stocksfield market. Armstrong claimed that as she bargained over the price of eggs with a local woman named Anne Forster, Forster had: "look't' her head." Three days later a mysterious man in ragged clothes came to her as she was moving cows from one field to another and told young Ann that Anne Forster was in fact a witch and wanted her to join her coven. Forster, she was told, would be the first to make a horse of her and ride her to a witches' sabbat. The ragged man described to her what would go on there, saying she could obtain whatever her heart desired simply by swinging on a rope she would find there. After he left, Armstrong fell into a trance and suffered fits, sometimes for days on end. During the course of these fits, she saw a vision which she later recounted to the justices of the peace and was taken as evidence of her having been bewitched. On Thursday, April 3rd, 1672, she claimed, Anne Forster had, as she had been warned by the ragged man, come to her and put an enchanted bridle over her head which changed the poor servant girl into the shape of a horse. Anne Forster then, sitting cross-legged upon her, rode the girl to a clearing near Riding Mill where others were gathered, 13 women and a tall black man they called their Protector.

The court records state: "which enchanted bridle, when they took it off from her head, she stood upp in her own proper person and see all the persons beforementioned dancing, some in the likenesses of haires, some in the likenesse of cats, others in the likenesse of bees and some in their own likenesse, and made this informant sit till they danced and every thirteen had a divell with them in sundry shapes. And at the said meeting their particular divell tooke them that did most evill and danced with them first and called every of them to account and those that did the most evill he maid most of."

When she next gave evidence, Ann Armstrong elaborated on the evil done by the coven. She revealed that on Collop Monday, February 10th, Michael Aynsley and his wife Margaret had come to

An Italian impression of witches dancing with the devil, engraved at the same time Ann Armstrong was accusing her neighbours of witchcraft (Picture courtesy British Library)

her and again used an enchanted bridle to ride her - this time to Allensford. Again the coven came together and confessed their wrongdoing. According to her testimony against Mary Hunter, the widow had "confessed to the divil that she had wronged George Taylor of Edgebriggs goods", in particular that "she had gotten the power of a fole of his, soe that it pined to death. And she had got power of the dam of the said fole and that they had an intention the last Thursday at night to have taken away the power of the limbs of the said mare." Her son, Anthony Hunter, also spoke to the devil, claimed Ann, and he "confessed that he had power over Anne, wife of Thomas Richardson of Crooked Oak, that he took away the power of her limbs and asked the divil's assistance to take away her life." And she accused a third person, Elizabeth Pickering of Whitonstall, who "had confessed to taking power of a neighbour's beast at Whittingstall and had killed the neighbour's chiuld."

Throughout that long, hot summer of suspicion, the confessions went on. On the next occasion the sabbat met, Armstrong claimed the assembled women called the Protector their God and he sat at the end of the table in a golden chair. Everyone seated around the table touched a rope which hung above it three times, and when they did so all the food they could possibly desire was brought to the table. But as the months of inquisition went on, the allegations levied by Armstrong became more and more fanciful. She reported she had danced before the devil in the shape of various animals and had ridden to the sabbat on eggshells and wooden dishes. At the end of every meeting, the witches pulled on the ropes and fine food tumbled onto their table: plum broth, beef, mutton, cheese, butter and ale. Lucy Thompson, she said, was given boiled capon, Anne Forster asked for cheese and Ann Dryden demanded currants and sweet wine. Those present had to report their misdeeds to the devil, who made much of those who had performed the most wickedness and beat those who had no evil-doings to report to his Satanic Majesty. Armstrong told the court she was offered a lease on her life to run for 60 years, during which time she would never want for money and one cow would provide as much milk as 10 normal animals. By the end of her depositions, she told how the witches' coven would gather to recite the Lord's Prayer backwards.

The evidence presented to the magistrates by Ann Armstrong shows her to be little more than a simple country girl. The demonic banquets she enjoyed probably say more about the limits of her imagination than the powers of darkness, with mutton, cheese and country dancing representing her idea of decadence. She claims to have sold her soul, not for all the riches in the world but for a good milking cow. Many of the stories she told owe a lot to the then widespread folklore of witchcraft and their familiars, evil spirits which took the form of animals, usually cats, and never strayed far from the witches' side. There were no orgies, no ritual murders and no cannibalism, but the stories brought the ever-present fear of the supernatural to bubble over into panic.

As the investigation went on, Ann Armstrong accused more than 30 people of witchcraft and named all 13 witches she had met at that first sabbat. She named Ann Forster and Mary Hunter, Mary's son Anthony and she led the justices to Dorothy Green. She named Christopher Dixon and his wife Alice of Muggleswick Park. She named Catherine Elliot and Elizabeth Atchinson, both of Ebchester, along with Isabel Andrew of Crooked Oak. The magistrates then returned to Edmundbyers to question spinster Annie Whitfield and John Whitfield, along with Michael Aynsley and his wife Margaret. One by one they were arrested. One of the alleged witches was brought before Ann, who collapsed in a swoon as soon as she breathed on her, a sign taken as further evidence of guilt. The trial began at Newcastle Assizes on April 2nd 1673 and was transferred to the Morpeth Sessions where it resumed a week later before Sir Thomas Horsley and Sir Richard Stote.

The depositions made by Ann Armstrong were read to the court and several of her neighbours were called to produce corroborating evidence. John March, the miller who had first heard Armstrong accuse Mary Hunter, told the court that he had indeed been travelling home at sunset one day and when he reached Bywell had seen a swallow. His statement to the court read: "There came a swallow which about forty times and more flew through the mare's belly and crossed her way before her breast and he struck at it with his rod about twenty times and wished to hinder it to so continue, until it went away of its own actions. And the mare went very well home and died within four days, and before she died was two days so mad that she was past holding and was struck blind for twenty-four hours before she died."

Then George Taylor, the Eddy's Bridge farmer whose stock was possessed by Mary Hunter according to Ann's earlier evidence, came before the court. He too confirmed that his mare and foal had been bewitched. The proof, he contested, was that although he fed them well, they did not thrive as well as those belonging to his neighbours. It was flimsy evidence - even by the standards of the day. Eventually, all were acquitted as the court accepted that the allegations were flights of fancy by an illiterate servant girl. But it came too late for Dorothy Green, taken from her Edmundbyers home all those months earlier when the finger of suspicion had been literally pointed at her by Ann Armstrong. She died in prison with the most heinous of accusations still hanging over her head.

A traditional belief in the supernatural has always existed throughout the villages of the Derwent Valley. Evil sprites were said to haunt many of the villages along the banks of the Derwent. In particular, many acts of mischief were blamed on the Hedley Kow, a mythical figure which was said to afflict the villages near

Hedleyhope and Hedley Hill and could change its shape at will. In the shape of their lover, the kow would lure young women from their homes at night, in the guise of a horse it would loosen reigns and upset carts, in the shape of a milking cow it would run amok and kick over the churns. The Hedley Kow figured in one of the most unlikely cases ever to come before Durham court when, in August 1729, Thomas Stevenson of Framwellgate gave evidence before Justice Burdess. He alleged that he was returning to Durham after business in Hedley and had brought along a guide for the journey over country roads late at night. At around 8pm, the pair had encountered an apparition, which was sometimes a man and sometimes a horse. This apparition, which he said was the Hedley Kow, took his bridle to lead the horse astray and then proceeded to beat both he and his guide black and blue through the entire course of the night until they arrived in Durham the following morning.

The kow was more mischievous than malevolent, allowing villagers to lay everyday mishaps at its door, but the Beldon Brag was more sinister. The brag was a spirit which appeared sometimes as a dog or horse, but most often as a guide with a lantern and lured travellers from the road onto the moors above Edmundbyers, before disappearing into the darkness and leaving its victim lost and alone among the ravines and bogs.

The witch trials of the 17th Century were not the only time the finger of suspicion was pointed at villagers. During the same century, Jane Frizzle lived at Crooked Oak Farm, close to Allensford, and although little is known of her she developed a reputation as having the power to bewitch men, women and cattle. The poet Dr Carr in his Ode To The Derwent wrote:

> *"Ghosts and witches came in for a share,*
> *"Though poor Frizzle has long breathed her last.*
> *"On broomsticks she rode through the air,*
> *"And scattered her pins as she passed."*

Elizabeth Lee, who died in 1792, was Edmundbyers' last reputed witch. She lived at The Riddings, which now lies below the Derwent Reservoir, and was held in such fear by locals that no-one would pass her door without a charm to ward off her evil powers. Even as late as 1824, local belief in the supernatural clung on and it was said that a visiting lay-preacher and faith healer by the name of Praying Johnny came to Edmundbyers and on his first day cured a woman "possessed of an evil spirit", who cursed, swore and danced at passers-by.

In an age of superstition, many unexplained phenomena were laid directly at the door of the Devil. In 1654, John Hunter, from Medomsley, was invited to a meeting of a then new religious sect which was growing fast in the Derwent Valley - the Quakers. On August 19th, he was invited to attend a meeting of the group at Benfieldside where, if we are to believe his account, the Devil himself appeared to the assembled Christians. He wrote: "At the earnest desire of some friends, I, with John Ward and Anthony Hunter, went to a meeting of the deluded souls called Quakers. I found about 20 persons all sitting silent. After we had sat a while, the Lord moved me to arise and call upon his name in prayer. I was no sooner up than my legs began to tremble and I had some difficulty to stand, but after I had prayed a short while the trembling ceased. While I prayed to God there was little disturbance, but when I cried in the name of Jesus Christ, the Devil appeared and roared to the deceived souls in a most strange and dreadful manner. Some of those present began howling, yelling and roaring and there was a strange kind of humming noise. Such a representation of Hell I never heard. After I had done praying (not opening my eyes before) I was amazed to see about one half of those miserable creatures so terribly shaken with such violent motions that I wondered how it was possible that some of them could live. This went on for a couple of hours and frightened dogs, swine and cattle and set them howling. Then the disturbance ceased, the minister left, but not before some of the Friends had soundly cursed him."

In all likelihood, the passage is not meant it be taken literally and instead pokes fun at the cacophony produced by followers of the new religion. On another occasion the Devil, who appears to have a particular attachment to Benfieldside, appeared at the opening of a new Christian meeting house in 1790 where he tried, according to one eye-witnesses: "to snatch away the keys which would imprison him forever." Other fairly implausible encounters with the Prince of Darkness are recorded in the dale. In 1750, John Redshaw lived at Coalgate Farm, just south of Muggleswick at the time another new religion was sweeping the Derwent Valley - Methodism. The farm was the first Methodist meeting hall in North West Durham and Redshaw was joined by his friend John Ridley, a weaver, for the first meeting. But during the course of the prayer meeting they claimed to have received a strange visitation. The Devil, in the shape of a big, black dog, came down the chimney of the farmhouse to disrupt proceedings. Undeterred, the two God-fearing souls stood their ground and called on the Holy Trinity to command the apparition to leave.On hearing this, the Devil then vanished back up the chimney in a sulphurous cloud of smoke.

But if many reports of supernatural goings on in the Derwent Valley can be dismissed as the imaginings of fervent believers, not all are so easily explained away. The most curious of all is undoubtedly the occasion when the Devil himself was reported to have appeared in Edmundbyers, one of the best documented reports of Satanic possession in English history. The story, which at the time was famous throughout the country, was originally printed in London in a pamphlet entitled "Most Fearful And Strange News From The Bishoprick of Durham" and sold far and wide. It dates to the days just before the outbreak of the Civil War when Puritanism was a growing force and absolute belief in Biblical good and evil was at its height. The story could have been put down to the hysteria of a simple farming family, stirred by fire and brimstone preaching and fuelled by a universal belief in the supernatural, but for the fact that so many witnessed the demonic possession which gripped the village for several days.

Stephen Hooper was a yeoman farmer who owned land in Edmundbyers and Hunstanworth and, although he wasn't rich, by the standards of his time he had a comfortable life. He was a sheep farmer, but also kept a few cattle and pigs and grew vegetables, with which he fed his family and was left with a decent surplus to sell at market and earn a little extra income. Hooper had a good reputation locally as a fair employer and, probably as a result of his fairness, his labourers worked well for him.

During the autumn of 1641, Hooper fell ill. His illness wasn't that serious, but it was sufficient to confine him to bed for several days and keep him away from his land. Consequently, his wife Margaret took it upon herself to supervise the running of the farm at Hunstanworth, a mile or two from the family's croft at Edmundbyers. Mrs Hooper was said to be less reasonable than her husband and less diplomatic. She quickly found fault with everything she saw and complained that the stone walls were badly built, the harvesting wasn't being done quickly enough, the stables weren't mucked out often enough and the labourers were all lazy. When she returned home, she complained to her husband about the state of the farm and told him: "May the Devil take me if I could not do better myself." If subsequent events are to be believed, that seemingly innocent remark was to have devastating consequences for Margaret Hooper and, indeed, her whole family.

For several days, life in the Hooper household returned to normal, or so it appeared. Mr Hooper's good health returned and he was soon back to his labours at the farm. But within days, it became apparent that all was not well with Margaret Hooper. She began to babble incoherently, making random outbursts about Hunstanworth farm. She began to show all the signs of being deranged, staring vacantly into space followed by rages against her family, cursing and using profane language which shocked her friends. As she sank deeper and deeper into her madness, she began to make wild gestures as if to ward off the invisible creatures which plagued her every waking moment. Quickly, the whisper spread throughout the village and wider countryside that Margaret Hooper was bewitched.

At a loss to explain his wife's sudden terrible condition, but fearing the worst, Stephen Hooper recited the Lord's Prayer over his stricken wife and asked her to pray with him. But the hapless woman raved all the more and began to foam at the mouth, her language and actions growing all the more violent every day. Her husband put her to bed, but her condition continued to deteriorate and she moaned as if in agony and thrashed around the bed. Eventually the bed itself began to move and everything else in the room, furniture and ornaments, shook violently as if in an earth tremor, terrifying the poor souls who came to nurse the distressed woman. As the room shook more and more, the bed-ridden woman cried out in her terror that the shaking was being carried out by the great bear which had followed her home from Hunstanworth farm on that fateful day.

After this terrifying episode, the patient began to recover slightly. She remained confined to bed with her husband praying over her exhausted body day and night as her family dared to hope that the worst was over. They were sadly mistaken. After a day or two, her condition worsened again and she once more began to rave, screaming, shouting and babbling but always, always fighting off the terrible invisible creatures which pawed at her. On November 15th,

1641, a Sunday night, she cried out in terror saying she could see a horrible snail-like creature which carried a burning firebrand. Her anguished cries woke the whole household, who rushed to her bedside and she asked each in turn if they could see the Devil. Each replied that they could not and, with a sudden calmness which struck cold terror into the hearts of each one, she told them: "You will see Him ... and very soon."

As they waited, there came a great rumbling sound from the distance which came closer and closer and louder and louder until the whole room trembled. Suddenly into the room burst a large, black beast. The terrible creature, described afterwards by the witnesses as "much like a bear without head or tail," leapt to the bedside of the now petrified Mrs Hooper. Her husband jumped to his feet to fight it off, beating it repeatedly with a wooden stool from the bedside.

But the beast did not so much as flinch and, as the deafening roar drowned out the screams of the family, it clawed at Margaret, striking her three times across the feet, then dragged the unfortunate woman from her bed. Then, according to the witnesses, the terrifying creature bent Mrs Hooper double into the shape of a wheel with her head bent forward to her feet and rolled her out of the room and down the stairs into the hall.

Mr Hooper and his friends cowered in the upstairs room paralysed with fear. For a full quarter of an hour, the god-fearing folk of Edmundbyers were gripped with terror as below a Hellish stench of sulphur and the glow of fiery flames wafted upstairs from the rooms where the creature held his wife. Then, slowly, they began to subside. Still the assembled crowd did not move and dared not follow, convinced by now the poor farmer's wife was dead. But suddenly Mrs Hooper's voice screamed out for help and her husband rushed to the stairs and called out: "Then in the name of God, come up to me."

Miraculously, she returned, bewildered but unscathed and climbed back into her bed. Four of her neighbours dropped to their knees and prayed, prayed as they had never prayed before, calling on the Lord to save them all from the vision of Hell they had all witnessed. But once more, as if commanded by unheard voices, Mrs Hooper rose from her bed and rushed to the window where she climbed up and sat on the sill, legs dangling outside as if to throw herself out. Below, in the darkness of the Durham night, her friends saw flames beginning to crackle and rise and the same stench as before, only viler so they could almost taste it.

In the middle of this inferno, a huge black monster began to take shape, reaching up from the ground to scrabble at her legs as if to pull Mrs Hooper from the ledge into its demonic clutches.

Those petrified souls in the bedroom prayed harder still, as Stephen Hooper called feverishly on the Lord Almighty to save his wife from the clutches of the Devil. At that moment, a candle, which had been burning dimly by the side of the bed, suddenly shone exceptionally brightly and a divine creature with the face of a little girl appeared in the room, described by the witnesses as "having a shining countenance". The crowd thanked the Lord as the child approached the window and raised a hand to the evil creature which was forming below to command it to begone. And with an eerie final

This woodcut, created in Somerset in 1614, tells an identical story to the horrors suffered by Margaret Hooper, a vision of a headless bear terrorises a bedridden woman while an angel looks on
(Picture courtesy of the British Library)

howl which could be heard across the moors, it shrank away into the darkness and, as the angelic child also vanished, the night was left still.

Margaret Hooper came round from her affliction immediately and, according to contemporary reports: "She asked forgiveness at God's hands of all that she had offended, acknowledging that she was sorely tormented by the evil spirit on account of her sins." Around a dozen people witnessed the events of that night, including her family, friends, neighbours and churchmen from the village. Stephen Hooper, Alexander Eglestone, John Sley. Anthony Westgarth, John Hooper, Alice Eglestone and several others would later swear to the truth of the terrible vision they had witnessed. Over the following months, the farmer's wife became something of a celebrity because of her close encounter with the forces of darkness and was visited, according to the same reports: "by godly and learned men from various parts of the country anxious to ascertain particulars of the case."

CHAPTER 14
THE RUNNING WOLF

IN the summer of 1687, a convoy of covered wagons slipped out of the town of Solingen in the German Rhineland under cover of night. Unnoticed by anyone, the procession made its way across country to the west. Inside were 19 men, their wives and families and every possession they owned, carefully gathered because there was to be no going back. The pilgrims, guided by their leader Clemens Hohemann, were undoubtedly afraid, for the penalties they faced if caught were terrible - but they were also filled with hope for a new, better life far away from the city walls they left behind. After several days of travelling they made it undetected to the Dutch port of Rotterdam where they took a ship over a calm sea to England. The settlers brought with them the secrets of their trade and, these German swordmakers, would pass into legend on the banks of the Derwent where they made their new home.

More than 300 years on, mystery still shrouds the flight of the Shotley swordmakers and what brought them to this quiet corner of England. According to local tradition, these German protestants were fleeing religious persecution in their own country. At that time, the French king Louis XIV had imposed the Catholic faith on his own country and threatened to invade his German neighbours to impose it there. But no such invasion had ever come. Certainly the German settlers were god-fearing folk - the homes they set up on the wooded banks of the Derwent bore religious inscriptions and the records of their church baptisms, weddings and funerals still exist.

The 19th Century historian The Reverend John Ryan wrote: "At Shotley Bridge, a colony of German sword cutlers, who fled from their own country for the sake of religious liberty, established themselves about the reign of King William. These quiet settlers, who brought with them the habits of industry, and moral and religious principle, easily mingled with the children of the dale, and forgot the language of their forefathers. Above the doorway of two decent houses there are German inscriptions (copied also into divers huge family Bibles) attesting the cause which drove these emigrants from their faderland to seek, on the green brink of the Darwent, protection under the equal law of that country which has ever proved an ark of refuge to the victims of religious or political persecution."

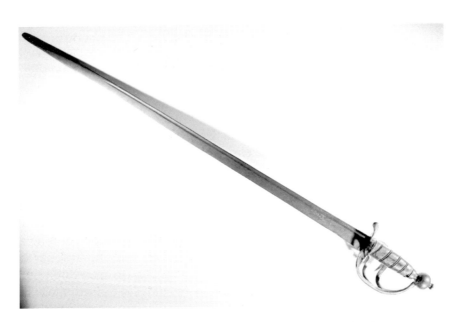

One of the few surviving swords made at Shotley
(Photograph courtesy of Beamish Museum)

So the descendants of the swordmakers certainly said it was religious persecution which forced them to abandon their homes and make a new life for themselves in an alien country. But it may well have been a much more worldly aim which spurred them on. In the 17th Century, important trades such as swordmaking were regulated by guilds - trade bodies which protected the secrets of their craft. The guilds dictated the number of tradesmen who could practice the craft and where they could do so. At that time, Solingen was one of the great swordmaking capitals of Europe and the knowledge of the craft was protected like a state secret. Solingen blades were among the very best in the world, stamped with the sign of quality - an image of The Running Wolf or Flying Fox. Among the very best of these was the hollow blade - invented in Solingen sometime during the 17th Century. The new sword blades had three faces, tapering to a razor sharp tip, and each face was hollowed out to give the weapon extraordinary flexibility, suppleness and strength. It was said that a Solingen hollow blade could be bent double so the tip touched the hilt and would spring back perfectly to its original shape, quality which brought significant wealth to Solingen.

As a result, the guild decreed that no Solingen swordmaker could leave the town to set up in business elsewhere - thereby protecting the secrets of all German blades, and this particular super-weapon, forever.

Enforced residence in Solingen may have seemed like an infringement of liberty to Clemens Hohemann, one of the leading swordmakers in the town, and enforced residence in a town already brimming with swordmakers may have seemed like an infringement of his economic fortunes. The grass on the banks of the Derwent began to look greener.

Then there is the mysterious involvement of a group of northern businessmen. John Sandford and John Bell, were both entrepreneurs from Newcastle. The pair were involved with the German swordmakers as soon as they arrived in England and the suspicion is that they may have even been secretly involved in enticing the Germans away from their homeland. The English swordmaking industry was poor by comparison and the prospect of making a fortune by attracting some of the best German smiths to Shotley may have led the mysterious pair to approaching Hohemann with an offer to work for them. Certainly the immigrants were unlikely to settle upon such a remote and unknown corner of the kingdom without being directed there by someone already living in England and there is some evidence to suggest that their workshops on the banks of the Derwent were set up before the swordmakers actually arrived, presumably by Sandford and Bell. In 1688, within months of their arrival in Durham, Sandford and Bell presented a petition on behalf of the company to King James II, asking for a patent to grant a monopoly in the manufacture of hollow blades. It included the plea: "At great expense they have brought foreign workers to England and they propose to make use of a mill unlike any other hitherto seen in His Majesty's Dominions." Three years later, on September 15th 1691, a charter was granted to The Governor and Company For Making Hollow Sword Blades in England. The charter includes mention of the dangerous flight of the Germans from their native land. "The swordmakers have been prevailed upon to expose themselves even to the hazard of their lives to impart to our said subjects the knowledge of their art and mystery."

But, even as the swordmakers were being welcomed to England, a furious hue and cry was underway in Germany. The Solingen authorities were livid that so many of their craftsmen had been spirited away from under their noses. On September 26th 1688, a full year after their flight, the court in Solingen issued an indictment against the fugitives:

"Having recognised that over a year ago Clemens Hohemann did entice away to the Kingdom of England various craftsmen here resident and bound by the district court, and furthermore did incite them to abscond, and as the infamy has become widely known and has been recognised as punishable in the highest degree, let him Clemens Hohemann, be charged here as a culpable seducer, together with all the persons involved."

The charge was pinned to the door of every swordsmith's home giving warnings to return to their place of work with six weeks and three days or else: "produce firm reasons for your refusal and defection, either personally or have at your disposal sufficient powers of attorney. Warning - do these things for, if you do not, immediately after the expiry of the appointed time, upon further representations being legally made to proceed against you, such proceedings will hereupon be taken, according to the law." The action threatened against them included removing all rights and privileges from their families and that, if any of them were found in Solingen's jurisdiction, they would be "punished on their bodies."

There was to be no going back. And so, in 1687, the Germans arrived at Shotley Bridge to start their new life. The village consisted of a few scattered houses on the wooded banks of the Derwent. The first mention of Shotley Bridge in history comes in 1356 when a flour mill stood next to the old stone bridge. The bed of the river produced the millstones and also provided a supply for the swordmakers while the water powered their mill. Away from prying eyes and with a plentiful supply of the raw materials their industry needed, it was a perfect location. Landowner Ralph "Mad" Maddison lived on the north bank of the river and at some point a pub was opened on the south bank, the Bridge End. Other farms and estates were nearby but no settlement of any great significance stood at Shotley, although Ebchester was just a short distance away.

The swordmakers set about constructing their own cottages near the site and expanding their industry, becoming along the way the first true ironmasters of the Derwent Valley. Despite the existence of furnaces nearby at Allensford and Blackhall Mill, the swordmakers both mined and smelted their own iron and steel. They diverted the river at Shotley to a mill race which powered the forge bellows and the tilt hammers at up to 150 strikes a minute. They made clearings in Chopwell Wood to roast their charcoal for the furnaces. They dug blackbands ironstone for the furnaces from a row of delft pits on the far side of Berry Edge, known ever since as Delves Lane. They may have also dug ironstone from Hownes Gill. This then had to be turned into iron and eventually shear steel for the blades. The ironstone was transported by horse to Shotley Bridge, or else to a special furnace which existed at Allensford where roasting kilns reduced it to iron. The swordmaking company also took lease of the old corn mill at Lintzford in 1694, probably with the intention of turning into another swordmaking mill, but the venture did not materialise and it was to be converted into a paper mill within 10 years.

But further mystery surrounds the swordmakers as they forged their industry on the banks of the river. Clemens Hohemann led 19 families away from Solingen - but not all of them made it to Shotley Bridge. Hohemann himself drops out of history somewhere between Solingen and Shotley. The leadership of the German settlers passed to Adam Ohlig, who changed his name to the more English Oley on his arrival, and Herman Mohll. These two became the most significant figures in the German community on the Derwent and it was they who drove along the new venture.

Business was, at first, good for the swordmakers. The firm produced 37 different varieties of swords, from three-foot long Large Latsons to 12-inch bayonets. They produced rapiers, cutlasses and scimitars and, according to local legend at least, their swords lived up to their reputation as among the best in Britain. There is an often-told story that one of Oley's descendants, challenged by a rival as to which could produce the better sword, turned up for the challenge seemingly empty-handed. While his rival boasted of the abilities of the sword he had brought with him, Robert Oley removed his hat and uncurled a sword from inside, so fine and flexible that it could be hidden inside his headwear. This reputation for quality and the efforts of Sanderson and Bell ensured that in the early years the business flourished.

It was a good time to be a swordmaker. Throughout the 17th Century, war had raged across the Continent of Europe, fuelled by the religious rivalry between Catholic and Protestant. In 1686, war had broken out between England, Spain and the Netherlands against King Louis XIV of France - the very tyrant who the German swordmakers would claim drove them to the shores of England a year later. This war would rage for another 11 years - giving a ready market for the weaponry forged at Shotley. But there were intrigues closer to home which promised to increase the demand for Shotley swords and which would eventually embroil the swordmakers themselves as well as others living in the Derwent Valley. In 1688, just a year after the swordsmiths arrived in England, the country saw the Glorious Revolution which swept the new Catholic King James II from power. Fearing a return to the centuries of bloodshed which had characterised English history, the king was forced from office by his court which offered the throne to his daughter Mary and her Protestant husband William of Orange. James made an attempt to retain the crown during an unsuccessful campaign in Ireland, which ended in defeat at the Battle of the Boyne later the same year. Thereafter, there were to be two further attempts to restore James' successors to the English throne by military uprising, in 1715 and 1745. Civil war once more threatened England and James' supporters, known as Jacobites, were under great suspicion. Most Jacobites came from Scotland or Ireland, but many Catholics in the North were supporters of the cause and, as will be seen later, the Derwent Valley had particular importance to the Jacobite cause.

The swordmakers of Shotley Bridge were sucked into this intrigue during a curious episode in 1703. Hermann Mohll, now the acknowledged leader of the group, had returned to Germany with his wife and two children for a year. The purpose of his trip is unknown, although it must have been important for him to leave for a full year while his colleagues ran the mill at Shotley. He arrived back in England aboard the Dutch ship Saint Ann which anchored off North Shields. At about 2am one Sunday, two men were rowing past the vessel when they were hailed from the ship and asked to take some bundles in their boat to a place of safety in the port. On the next tide, a crewman from the Saint Ann would join them and they were to take the bundles up river to Gateshead. At first, they complied but grew suspicious and alerted the authorities in North Shields. The bundles were searched and found to contain swords. Then a group of fishermen at South Shields netted a haul of more bundles, seemingly thrown over the side of the Saint Ann to be collected later. These too included swords. In all, 46 bundles of swords were recovered, quite a haul of weapons. A letter sent by Justice Villiers to the Secretary of State the Earl of Nottingham referred to find as containing swords: "the blades being hollow, a weapon which at this time was made nowhere else in England except at Shotley Bridge." Mohll, facing possible charges of smuggling, found himself in deeper trouble when the Saint Ann was searched and was found to contain 20 Scottish and Irish soldiers, almost certainly Jacobites - supporters of James Stuart's claim to the English throne. Hermann Mohll was arrested under suspicion of treason - the allegation that he was smuggling weapons: "at the instigation of some known friends of the Stuart family in the neighbourhood of Newcastle." It was a charge which carried the death penalty and he was thrown into Morpeth Jail while investigations were carried out.

Things looked bleak for Hermann Mohll - a foreigner found trying to conceal a large quantity of smuggled weapons in a boat brimming with armed traitors. Yet, remarkably, little over a month later he was freed to return to Shotley Bridge. His colleague Henry Wooper gave evidence to the court that Mohll was an honest man and had been in Germany while the Shotley works was closed down until word was sent to him to return. Newcastle cutler Thomas Carnforth declared he had known the German for 14 years and said he believed Mohll to be "a very honest man." The depositions were accepted and Mohll was freed to return to Shotley.

But, if Mohll was not smuggling weapons for the Jacobites, then what was he doing? One possible answer appears to be that some of the swords stamped with Shotley's famous name and Running Wolf symbol were not made in Shotley at all. It may well have been that Mohll had returned to Germany to buy swords and smuggle them into England, avoiding paying import duty, and having them stamped with Shotley's famous symbol on his return. Mohll returned to his Shotley works where he lived until his death in 1716. But, interestingly, one cache of Shotley swords went undiscovered for more than 100 years. In 1815, at the height of the Napoleonic Wars, soldiers scouring the North-East for evidence of French invasion uncovered a concealed room hidden in a chimney stack at Danby Hall and inside was a large number of Shotley-made swords and documents indicating they were intended for use during the Jacobite rising.

The year after Mohll's release from prison, the swordmakers appointed William Cotesworth as their agent. Cotesworth was an extraordinary figure who, in an age when social standing was determined at birth, rose through the ranks of society from the son of a yeoman to become one of the most powerful landowners and coal owners in the region. Cotesworth began life as a merchant, trading in everything from candles to chocolate, and achieved spectacular success, some of which rubbed off on the sword makers. Between November 1710 and August 1712, the company sold 19,000 blades, each marked with the symbol of the Running Wolf and the mark Shotley Bridg. By the end of that period, the entire output of the mill - some 1,600 dozen blades a year - was being sold through Cotesworth, although the fact that he was buying them at 6d a dozen less than in previous years was an indication of troubles to come for Shotley.

The death of sword making at Shotley Bridge came slowly. By the time Adam Oley, the last of the original settlers, passed away in 1726, the mill had changed hands and was in some financial difficulty. Demand for swords was slowing now as firearms became the Army's weapon of choice and a period of peace reduced the demand still further. Cotesworth blamed the business decisions made by the original partners. In 1724 he wrote: "Those of the Sword Blaide Company that were there concerned are all in adversity and misfortunes by hastening to be rich." The settlers' descendants continued the business, but great fortunes were not to be made and many left the village to seek work elsewhere, including Sheffield - where the steel industry was taking off. Eminent visitors reported that all was not well at Shotley Bridge. The Swedish steelmaker Angerstein came to the village in 1754 during a tour of the iron-making plants in the Derwent Valley and made some astonishing observations, reporting that the swordmakers were openly quarrelling among themselves which he put down to "German laziness and arrogance". Other settlers, he said, turned to the bottle more often than work.

The Oley family continued to run the business and in 1787, William Oley completed the construction of Cutlers Hall, his home which still stands today. By the early 19th Century, the once-proud sword mill had diversified into making scythes, sickles and agricultural implements to make ends meet. Robert Mole, the descendent of Hermann Mohll, eventually moved his business south to Birmingham - leaving just the Oley family left to carry on the trade. In 1889, Robert Mole's company was taken over by his great rival Wilkinsons, which later adopted the name Wilkinson Sword and adopted the crossed swords symbol of the Shotley swordmakers. The last of the Shotley swordmakers was Joseph Oley, born in 1806 the grandson of William Oley. He carried on producing swords until 1840, ironically the same year that the Derwent Valley's other great metalworking industry was born at Consett. Demand had reached such a low that he finally closed down the forges for good and the old mill was given over to the grinding not of swords but of corn. Joseph Oley became an auctioneer and lived in Shotley until his death in 1896 at the age of 90. His gravestone still stands in Ebchester churchyard inscribed: "He died in the Lord - The last of the Shotley Bridge swordmakers."

Joseph Oley, the last of the Shotley swordmakers
(Photography courtesy of Beamish Museum)

*Espershields Woods from across the Derwent Reservoir
(Picture by Brian Clough)*

CHAPTER 15
MAD MADDISON

SUBMERGED deep beneath the calm, lapping waters of the Derwent Reservoir lie the ruins of Espershields Farm. As the birds cry at dusk on a summer night and the gentle waves lap the shoreline, it is difficult to envisage that it could be anything other than serene and peaceful. But it was here that the madness of Ralph Maddison first showed itself. At one time, there stood a great oak forest at Espershields. In a fit of rage, Maddison burnt the entire forest, tinder dry after a long hot summer, to ashes in an inferno which threatened to engulf neighbouring farms and could be seen for miles around. It was an act of lunacy which made Maddison the most feared figure in North Durham. At first, many considered Maddison to be little more than a rogue, whose eccentricities verged on the endearing. But as he spiralled ever deeper into insanity, Maddison's moods became darker and ever more dangerous. Drunken bravado became recklessness, recklessness became arson and arson eventually became cold-blooded murder. His descent brought terror to his neighbours in Shotley Bridge and throughout the Derwent Valley and earned him the nickname by which he is still known - Mad Maddison.

Ralph Maddison was born in the middle of the 17th Century to a prosperous landowning family, far from rich but sufficiently well off. The family's land lay on the north bank of the Derwent at Shotley Bridge and was to be inherited by the young Ralph. But from an early age he displayed the flaws in his character which were to ensure he would never fully enjoy his inheritance and the failings of his own family were to contribute to his decline. As a child, Maddison was uncontrollable. He was spoilt by his family and rather than discipline his unruly child, his father found his son's mischievous tricks amusing, while his insolence and habitual disobedience were looked on as signs of strong character. Unchecked, the boy became ever more wayward as he grew into manhood.

Maddison's relentless pranks and mad antics soon began to tire his neighbours and visitors to the family homestead became few and far between. As he aged, Ralph's humour became increasingly malevolent. He turned to petty theft, criminal damage and minor violence - simply for the fun of it. Several stories survive of his wayward behaviour. It is said that one day as he rode along the banks of the Derwent at Allensford, in the days before there was a bridge and the river had to be crossed by a ford, he came across an old woman. The river, while not in flood, was full and she was stuck on the bank unable to cross. Maddison stopped and offered to help the old woman across on the back of his horse. Grateful to the charming stranger who had come to her assistance, the old woman climbed on and thanked the Good Samaritan, telling him it was a pleasure to meet such a man when there were scoundrels such as Mad Maddison around. Maddison said nothing, but walked his horse to the deepest part of the river where he unceremoniously pushed the old woman into the waters and rode off laughing. His victim was washed downstream before she somehow managed to scramble to the bank side, more dead than alive.

So the legend of Mad Maddison grew. On another occasion near his home in Shotley Bridge, a farmer's wife had hung out two pieces of linen to bleach. Maddison stole one and was about to make off with it when the woman emerged and berated him as a thief. Maddison told her: "Then I will have both for it is as well to hang for a hog as a halfpenny" and returned for the second piece of cloth. There were some occasions, however, when his neighbours got the better of him. Among his favourite pastimes as a young man was to overturn stacks of hay and corn. In a world where a good harvest was vital to farming families, this went beyond mere annoying vandalism, especially as Maddison was particularly fond of doing so when rain was likely and would destroy the crop so carefully gathered. Dozens of haystacks fell victim to him until one farmer, aware of who was responsible for the destruction, built his haystack around the stump of a tree. Maddison attacked it and tried repeatedly to overturn the stack with all his might but was unable to budge it and, finally convinced that witchcraft was protecting the stack, ran off.

As he grew into middle age, instead of calming down his escapades became ever more sinister. As a prosperous landowner, he should have been a respectable figure and, indeed, at one stage was warden of the district and saw service fighting mosstroopers. But the first death which Ralph Maddison had on his conscience was within his own family.

He had a daughter, who eventually got married. Maddison took his new son-in-law drinking to the Bridge End Inn, now known as the King's Head in Shotley Bridge, which was his local. After a bout of heavy drinking, the younger man ended up in a particularly bad state and needed to be returned home to Shotley Hall. Maddison sent for a horse, the wildest he owned, which was famed locally for its speed and strength. His drunken son-in-law was unceremoniously loaded into the saddle facing the wrong way, so that he was looking towards the horse's tail. According to the story, Maddison then fixed a swish of thorns to the horse's flank. The bewildered animal bolted. Off it raced at breakneck speed with the poor rider balanced precariously and clinging on as best he could.

As Maddison laughed, the pair raced away into the distance away from Shotley Hall. They had reached Black Hedley before the mount eventually threw its young rider who was killed outright. No charges were ever brought against Maddison, but it was a warning of what was to come.

His daughter remarried very quickly after the incident, and John Elrington of Acton became his new son-in-law, although it appears

The King's Head pub in Shotley Bridge, known in Ralph
Maddison's time at The Bridge End
(Photograph courtesy of Beamish Museum)

Maddison thought no more of him than he did of his daughter's first husband. Elrington owned land, 300 acres at Acton and Cronkley in the upper reaches of the valley, which was too tempting a prospect for his father-in-law to pass by. Somehow, Maddison persuaded his new son-in-law to hand over the property to him and become a tenant on his own estates, paying rent of 50 shillings a year. When Elrington began to struggle to pay the rent, Maddison and his son Joseph threatened violence to make him pay up. On one occasion, Maddison flew into a rage and fired a pistol at his son-in-law, although the shot missed its target. The feud between the increasingly deranged Maddison and Elrington was to have dramatic consequences.

Maddison, helped by a gang of his family and friends, burnt down Elrington's farm at Acton and escaped with his livestock to settle the supposed debt. But the blaze spread and engulfed Espershields Wood, which stretched for miles along the banks of the Derwent from the farm to Newbiggen, above Blanchland. The destruction was huge and left Elrington with no choice but to prosecute his errant father-in-law for arson and larceny. The prosecution did little to endear the two men to each other and Elrington was eventually forced to flee and seek protection from the justices at Newcastle from the wrath of his father-in-law. The proceedings were eventually heard in May 1681 and evidence emerged in court of Maddison's reign of terror over the Derwent Valley including a three-year campaign of arson against his enemies which had seen him use gunpowder to set fire to houses in Benfieldside and stables at Iveston. As well as accusing Maddison of starting the devastating fire at Espershields, Elrington's deposition said: "That Ralph Maddison, Joseph Maddison (his son), Thomas Pattyson of Unthanke and Robert Thompson, did come to this informers house at Acton and did carry away four oxen, six cowes, young beasts and five score tenn of weathers, yewes and hogges. Ralph Maddison did confess to this informer that in March 1678 he burnt Joseph Rawe's house at Benfieldside and Nun's House stable with match, gunpowder and tow." Neighbour Isaac Ward gave evidence at the trial that Maddison had been in a quandary over which of Elrington's properties to destroy first, those at Acton or Cronkley. Joseph Maddison was acquitted but his father was convicted and the court ordered he be branded, burnt on the hand with a red-hot iron, for his crime, although it appears the sentence was never carried out.

The prosecution did not bring Maddison to his senses, but his luck would finally run out in 1694 when he quarrelled with Lord Atkinson, the Laird of Cannyside Wood. Although grandly titled, Atkinson was a minor landowner. The origins of the argument are unknown but the outcome is certain, Maddison killed Atkinson close to the Bridge End Inn and then returned to his home with his guns. There he barricaded himself inside, threatening to shoot dead anyone who approached. No constable would go near him and his fearsome reputation ensured no citizen would volunteer to help in his capture. The authorities sent out for soldiers from Durham to capture the fugitive and, when news reached Maddison, it appears that for the first time in his reign of terror, his nerve cracked. Fearing the game may finally be up, Maddison saddled his best horse and fled from his pursuers. Up the Derwent Valley he raced, past Eddy's Bridge, hoping to reach the moors and the wild open spaces where he could escape into Cumberland. But, as he entered Muggleswick Park on the edge of safety, his horse halted and refused to go further. The beast, normally so reliable and swift, would not be budged despite the increasingly frantic use of Maddison's spurs. With the detachment of soldiers now almost upon him, Maddison dismounted and ran for cover into a nearby wood, hiding inside the trunk of an old yew tree.

It was no use. Abject and terrified of the certain noose which awaited him, Ralph Maddison was found cowering in the tree hollow. The man who had held all the Derwent Valley in fear for so long was dragged from his hiding place, bound hand and foot and escorted to Durham by the soldiers. At the forthcoming Assizes, he was tried for murder and convicted. In front of Durham Jail on September 16th, 1694, Ralph "Mad" Maddison was hanged by the neck until dead.

CHAPTER 16
JACK ANVIL

AN INFANT steel industry was growing in the Derwent Valley led by one of the most extraordinary figures of the 17th Century - Ambrose Crowley. He was born at Stourbridge in 1658 and began his working life as a common blacksmith but, over the next few decades, would establish himself as one of the foremost industrialists of his day. In an age when status was very much determined by birth, Ambrose Crowley would rise to the very top but had to endure the open derision of polite society.

At the age of 16, he was apprenticed to Clement Plumpstead, an ironmonger in the City of London and the teenage boy lived in the great metropolis for seven years while he served his time. In 1681, at the age of 23, the newly-qualified Crowley opened his first business in Carey Lane, London, making and selling nails and frying pans. Within the year he married Mary Owen, the daughter of a wealthy Shropshire landowner - a woman who would appear to have been significantly above his station in those class-conscious times.

Trouble seemed to dog Crowley's early progress and later evidence would suggest that he held forthright views at odds with the mainstream which he was not afraid to air. He left London after an unspecified disagreement with the ironmasters of Birmingham, who controlled the flow of raw materials to the metalworkers of the capital, and headed north to Sunderland where, aged just 24, he opened his own ironworks in 1682. There were problems from the start at Crowley's plant on the Wear - a shortage of land for expansion, a shortage of suitable trees for the production of charcoal but most importantly a shortage of skilled labour capable of operating the works. The ever-resourceful Crowley resolved his problem by recruiting up to 100 foreign workers to come to Sunderland, many from Liege in Belgium, then a centre of the nail-making industry. The arrival of these Catholic immigrants provoked such hostility with the local authorities that Crowley eventually turned to the king for support and the Bishop of Durham was asked to mediate in the dispute. The wrangling was enough to force Crowley to give up on Sunderland and look elsewhere for the perfect site for his ironworks. He found it on the Derwent.

The remains of Crowley's great ironworks at Winlaton
(Photograph courtesy of Beamish Museum)

The Derwent Valley had everything he needed - a fast-flowing river to drive the forges and mills, nearby Chopwell Woods provided the charcoal, there was a plentiful supply of coal and labour and it was close to the Tyne so iron could be landed from Sweden and finished products could be shipped out. In 1690, Ambrose Crowley established his offices in Winlaton - the first step in a great enterprise which would become known the world over. The following year, he took over the corn mill at Winlaton Mill, then a tiny village of around a half a dozen houses with a population of less than 20, and built a forge and grinding mill. Skilled workers were brought in from London and, by the turn of the century, a steel furnace was working at Winlaton. The works produced a variety of iron products, mainly nails, files and small tools and the business flourished. In 1701, he opened a warehouse in Blaydon where the keel boats would load up and take the goods down to the ships waiting further down the Tyne.

It was evident that Crowley had hit upon a winning idea and it did not take long for the opposition to try to cash in. A partnership of three business rivals, including a former employee of Crowley's Sunderland works, set up in opposition at Swalwell and poached many of his workers. The venture lasted five years until 1707, when Crowley bought them out and added Swalwell to his ever expanding empire.

The new works at Swalwell specialised in larger implements, including huge anchors and mooring chains for the Admiralty, engine pumps and agricultural tools. He agreed lucrative contracts to supply the famous East India Company and, in the Americas, the plantation slaves were bound by chains made on the Derwent and dug the Virginia earth with Crowley's hoes. His Swalwell warehouse sold his products for consumption in the country and a second warehouse at Greenwich sold to the rest of the world. New villages grew up at Winlaton and Swalwell to house his workers, known by the nickname of Crowley's Crew, and at their height 300 people were employed by the Winlaton works alone. By 1770, when his descendants were running the business, the ironworks was the largest manufacturer of its kind in Europe and it even possessed a small fleet of ships which made up to 10 trips a year to the Baltic and brought Swedish iron back to the Derwent.

A poem written about Crowley's ironworks records:

Incessant, day and night each crater roars
Like the volcano on Sicilian shores
Their fiery wombs each molten mass combine
Thence, lava like, the boiling torrents shine
Down the trenched sand the liquid metal holds
Shoots showers of stars and fills the hollow moulds.

Impressive as Crowley's achievements as an entrepreneur were, it was his remarkable methods as an employer which mark him out from the others of his generation. The villages of Swalwell, Winlaton and Winlaton Mill had their own peculiar courts alongside what amounted to an early form of the welfare state - although the price to be paid was an incredible degree of interference in the everyday lives of his workers.

Crowley had three factories at Winlaton and two at Winlaton Mill, each built in a square around a central courtyard where the workers lived - and every element of life inside the square was governed by the rules laid down by Crowley. They worked 80 hours a week - from five in the morning until eight at night, or seven on Saturdays, with two meal breaks. Timekeepers slept in their offices to ensure the 5am bell was rung to summon the labourers to work and they also carried out spot checks during the day to make sure there was no slacking. Crowley insisted he paid wages for a full working week and not: "for being at taverns, alehouses, coffee houses, breakfast, dinner, playing, sleeping, smoking, singing, reading of news history, quarrelling, contention, disputes or anything else foreign to my business, any way loitering or employing themselves in any business that doth not altogether belong to me." To make sure the message got across, Crowley ordered that the windows in his factories be built at such a height that the workmen could not see out of them, ensuring there would be no distractions from the matter in hand.

Crowley's reach did not end at the factory gate. Each square was governed by a warden, who strictly regulated all aspects of life under a system of 117 rules contained in Crowley's Law Book. The warden ensured that all visitors were gone by dark and the gates into the square were locked. He ensured that everyone was home by 9pm on Sundays and 10pm on other days. No hawkers or drunks were allowed into the squares, or anyone disturbing the peace. Fines were to be imposed on any residents found gambling, fighting, using obscene language throwing stones or making any disturbance. Children who broke the rules were to be whipped by their own parents - or else the parents would themselves by fined.

Crowley held drinking in particular contempt. He ordered his wardens "to Pry and Enquire" into the drinking habits of his workmen and resolved that anyone discovered drinking before noon was to be fired on the spot: "Whereas Mr Crowley hath made it his observation that Morning Drinking hath been of fatal consequence to all that have made a practice of it (1) it is of all things the most destructive to business (2) it destroyed health, memory and understanding (3) produceth nothing but folly and madness (4) it wastes the only time to do business in."

But, if his law book appears heavy-handed today, much of Crowley's system was remarkably enlightened by the standards of the time. To settle grievances, a court of arbitrators was established as an alternative to the expensive and time-consuming law courts, which were out of the reach of most working men. The court of arbitration sat every ten weeks and comprised the chaplain, two members appointed by Crowley and two members appointed by the workforce. It adjudicated on disputes, heard appeals and preserved good order in the villages. The court had the power to levy fines, not just for breaches of the law but also for moral conduct. The money raised through fines was spent on improvements in the villages.

Most importantly, Crowley also set up a rudimentary system of sickness insurance, weekly pensions were paid to the old and disabled and a workman's family were provided for on his death. Schools were established at Winlaton, Winlaton Mill and Swalwell where the workmen's children were taught reading, writing and accounts. Children attended school from 8am to 4pm in the winter and 6am to 5pm in the summer, with a two-hour lunch break, six days a week. The only holidays the children had were Sundays, holy days and the 12 days of Christmas. Crowley issued specific orders to his schoolmaster to keep the children at their desks all day, regardless of what travelling entertainment may be in town: "He shall not upon any account of races, cock-fighting, rope dancers or stage players dismiss his scholars. He is to make his scholars shew due respects to their superiors and especially aged persons and to correct such as he finds guilty of lying, swearing or such like horrid crimes, but above all things set a good example before the children. He is to carry it with an even hand to all his scholars and not to despise any for their poverty."

A surgeon, William Rayne, was appointed to attend to the workers and their families. The doctor had to attend the factory every day in case of accidents and also provided free medicines, although John Crowley, the son of Ambrose, later complained that the villagers would feign illness in order to sell their medicines elsewhere. However, it appears that Dr Rayne, who would later be succeeded by his son John, was to be kept very busy. A mystery illness swept through Winlaton in 1710 which led to the death of 40 children, although it would have been many more were it not for the medical help offered by Dr Rayne. The village was also at the centre of a smallpox outbreak in 1741 which had dreadful repercussions. Between July of that year and January 1742, smallpox carried away almost 200 people including 43 children and left many more blind or disfigured. At its height, four people a day from Winlaton were being buried at Ryton Churchyard.

Ambrose Crowley was knighted on New Year's Day, 1706 and the following year was appointed sheriff of London. By the time of his death in 1713, Sir Ambrose had been elected MP for Andover and was an alderman of the City of London - where he had served his long apprenticeship all those years earlier. But Sir Ambrose never once forgot his roots as a blacksmith and above the door of his offices in Thames Street, the centre of his colossal business empire, hung a picture of the old leather jerkin he had worn as an apprentice smith.

Despite his remarkable achievement, Crowley was ridiculed by polite society. He was viciously satirized in The Spectator magazine in a thinly-veiled attack entitled The Story of Sir John Anvil, a man who, despite his success, could never truly rise above his humble beginnings. The sneering article said that Sir John: "began the world with a small parcel of rusty iron and being gifted in the acquisition of wealth was knighted in his 35th year and, being intent on making a family with a dash of good blood in their veins, married a woman of fashion who changed his name to Enville and confined her husband to the cockloft when she had visitors of quality." The story went on: "She thought herself his superior in sense as much as she was in quality and therefore treated him like a plain well-meaning man. She even dictated to him in his own business, set him right in points of trade. In short, he was so much out of his natural element that to recover his old way of life he would be very content to begin the world again and be plain old Jack Anvil."

After his death, the ironworks passed first to his son John and then to his granddaughter Theodosia. Gradually, the social insurance system which Ambrose Crowley had established was eroded. At the same time, it became clear that for all his attempts to regulate the conduct of his workforce, Crowley's Crew were not to be content with their lot and, for the next 100 years, appeared to be at the centre of every revolutionary movement to impact on the North. Winlaton and Swalwell acquired a reputation as hotbeds of revolutionary agitation. In the summer of 1740, bread riots broke out in Newcastle, described at the time as the worst outbreak of violence the city had ever seen. The combined effects of an economic depression, a poor harvest and a severe winter had left the people hungry while seeds rotted in the ground and farm labourers were being laid off. When magistrates failed to release enough low-price grain, a full-scale riot broke out and The Guildhall was besieged by an angry mob. Shots were fired into the crowd, leaving one man dead and dozens wounded, but the shooting merely served to inflame passions and the rioters broke in and ransacked the city's treasury. Warrants were issued for the arrest of known troublemakers and the authorities appear to have decided the ringleaders of the riot came from Crowley's Crew. Hundreds were thrown in jail, some arrested as they fled north to Scotland and, in the end, seven men were transported to the colonies for their part in the riot while many more received lesser sentences.

The presence of hundreds of disgruntled workmen at Crowley's ironworks with the knowledge and means to make their own weapons posed a constant threat to those charged with upholding law and the existing social order. This intensified after the Peterloo massacre of 1819, when a detachment of militia charged with sabres drawn into a crowd of peaceful protesters in Manchester. Eleven people were killed and 400 wounded, sparking outrage across the country. The protest, calling for working men to be given the vote, was in part organised by the Manchester Corresponding Society, an organisation set up to represent radical opinion in a time when political parties were illegal. In the aftermath, delegates from Manchester travelled to the Derwent to establish such corresponding societies in Swalwell, Winlaton and Blaydon. Meanwhile, the radicals of Crowley's Crew were having an influence on their near neighbours. In the months after Peterloo, striking miners at Ryton decided that, in order to protect themselves against a similar fate to that suffered by the cotton workers of Manchester, they would take middle-class women as hostages to form a human shield against the swords and bullets of the militia, although it appears the threat was never carried out.

By the middle of the 19th Century, by which time the Crowley family had sold the ironworks, Swalwell and Winlaton had emerged as a centre of Chartism, the next great movement for democratic reform. The Chartists demanded that all men have the vote and staged a series of great demonstrations and mass petitions of Parliament to press their case. On at least one occasion, the women of Winlaton held afternoon teas in The Highlander pub to raise funds for the Chartist cause. But as well as these peaceful protests, Chartism also had a more extreme wing which threatened revolution and it was said that the men of Crowley's factories were particularly militant in the movement, preparing weapons including pikes, rudimentary hand grenades and guns at the ironworks for distribution around the north in the event of revolution.

In August 1839, the Chartists staged an abortive rising in Newport in which 24 protesters were shot dead by soldiers. The Chartist leaders claimed to be ready to mobilise thousands of armed working men and claimed to have 700 armed men in Winlaton ready to go into battle. Whether true of not, the claim certainly alarmed the magistrates who, within days of the Newport Rising, sent troops to Winlaton and Swalwell to search for weapons where it was said the villagers mobilised 14 canons to keep the soldiers at bay while the weapons were spirited away.

Crowley's works was the largest and most important of a string of ironworks growing up along the banks of the Derwent at the turn of the 18th Century. Nothing remains of Crowley's great concern, but further up the river at Derwentcote stands a small furnace which is now among the most important industrial monuments in the country - the only complete cementation furnace in Britain which helped to kick start the Industrial Revolution.

A mill has existed at Derwentcote since the time of the civil war, but the forge which made its name probably dates only to 1719.

Alderman Ralph Reed of Newcastle was the first owner of Derwentcote forge in partnership with his brother-in-law William Thomlinson and other family members. Reed recruited forge workers from Ireland - of whom George Bevins and John Lavender are thought to be the first - to bring their expertise to the Derwent Valley.

From the start, the fortunes of the Derwentcote forge were closely linked with those of the nearby furnace at Blackhall Mill. There, a furnace had been set up back in 1687 by Dennis Hayford which was operated by German-born William Bertram. Bertram holds a unique place in the industrial history of Britain and was, for many years, the only man in the country who produced the metal known as German or shear steel - bar iron converted in cold blast furnaces into a steel which could be forged repeatedly. Bertram and his furnaces were closely connected with the swordmakers of Shotley Bridge, the sword mill and the furnace were opened in the same year and Blackhall Mill supplied shear steel to be turned into the famous blades. Bertram may even have been among those who made their flight from Solingen - although there is also some suggestion that he was responsible for the primitive blast furnace and bloomery which existed upstream at Allensford and which opened some years earlier. The Allensford furnace, which was also used by the Shotley swordsmiths, was in operation from 1670 until 1710 and Bertram certainly operated it for some of that period.

Only a handful of men were required to operate the small-scale ironworks at Derwentcote and Blackhall Mill - but several generations of the same families found work at the two ironworks, sometimes dividing their entire working lives between the two sites. Initially, Derwentcote had consisted of a forge, dam, mill race and smith's workshop, but once the furnace was built in the 1740s, the two works were almost identical.

At Derwentcote, iron bars imported from Sweden would be placed in chests made of firebrick and packed down with charcoal brought from Chopwell Woods, then sealed with dry sand. Locally-mined coal would provide the fire, with heat and flames carried around the furnace by a system of flues before escaping into the air through the distinctive conical chimney. It was a simple process - but would take days to complete. Firstly, a furnaceman and his assistant would climb down through heat and ash into the tiny

Blackhall Mill foundry in 1912
(Photograph courtesy of Gateshead Libraries Service)

spaces of the furnace to load between 10 and 14 tonnes of the metal, charcoal and sand into the sealed chests. It would take them about six hours working in the most claustrophobic of conditions to load the iron, then the fires were lit. Within about 15 hours, the chests full of iron would be red hot. For five days and five nights, the furnace would super heat the metal as assistants stoked the fires to keep the temperatures up. Finally, the furnace had to be left to cool, for anything up to 10 days, before the furnacemen could return for the metal, which had been transformed into blister steel - so called because the impurities blistered to the surface during the roasting.

The process had been invented in Germany in the 17th Century but Tyneside had by this time emerged as the European centre of the industry and Derwentcote was one of the most important furnaces. At a time when only 1,000 tons of blister steel a year were being converted in the whole of England, Derwentcote was producing more than 100 tons.

Ralph Reed's partners sold Derwentcote in 1733 to a four-strong partnership of Newcastle businessmen, who were instrumental in opening the all-important furnaces and expanding the operation. But their involvement ended in protracted legal proceedings, complicated by the bankruptcy of one partner and the deaths of two others, which dragged on for six long years. Finally, in 1753, Derwentcote passed into the hands of a Mr Hodgson of Newcastle. Under his ownership, the links with Blackhall Mill grew ever closer - Derwentcote began to use the trademark devised by Hayford to denote Bertram's famous steel, one of Bertram's apprentices is listed as making German steel at Derwentcote and the roll-call of workers shows more and more the same individuals were working at the two works. By the middle of the 19th Century, both furnaces were being leased by the Cookson family - a famous clan of ironmasters who owned works from Chester-le-Street to Cumbria. One descendant of the Cookson family would go on to be chairman of Consett Iron Company during the 20th Century.

The Cooksons gave up their interest in Derwentcote in 1872, by which time its days were over. Such furnaces had been superseded by great metal producing machines such as Consett. Derwentcote passed through a series of owners until its final closure in 1891, Blackhall Mill limped on until 1916. The future of iron and steel making lay elsewhere in the Derwent Valley.

CHAPTER 17
THE DERWENTWATER LIGHTS

ON his last night on earth, after just 27 tragic years, the Earl of Derwentwater gazed silently out of the window of his prison cell in the Tower of London at the night sky. A crowd was gathering in the capital's dim and overcrowded streets for the morning's execution and, for a moment at least, they forgot their drinking as their eyes were drawn to the Heavens. Hundreds of miles north, on the banks of the Derwent, his friends and family also looked upwards. The Northern Lights burned especially bright that night. Vivid reds, yellows and blues streaked across the night sky in an amazing astronomical light show. The crowds, briefly distracted, turned back to their gin and beer, the family returned to their prayers and the earl returned to his quiet contemplation. In the lane between Shotleyfield and Kiln Pit Hill, a thundering of hooves was heard for the third night running. Cowering in their homes, the fearful villagers saw the spectre again, the Derwentwater death coach, driven by a headless coachman, made its way along the night roads to the family's ancestral home.

Later that night, the young earl sent for the undertaker Stephen Roome to make arrangements for his own funeral. Derwentwater asked that a silver plate be fixed to his coffin and be inscribed: "that he died a sacrifice to his lawful sovereign." Considering such a request tantamount to treason, Roome refused the earl's final request and the undertaker was unceremoniously dismissed from the cell.

The following day dawned fair. The earl dressed carefully in a coat, waistcoat and breeches of black velvet, he pulled on stockings to the knee, his shoes and a wig of uncommonly fair hair which cascaded down to his chest. Outside in the streets, the first conversation of the day turned to the previous night's spectacular lightshow. For more than 200 years afterwards, the dazzling display would be known as the Derwentwater Lights. Finally, he appeared before the crowds at the Tower, his handsome face raised to the crowd. Pale with fear, he spoke falteringly: "Being in a few minutes to appear before the tribunal of God where, though most unworthy, I hope to find mercy which I have not found from men now in power, I have endeavoured to make my peace with His Divine Majesty by most humbly begging pardon for all the sins of my life."

But as he spoke, the young earl visibly grew in confidence and with a voice ever more steady he told the crowd: "I intended to wrong nobody, but to serve my king and country and that without self-interest, hoping by the example I gave to have induced others to their duty and God." Derwentwater briefly bowed his head then walked over to where Marvell, the hooded executioner, stood leaning on his axe by a block covered in black serge. The earl examined the block closely and, noticing it had a rough, splintered edge where he might nick his neck, asked the executioner to chip it smooth. The condemned man then produced a small leather purse containing several guineas which he passed to the executioner as payment for a clean death. His close friend and co-accused Lord Kenmure was first to go. He tipped Marvell eight guineas but, as the drums rolled, he struggled and it took two blows to kill him. Then Marvell turned to Derwentwater.

The Catholic priest Father Pippard was there to witness the execution. He later wrote: "The very executioner knelt down and prayed and wept like a child and I heard him say: 'No Caesar could die greater. I ask your lordship's forgiveness'. 'With all my heart' said the young lord. 'I forgive all my enemies, the most malicious of them, and I do forgive you." Derwentwater lay down on the scaffold and prostrated his neck on the block, still wet with blood, as the drums began to roll once more. Three times he recited his final prayer: "Dear Jesus, be merciful to me" and on the third occasion, the axe fell. On the morning of February 24th, 1716, James Radcliffe, the 3rd Earl of Derwentwater, convicted traitor, was executed with a single blow to the neck.

James Radcliffe was born on June 28th 1689 and spent his early years in Paris among the Jacobite court, a childhood friend of James Stuart, son of the exiled King James II of England. When the former king died in 1701, the mantle of Pretender to the English throne fell to his son. So, from an early age, James Radcliffe was associated with the Stuart cause. At the age of just 17, his own father died and he inherited his title as 3rd Earl of Derwentwater even though he had barely set foot inside England during his short lifetime. Although the ancestral title derived from the family's lands in present day Cumbria, the family also owned extensive lands on the banks of the Derwent and in 1710, when the earl came of age, he returned from France to live at Dilston Castle on the banks of The Devil's Water between Hexham and Blanchland.

The execution of the Earl of Derwentwater on Tower Hill

The earl became a hugely popular figure on his estates where he was held in very high regard by his tenants. Derwentwater owned extensive lands on the north bank of the Derwent, including at Allensford, Mosswood, Shotley Bridge, Shotleyfield, Kiln Pit Hill and Whittonstall. The earl was said to be as at home in the lowly cottages scattered across the Derwent Valley as his own castle. The young lord also owned, among other property in the area, Healeyfield Lead Mine at Castleside where he was a regular visitor. During his visits he would stay at Dene Howl farmhouse, owned by a farmer named Mr Shirley, where the earl would dine with his friends long into the night. Young and handsome, dashing, and cosmopolitan, he was a breath of fresh air among the stilted squires of Northumberland and Durham. A rhyme coined at the time shows his popularity among the ordinary folk on his lands:

> "O Derwentwater's a bonnie lord,
> "And golden is his hair
> "And glintin' is his hawkin' eye
> Wi' kind love dwelling there."

The new earl was also close friends with Thomas Forster. Forster came from an ancient landed family and owned Bamburgh Castle, but derived most of his £530 a year income from his extensive lands around Blanchland, centre of the growing lead mining industry. The young Thomas was educated by his private tutor Mr Hilyard at Blanchland and he remained a regular visitor to the village. A contemporary description portrayed him as: "of middle stature, inclining to be fat, well shaped except that he stoops in his shoulders, fair complexioned, his mouth wide, his nose pretty large and his eyes grey." Thomas Forster may have lacked the handsome features of his friend, the earl but they certainly had one thing in common - the Forsters too were supporters of the Stuart family's claims on the English throne.

Events far away were to catapult these two country landowners onto the national stage. In 1714, William's successor Queen Anne died, leaving no heir. James Stuart claimed the Crown, but the throne was instead offered to George I, a German cousin of King William who had never set foot in England and spoke barely a word of the language. Within a year, the Jacobites made their move. Plans for James Stuart to land in Plymouth in the summer of 1715 and stage an English insurrection centred on Bath were abandoned at the last minute when the plot was uncovered. There was even talk of a landing on Holy Island followed by a march on Newcastle, while in Scotland, the earl of Mar, a long-standing supporter of James Stuart, began to raise an army and openly threatened rebellion. The time had come for all Catholics and supporters of the Stuarts to decide which side they were on.

On September 6th, Mar raised his standard at Braemar with an army numbering just 500. The army may have been small but the Highlanders flocked to the banner and, by the end of the month, Mar had captured Perth with a force of 5,000 men and all of Scotland stood at his mercy. In England, the pressure was mounting on Jacobite supporters to show their hand. There was a widespread feeling of pessimism among the English Jacobites, possibly because of the abject failure of the proposed Bath rising only months earlier. On September 21st, 1715 a message was sent to Parliament from King George himself declaring that he had just cause for suspecting Forster, Derwentwater and four others of plotting to support the invasion of the kingdom in the interests of the Pretender. The king therefore asked for the approval of the House to arrest the six as conspirators against the Government. Events were now moving fast.

The 3rd Earl of Derwentwater James Radcliffe
(Picture courtesy The Northern Echo)

The earl of Scarborough took it upon himself to organise the defence of the north against the rising and raised all the leading families in Durham to arm their servants and tenants to defend the king. Scarborough raised two troops of horse, one to patrol the south of the county while the defence of North Durham was handed to Captain James Clavering of Axwell Park.

Meanwhile, Derwentwater was dithering. The rising had broken out and a warrant had been issued for his arrest but for some time he tried to stay out of the rebellion. Now he was involved in a deadly game of cat and mouse with Captain Clavering, whose men pursued him through the dale. The earl went to ground and sought refuge in the humble cottages on his estates where he was hidden by his tenants. According to legend, the earl was hiding on his Whittonstall estates when Clavering was tipped off and sent his men to arrest him. The earl was spotted as he rode his grey mare on the hill above Greenhead and Unthank Farm and was chased at breakneck speed by a posse which began to close in. One of his farmers appeared and showed the earl the entrance of a nearby drift mine which he rode into and hid, while the loyal tenant pointed his pursuers further down the valley. The spot is still known as Grey Mare Hill today. The earl's mind was finally made up when, during a night time visit to Dilston to confer with family and friends, his wife told him: "It is not fitting that the Earl of Derwentwater should continue to hide his head in hovels when the gentry are up in arms for their lawful sovereign." The countess then passed her husband her fan and said: "Take that, and give me your sword."

The following day, October 6th 1715, the renegade Earl of Derwentwater and a small band of followers gathered on the banks of the Derwent and rode off for their date with destiny. That morning, word reached Lord Widdrington, of Stella Hall, near Blaydon, that the long-awaited rebellion had broken out. William Widdrington was a 37-year-old gentleman landowner living in enforced retirement as a Catholic who was barred from Parliament, the professions or the Army. His wife, Lady Anne, had died the previous year and his family's long association with the Catholic cause compelled him to one last great adventure. He gathered together his brothers, 30-year-old Charles and 23-year-old Peregrine, for breakfast, along with family chaplain John Wilson and all the friends and estate tenants he could muster.

There he toasted the success of Derwentwater and the rebellion with whiskey, and rode off to join the growing band of rebels.

North Durham was soon awash with armed men and spies criss-crossed the county by night. Clavering sent men to Dilston to spy on Lady Derwentwater to see if she would betray her husband's plans. Suspected rebel sympathisers were arrested, including George Hartford, known as Brave George, who was arrested at Stanhope and taken under armed escort to a house in Cornsay where he was held for several days until he could be removed to Durham Jail. Clavering's men roamed the countryside looking for rebels: they seized a pack horse at Teesdale, heading north and loaded with pistols for the rebellion; guards were positioned at Allensford and Eddy's Bridge and the captain sent a squadron of militiamen to Shotley Bridge, to watch for any attempt the rebel army might make to enter County Durham and also to intercept rebel messengers crossing the river. Captain Clavering's accounts show that between October 12th and 14th, he paid 15s to his spy, known only as HH, to take messages to the watchmen waiting at Allensford and issue them with further orders.

At around the same time, he paid almost as much to the constable of Muggleswick to search premises in the parish after reports reached him that several strangers had been spotted there. When a rumour reached him that the Jacobites were to seize horses at Lanchester, Clavering ordered the constable to take the 39 mounts to stables in the safety of loyal Gateshead. Clavering also kept a close eye on the lower reaches of the Derwent. John Wilson, the luckless priest of Stella House, was taken and John Crowley, the son of Ambrose Crowley and now head of the great ironworks, was arrested and questioned before being released. Clavering also reported that there were 200 Catholics at Blaydon and Winlaton ready to join the rising and he had his men pay close attention to both villages for signs of disloyalty.

But by then the rebels had left the Derwent Valley. Derwentwater, Widdrington and Forster considered attacking Newcastle to capture the arms stored there. But, during the weeks of dithering, the king's men had reinforced the garrison and, faced with superior numbers, the rebels decided to head to Northumberland where they would recruit more men. They marched north to Warkworth and then to Morpeth, which they captured on October 13th - a week after the rebellion had broken out in England. By the time they entered Morpeth, the little band of rebels had swollen to 330 men, although Clavering sent an intelligence report to his masters describing the army as being made up of "mean men".

But in the seven days it had taken to raise this force, the Government had not been idle. The Durham militia was moved to Newcastle and the capture of the city - with all its arms and ammunition - was judged to be beyond the rebels. Instead, they moved to Hexham and spent three days there recruiting more men, including horsemen from the Scottish Borders under Lord Kenmure. Finally, word reached the rebels that Mar had ordered 1,000 men commanded by Brigadier Mackintosh to march south to link up with the northern rebels. Derwentwater and his colleagues went to meet them, reaching Rothbury on October 20th, Wooler the following day and finally Kelso on October 22nd, where the two armies linked up.

It should have been a moment of triumph. The rebel army at Kelso now numbered around 3,000 men, including around 600 horsemen. However, the fateful decision was made to place Forster, a man with absolutely no military experience whatsoever, in charge of the entire enterprise. The English contingent, short of arms and without artillery, wanted to return to their initial plan of capturing Newcastle. But on the same day they reached Kelso, General Carpenter with several regiments of dragoons had reached the Tyne and it was accepted by most that an attack was unlikely to succeed. The Scottish contingent suggested two other options, a move against Dumfries, which again was heavily guarded, or the most obvious tactic, striking north against the last remaining Royalist forces north of the Border at Stirling, which would have united the two Jacobite armies and captured the whole of Scotland.

Both options had their advantages but instead Forster settled on an extraordinary plan. Convinced the whole of the north was itching for the opportunity to rise up in support of their cause, Forster decided he would invade England - launching an attack on Manchester where he would find willing supporters among the Catholic population of Lancashire. It was such a spectacularly bad strategy that 500 of the Highlanders immediately packed up and headed home. In the meanwhile, General Carpenter had left Newcastle with three regiments of dragoons in pursuit of the Jacobites.

On October 27th, three weeks after the rising had broken out in the north, the small but proud rebel army left Kelso for Jedburgh and, on November 1st, crossed into England. Just north of Penrith, a rabble of unarmed countrymen turned out to fight but, on seeing the strength of the invaders, turned and fled - a victory which gave false hope to the Jacobites. They marched through Appleby, Kendal, Kirby Lonsdale and Lancaster expecting to find recruits in every town - but precious few came and in fact their numbers dwindled as some, realising the hopelessness of their cause, deserted. On November 9th, the Jacobite cavalry reached Preston - then a busy market town straddling the River Ribble. Two troops of Royalist dragoons guarding the town withdrew as they arrived and the following day the Jacobite infantry caught up and occupied the town, planning a day's rest before their victorious march on Manchester.

But the news they received there was not good. It came as a surprise to learn that General Wills was nearby at the head of five regiments of Royalist cavalry and three regiments of infantry. Moreover, they received news that General Carpenter was closing in behind them. Forster's inexperience came to the fore. It was said that on realising they were cornered and that no help was coming from the people of Lancashire, he went to pieces, issued a series of contradictory orders and counter orders, then retired to bed leaving his bewildered subordinates to organise the defence of the town as best they could.

The only way into the town was along the narrow country lanes, hemmed in by steep banks and hedges. These tiny lanes would have made the perfect spot for an ambush, but the Jacobites did not dare commit their outnumbered forces in open countryside and instead set up barricades at the entrances to the town. Snipers took up position in the houses and their six pieces of cannon were deployed to overlook the approach roads. On the eastern edge of the town, Brigadier Mackintosh was in command of the barricade near the church and Derwentwater's men were spread out in the churchyard, using the gravestones and church wall as cover. Other barricades were set up on the Liverpool road and the Lancaster road, the houses were fortified and snipers were put into position to command the lanes and open fields beyond. By noon on November 12th, the rebels had laid their defences as best they could.

As the drums sounded, General Willis ordered his first tentative attack. A detachment of dragoons, backed by infantry, thundered down the lane towards the barricade at the church - but they were driven off in a hail of gunfire by Derwentwater's men in the churchyard. However, the main attack was now underway on the Wigan side of the town. Ranks of redcoats launched a fierce attack on the barricades, but came under withering fire from the Jacobite sharpshooters hidden in the houses overlooking the lane. They were forced to retreat without laying a foot inside the town and the spirits of the defenders soared.

It was a momentary respite. The double barricades manned by Mackintosh's men were flanked by two large merchants' houses. These became the scene of the fiercest fighting as the redcoats battled their way inch by inch across the gardens and finally managed to capture one of the two townhouses by early evening. Then another all-out assault was launched against the barricade, supported by the redcoats now inside the edge of town. Casualties were beginning to mount among the defenders and Mackintosh was forced to call for reinforcements from Derwentwater's men in the churchyard to man the barricade as enemy infantry took up positions in the fields and let loose volley after volley of musket-fire towards them. Finally, as dusk fell, the attack was seen off and General Willis withdrew his men.

The still of the night was punctuated by the regular whip-crack of sniper fire from both sides as the rebel commanders took stock. After a day of intense fighting, the line had held but 18 Jacobites had been killed and 25 were wounded, while in the fields, lanes and gardens around Preston 200 redcoats lay dead or wounded. But the situation was hopeless. Now that the house near the church barricade had fallen, it appeared only a matter of time before Mackintosh's position was overrun. The English army could expect to receive reinforcements soon, whereas it became clear from interrogation of the few prisoners the Jacobites had taken that none of the soldiers were about to desert. Under cover of darkness, hundreds of disillusioned rebels quietly melted away from their posts, forded the River Ribble - which had inexplicably been left unguarded - and disappeared into the night.

Early the following morning, General Carpenter's dragoons finally arrived from the north and sealed off the final exit. The remaining rebels were now trapped. Derwentwater argued vehemently that they attempt to fight their way out; the Highlanders argued simply that they stand and fight to the last man. The final say went to Forster and, to the subsequent fury of his comrades, he decided that to prevent further bloodshed, the rebel army would surrender. It was a decision for which Forster almost paid with his life there and then, as a witness named Patten later recalled: "Many exclaimed against Forster and had he appeared in the street he would certainly have been cut to pieces. As it was, he would have been killed in his chamber by Mr Murray had not I, with my hand, struck up the pistol with which he had fired at him so that the bullet went through the wall of the room."

In the early afternoon, the English marched into town and disarmed the rebels in the Market Square. Dozens, mainly Highlanders, were shot dead on the spot. An estimated 700 were taken prisoner, including 56 loyal men from Derwentwater's estates in Northumberland and Durham and another 16 from Widdrington's estate at Stella. The rank and file were treated with considerable savagery - they were beaten, stripped of their shirts and imprisoned in an unheated church until a more permanent home could be found for them. Among those captured were Joseph Maforshead, a poor cobbler from Ryton, John Willson, a carpenter from Whickham and Alex Robinson, a seaman from Ryton, along with countless others from the banks of the Derwent who had joined the great adventure and now found themselves imprisoned in stinking cells across Lancashire. Facing the prospect of a trial for treason and the gallows, around 500 took the option of immediate transportation without trial. At least one ship crammed with Jacobite rebels mutinied during the long voyage across the Atlantic and the prisoners made it to the safety of the French Colonies, but for most they would see out their remaining days not on the banks of the Derwent but on a Virginia plantation.

The lesser gentry were held prisoner in Chester Castle in overcrowded cells where disease spread like wildfire. They were held 80 to the room, three per bed, for months. By February 1716, they were in: "a most miserable condition, being crowded like beasts in a fold, having a raging fever amongst them and daily dying with ill useage." The senior officers, however, were to be brought to trial. After being held for a day or two in the finest houses Preston had to offer, from which several of Derwentwater's personal servants escaped, the orders arrived that the ringleaders of the rebellion were to be brought to London to answer for their treason.

The English took no chances. The Jacobite officers were shackled and taken to London at bayonet point, escorted by a troop of cavalrymen, five soldiers for every prisoner. Humiliated in battle, they were to be humiliated in captivity as the solemn procession made its way south. At the head rode Derwentwater with a priest alongside him, the other officers behind. Each, though in chains, was mounted on a horse which was led by an English infantryman. Two cavalrymen rode alongside each Jacobite, swords drawn to prevent escape. If they had dreamed of being welcomed to London by a population liberated from a tyrannical king they were sadly mistaken. Every village along the way emptied to howl abuse and hurl missiles at them from the side of the road. On reaching the capital, they were treated to a grisly sight - three rebels hanged early in the day had been disembowelled and their innards put on display in a box at the entrance to the city. It turned Forster's stomach so much he was unable to eat for days afterwards. It was also the last thing the two friends would see together as they were to be split up: Derwentwater was thrown into the Tower of London where he would spend his last days while the disgraced Forster was taken to Newgate Prison.

Their only hope now lay with the success of the rebellion in Scotland - but on the very day the English rebels were fighting in Preston, the tide was also turning north of the Border. Mar's army fought an inconclusive action at Sherrifmuir and forces loyal to King George were closing in. As disenchantment in the ranks grew and the number of desertions rose, the Jacobites left Perth, pursued through the winter snows by the redcoats. In the first week of February, the leaders boarded a ship to take them back to exile in France.

The rising was over and with it came the end of Derwentwater's hopes. Five days after Mar fled over the water, the earl and Forster were put on trial for treason, were convicted and condemned to death. The sentence read to Derwentwater was chilling: "You must be hanged by the neck but not till you are dead, for you must be cut down alive then your bowels must be taken out and burned before your face then your head must be severed from your body and your body divided into four quarters and these must be at the king's disposal."

All three Widdrington brothers pleaded not guilty, but later changed their minds and threw themselves on the mercy of the court. Lord Widdrington described the rising as "rash folly" and a "miserable expedition. He told his judges: "Your lordships see before you an unfortunate man who after leading a private and retired life for many years has by one rash and inconsidered action exposed himself and his family to the greatest calamities and misery." He added: "As to the insurrection in Northumberland, I only heard of it accidentally the night before it happened and being soon after informed that all my neighbours and acquaintances had met in arms, a crowd of confused and mistaken notions hurried me at once into a precipitate resolution of joining them."

But if hope appeared to have gone as the rebels languished in their condemned cells, they had reckoned without an extraordinary young woman. Dorothy Forster was 29-years-old when she heard of her brother's arrest. She left Blanchland with a local blacksmith, named Purdy, and headed for London to rescue her incarcerated brother. After attempted bribery failed she finally managed to get an impression of the keys to Newgate Prison by pressing them into a piece of clay she held in her hand. She returned to Newcastle, had a new set of keys cut, and went back to London where she was able to pass the copied keys to her brother. Coolly, Forster and Mackintosh invited the governor of the prison for a drink, locked him in his cell and sauntered out of the prison, Forster leaving his dressing gown on the doorstep of the jail. Within 24 hours, they were in Calais before the hue and cry could be raised. The authorities were furious that such a figurehead of rebellion had escaped their clutches and put a price of £1,000 on his head. In the meantime, Forster was expelled from Parliament and his estates in Blanchland and Bamburgh were sold off.

To avoid his recapture, Forster's friends spread the rumour that he had died shortly after his escape. To add to the deception, a sealed coffin full of sawdust was brought home from France to be buried at the family vault in Bamburgh. Forster eventually died a free, if disillusioned, man at Boulogne, in September 1738, and his body replaced the empty coffin which had earlier been interred.

The Widdrington brothers also escaped the block and eventually all three received a Royal Pardon. Peregrine, who was aide-de-camp to Forster during the abortive campaign, contracted spotted fever in prison but survived. William, Lord Widdrington, lived out his retirement in Bath and died in 1745, the year of the next great Jacobite rising, leaving a son, Henry. Charles Widdrington left for France and died a free man in St Omer in 1756.

But, for Derwentwater, there was no swashbuckling escape. He spent the two weeks between trial and scaffold locked in the Tower. His sentence was commuted to simple beheading but there was to be no hope of reprieve. As the date of his execution drew nearer, the Derwentwater death coach was seen ever more regular on the country roads of the Derwent Valley. For three consecutive nights before the execution it made its way from Shotley up through Kiln Pit Hill and on through the night, pulled by two headless horses and driven by a headless carriage driver. And as the Derwentwater Lights created a spectacular backdrop to its spectral journey, it made its way towards what would be his final resting place at Dilston. On the night of the execution, the Devils Water was said to have bubbled blood red.

After the execution, his servant Francis Wilson wrapped the earl's severed head in red velvet and his body in a black cloth for the long journey home. With the help of a bribe, Wilson managed to smuggle the body out of the Tower and took it to a safe house in Romford. Secretly, journeying only by night and resting by day, the earl's friends, including Mr Shirley of Healeyfield, brought the body back home to be buried among the people who loved him.

As they reached the borders of Durham, the Derwentwater lights were seen once more illuminating the night sky. One contemporary observer noted that: "The entire sky was suddenly lit up by fiery brilliance, with streamers of flame and colour flashing from east to west." The final day was spent resting at Dene Howl Farm - the Healeyfield house where the earl had spent many a happy night celebrating with his friends. Finally, with only a handful of mourners, they reached Dilston Castle and buried the Earl of Derwentwater at night.

Although the earl was now dead and buried, his supporters scattered across the prisons of England and the plantations of the New World, the fear of the Jacobites went unabated. Rumours of rebels swept the North every few months. In the spring of 1718, this alarm reached new heights. In March, Colonel George Liddell wrote to landowner William Cotesworth of his fears that the rebels were preparing to raise the standard once more. "There were 50 or 60 armed horsemen rode thro Winlayton I believe the fact to be true," he wrote. "There were 30 seen after that. Since I began this I had one from Winlayton on a little business who told me that last week six gentlemen well mounted and armed and with blue coates and green cockades rode thro that town in the evening southward. The rebels meet and cabal frequently and brag of their having been in the rebellion. I am satisfied we shall have another Brush this summer."

The following month, Liddell's warnings were even more stark and he pointed the finger of suspicion at some of the leading Catholic landowner's of the day, including George Silvertop of Minsteracres, who he suspected of preparing men and horses for a Jacobite army. "There is certainly some villainy afoot, we have it from all quarters," he wrote. "I met a man from Bladon, he was with Dr Finney and his curate last night, where he could not but observe some things remarkable. He says Dunn and Silvertop's colliery waggon horses are so nicely fed and kept that their workmen cannot but notice it. One Cook, a vile Papist at Winlaton, in his liquor told his landlord that in a little town he would see brave sport, which his landlord thought was a horse race at Derwenthaugh, but the other replied it was otherwise game than that."

The threat of a second rebellion came to nothing. Indeed, when the Jacobites did return to battle, in 1745, the North was noted for its loyalty to the Crown.

If it was to be the end of the Jacobite cause in the North, it was not the end of the tragedy for the Derwentwater family. The earl's estates were confiscated in 1716 and his widow left to make a new life for herself and her son in Europe. She died just seven years later at the age of 30 in Belgium and her son John, heir to the Derwentwater title, died in a riding accident in France aged just 19. Dilston Castle fell into ruins and the stones were taken for building materials. Within a generation, the dashing earl had become little more than a fading legend.

And there the story could have ended were it not for a remarkable woman more than a century later. In the middle of the 19th Century, an eccentric middle-aged woman turned up in Blaydon with a fantastic story. She claimed to be The Lady Amelia Matilda Mary Tudor Radclyffe, Countess of Derwentwater and rightful heir to the

The Countess of Derwentwater, wronged heiress,
wicked charlatan or deluded fool
(Photograph courtesy The Northern Echo)

*The ramshackle camp in which the Countess of
Derwentwater made her home near Dilston
(Photograph courtesy of The Northern Echo)*

earl's estates. The mysterious woman claimed that John, the earl's son, had not died in 1731 at all. The reported death, she claimed, had been a family ruse to put the authorities off the scent. John, she claimed, had survived, fled in secret to Germany where he had married and gone on to father 11 children, dying in 1798 at the ripe old age of 86. She, as his eldest surviving granddaughter, claimed she was entitled to all his Northumberland estates. It seemed an outlandish claim, but she produced various pieces of jewellery, pictures, plate and furniture which she said had been spirited away from Dilston Castle by the family while the earl was held in the Tower and held in trust for successive generations. These, she claimed, proved her claim to the Derwentwater title. The Newcastle Weekly Chronicle, one of several newspapers to champion her claims, said: "Her evidence places her lineage beyond all question." Others argued she was a fraud - there were claims she was in fact a West Country servant girl who had acquired the heirlooms in an

168

antique shop and was chancing her arm. Intriguing as the trinkets were, they cut no ice with the authorities and although she petitioned Parliament for her claim to the lands to be recognised, it was rejected.

But, the Countess Amelia was not a woman to be easily dissuaded. Wronged heiress, wicked charlatan or deluded fool, she began her lonely battle for what she argued was rightfully hers. On September 27th, 1868, an unusual procession made its way to the tumbledown ruins of Dilston Castle. In a coach drawn by four horses and attended by four footmen in red jackets, breeches and tights, rode the Countess Amelia. In a regal black satin dress and hat, and carrying the 3rd earl's rapier, she was attended by her faithful servant Harry Brown. Brown, an auctioneer from Shotley Bridge and county court bailiff, was descended from tenants who had farmed the riverbank at Shotley Bridge under the earl. His devotion to her cause knew no bounds and as Countess Amelia pursued her claim like a Victorian Don Quixote, Harry Brown followed her exploits around the countryside like Sancho Panza.

Tarpaulin was stretched across the top of a roofless room of the dilapidated building and the countess announced to her bemused neighbours that she was taking up residence once more in her castle. Brown and the footmen fetched bales of straw to plug the gaps in the windows, framed oil portraits of long-dead members of the Derwentwater dynasty were hung on the moss-strewn walls and the ancient flag of the Radcliffe clan was hoisted once more on a specially-installed flagpole. There, as the cold autumn wind howled around the broken stones of the ruined mansion, the Countess Amelia held court for three days, now dressed, incongruously, in the uniform of an Austrian soldier. Finally the authorities arrived to eject the countess from her family seat. Still wearing her military cloak and her sword in its scabbard, she was unceremoniously dumped by the roadside. There she stayed for another 35 days, first in a tent and then in a wooden shack built by her friends from Blaydon to keep her safe from the worst ravages of the Northumberland weather. Eventually, Hexham Highways Board declared her hut an obstruction and demolished it, fining her 10 shillings in the process, and Lady Amelia temporarily abandoned her crusade.

The campaign captured the public imagination and newspapers clamoured for every detail of the incredible story. In the early days of 1870, she resorted to ever more extreme measures to press her claim. Harry Brown went to South Newlands Farm near Shotley Bridge where he demanded the then astronomical sum of £270 in back rent which, he said, the farmer owed the countess. When, not unsurprisingly, the farmer refused, Brown and the countess helped themselves to livestock to cover the debt and rode off. A body of mounted men intercepted them at South Newlands and recaptured most of the stock, but Amelia rode off to Consett where she sold some of the beasts. As she entered the town she was cheered by her supporters among the townsfolk and went on to the Railway Inn, where she used the proceeds of the sale to buy beer for everyone, declaring to thunderous applause that there would be much more when she finally won her claim. But, despite the support she had among the population of Consett, particularly among the Irish labourers, she was promptly arrested by the police.

The Countess Amelia and her faithful retainer Harry Brown, along with several other supporters were tried for their part in the South Newlands raid on February 23rd, 1870 at Newcastle Crown Court before Mr Justice Brett and found guilty. All were cautioned apart from the luckless Harry Brown, who was sentenced to nine months' imprisonment with hard labour, a tough sentence for a man then aged 60 years old. The Countess herself was declared bankrupt over the £500 of livestock taken in the raid on South Newlands Farm and spent a brief spell in the debtors' prison at Newcastle.

In 1874, she carried out a second raid to demand rent at Whittonstall and the following year she again camped out to demand her rights, this time at Blackhill. But no-one was listening now. The press and public had grown tired of the whole charade. The Newcastle Journal wrote of the: "highly ludicrous but decidedly inconvenient audacities of the countess and her abettors." The Telegraph simply wondered why she had not been committed to a lunatic asylum many years ago. Finally exhausted after her campaign, the Countess Amelia died of bronchitis on February 26th 1880 at the Jacobean Dial House on Cutlers Hall Road in Blackhill and was buried in Blackhill Cemetery. To the end, she insisted on the justness of her claim, without convincing anyone of her cause - with the sole exception of Harry Brown. He died at Iveston in November 1891, aged 81, having suffered immense troubles for the woman he believed in. History does not record whether the Derwentwater lights shone on the night the Countess Amelia died.

CHAPTER 18
BEYOND THE GRAVE

ONE of the most extraordinary stories to come from the Derwent Valley could probably be dismissed as superstitious nonsense were it not for the impeccable credentials of the witness who recorded it. The Reverend John Wesley, founder of Methodism, detailed in his journal the incredible tale of the death of Robert Johnson, as related to him by those who were present and witnessed the events.

Robert Johnson's last will and testament, which plays a pivotal role in the strange events which follow, was drawn up in 1757 although, curiously, the records of his burial have since been torn from the parish register. Johnson lived at Ebchester Hill in the building which is now St Mary's Convent, and had a son, Cuthbert, who married a local girl against the express wishes of his father.

The Reverend Wesley wrote of Robert Johnson: "At this time, he was so enraged that he wished his right arm might burn off if ever he gave or left him sixpence. However, in March last, being taken ill, he made his will and left him all his estate. The same evening he died. On Thursday 10th, his widow, laying her hand upon his back, found it warm. In the evening, those who were with him went into the next room to take a little refreshment. As they were eating, they observed a disagreeable smell but could find nothing in the room to cause it. Returning into the room where the corpse lay, they found it full of smoke. Removing the sheet which covered the corpse they saw (to their no small amazement) the body so burnt that the entrails were bare and might be seen through the ribs. His right arm was nearly burnt off, his head so burnt that the brains appeared and a smoke came out of the crown of the head, like the steam of boiling water. When they cast water upon his body it hissed just as if cast upon red-hot iron. Yet the sheet which was upon the body was not singed, but that under him with the pillow-bier and pillow, and the plank on which he lay, were all burned and looked as black as charcoal.

"They hastened to put what was left of him into the coffin, leaving some to watch by it. But after it was nailed up, a noise of burning and crackling was heard therein. None was permitted to look into it, 'til it was carried to Ebchester churchyard. It was buried near the steeple. As soon as it was brought to the grave, the steeple was observed to shake. The people hastened away, and it was well they did, for presently part of the steeple fell; so that had they stayed two minutes longer they must have been crushed to pieces. All these circumstances were related to me and my wife by those who were eye and ear witnesses."

But the remarkable story of Robert Johnson and his burning body was not the first supposed message from beyond the grave to be recorded in the Derwent Valley. Another even more incredible tale - this time with grim results - was told at Durham Assizes court before Judge Davenport during 1632.

The court heard that during the previous summer, a teenage girl named Ann Walker was living in Lumley, near Chester-le-Street, where she was housekeeper to her uncle John Walker, the local miller. During those summer months, a relationship developed between the two and young Ann fell pregnant. As her condition became known, Ann left Walker's house and moved in with an aunt, known as Dame Caire, who also lived in the town. Although Ann did not reveal the identity of the baby's father, Walker was determined to rid himself of the inevitable scandal which would follow and so enlisted the support of his business partner Mark Sharpe to help him in his evil enterprise. The pair owned mills not only at Lumley but also at Lockhaugh, on the Derwent near the present day Winlaton Mill, and between them they hatched a terrible plan.

In the autumn, before signs of her pregnancy were beginning to show, the court heard that Walker told his niece that Sharpe would take her to see a midwife in Northumberland. Late one night, Sharpe called on her and, innocently, she set off with him along Clockburn Lane towards the mill at Lockhaugh - a route the millers knew like the back of their hand. Somewhere close to the Derwent, Sharpe produced a pick axe and murdered his young charge in cold blood, then threw her lifeless body down a nearby pit shaft before returning home as if nothing had happened. Walker explained the disappearance of his niece to curious villagers by saying she had gone to Lancashire to visit her family. Weeks passed by and it appeared that the pair had, literally, got away with murder - until an extraordinary turn of events occurred.

Kiln Pit Hill Churchyard (Photograph by Brian Clough)

On Christmas Eve, 1631, James Graham - another miller who worked two miles from Lumley - was working alone. Having put the corn in the hopper he came downstairs where he was confronted by a hideous ghostly apparition. It was a woman, her hair hanging down and matted with blood,. She threw back her cloak to reveal a baby at her breast and five gaping wounds on her head from which fresh blood trickled down her face and neck. She fixed him, he later said, with a stony stare which froze his blood. The terrified miller cowered and asked the apparition what it wanted of him. She replied: "I am the spirit of Ann Walker and one night was sent away with Mark Sharp who slew me with a pick and gave me these five wounds and afterwards threw my body into a coalpit." The ghost added that her blood had soaked Sharpe's shoes and stockings and, after trying to wash them clean in the Derwent, he had hidden them in the riverbank. She asked the miller to go and find the evidence to bring her killers to justice and then departed. Graham immediately checked the mill doors and found them, as he had left them, bolted from the inside.

Whether Graham doubted his own sanity, whether he did not want to get involved with the law or whether the prospect of a lengthy

173

Christmas Eve journey to the Derwent at the behest of ghost did not appeal, he did not do as she asked and instead went home. So the spirit of Ann Walker returned to haunt him night after night. Each time she repeated her exact words and asked what he had found on the banks of the river - each time she grew angrier and angrier as he revealed he had not done as she commanded. Eventually - after several appearances by the spectre - Graham plucked up the courage to go to the authorities and, in the company of the magistrates, he went to the banks of the Derwent. There they found the evidence just as she had told them, her body was found in a pit shaft with five clear wounds to the skull, bloodied shoes and stockings belonging to Mark Sharpe were found in a hole in the banks of the river.

John Walker and Mark Sharpe were arrested and were tried for murder. The only evidence at the trial came from James Graham - and Ann Walker. Walker and Sharpe were convicted and eventually, in August 1632, hanged for their crime.

Liberty towers over the Gibside estate
(Photograph by Brian Clough)

CHAPTER 19
LIBERTY AND LICENSE

HIGH above the Derwent Valley at the top of a stone column stands the figure of Liberty, gazing down over the lush Gibside estate with its carefully manicured gardens, its stately avenues of trees and its grand stone mansions. The statue has seen lords, ladies, kings and emperors pass beneath - men who literally changed the world around them and created these tranquil gardens from the wild wood. Its walls kept at bay the ever encroaching world of industry outside as the waggonways and grimy pit villages crept ever closer to this oasis of gentility. But Liberty has also looked down on the darker things which took place within these walls, on licentious behaviour behind closed doors and acts of the deepest depravity among those in high places.

By the end of the 17ᵗʰ Century, the young Elizabeth Blakiston was heiress to Gibside. In August 1693, she married Sir William Bowes, sucsessful and owner. Although he was older than his bride, by all accounts the marriage was happy. Elizabeth spent the next 13 years in an almost permanent state of pregnancy - giving birth to no less than 10 children. It appeared idyllic - but tragedy was to dog the family for the next 100 years. Two of Sir William and Elizabeth's children died in infancy, leaving four boys and four girls. Sir William himself died in 1706 at the age of 50, leaving his widow to bring up the family of eight alone. Lady Bowes, as she was now known, appeared to run the family admirably and when her own father Sir Francis Blakiston died in 1713, she was left with sole control of the Gibside estates until her eldest son should come of age and inherit the title - in accordance with the property laws of the time. The formidable Lady Bowes was equally adept at running a country estate as she was at raising a large family and threw herself into local commerce and politics with the skill of an old hand, although she did develop a reputation for being close-fisted along the way.

But if her business affairs were going well, Lady Bowes' family life was about to go hideously wrong. Smallpox, the scourge of rich and poor alike, visited the Derwent Valley and claimed the life of her eldest son John at the age of only nine years. Her second son, William Blakiston Bowes, also died of smallpox at the age of 24 and her third, Thomas, died of a fit in 1722.

So it was that George Bowes, a man never expected to inherit the title, lost five siblings by the time he was 21 years of age and became the heir to the family fortune, the first man born of the Bowes family to inherit the Gibside seat. George Bowes was born in 1701 and was five when his father died. By the time he came of age he had already developed something of a wild reputation. He was described as rash and autocratic both in his business dealings and his family. Although he had quite a talent for commerce - he was the driving force in the coal cartel known as the Grand Allies which broke the monopoly of the London coal traders - he was held back by his lack of tact in business dealings where he could appear blunt to the point of rudeness. He was also impetuous, running away from home at the age of 18 to become a captain in the Army and had to buy out his commission three years later when he inherited on the death of his brother.

His fiery temper was becoming a liability for a young man whose high-handed manner and determination to get his own way earned him the nickname The Count. But if his character had flaws, he was extremely handsome and was noted for it throughout society. For several years, he enjoyed the carefree life of a gentleman, surrounding himself with a group of young bucks from high society. George Bowes is generally credited with having introduced fox-hunting to County Durham with a pack of hounds based at Gibside and he spent much time engaged in horse racing, owning several famous mounts. Indeed although he was a noted student of architecture, his main interest appeared to have been gambling and he spent many late nights at the card tables in Gibside. George Bowes threw himself into the round of society balls and events with wild abandon and the behaviour of the dashing heir became something of a talking point across the north. In July 1729, Edward Wortley Montague wrote to his friend: "We hear no news here but of the gaieties of my two partners Sir H Liddel and Mr Bowes who are so much taken up with feasting and balls that I have had a good deal of difficulty to get them to settle to business."

To date the rakish George Bowes had shown himself to be a high-handed and fiery-tempered rogue who enjoyed a healthy appetite for the pleasures of life. But it was his marriage which, to modern eyes at least, appears distasteful. In early Eighteenth Century England, as has already been seen with regard to his brother William Blakiston Bowes, it was considered entirely proper for marriage negotiations to centre on hard cash. To that extent it was only natural by the standards of the time that when George decided to marry, financial considerations should come into play. In 1720, the 19-year-old George decided to marry Eleanor Verney, who was to come into the not inconsiderable sum of £15,000 when she married and discussions took place to arrange the wedding. The bride-to-be was only 10 years old when the deal was done and the couple had to wait until the ceremony could take place, when Eleanor had reached the grand old age of 14. On July 20th, 1724, shortly before their eventual wedding, George wrote to his child bride: "I am not able to bear the cruel absence of my angel any longer without having recourse to pen and paper for relief of my tortured heart which can at present find no other way to ease itself." On the 1st of October 1724, Eleanor was sent to marry her new husband.

She died just two and a half months later, still aged 14 years. Despite the hard financial bargaining which took place ahead of the wedding, George Bowes appeared to be genuinely upset by the death of his love. Nevertheless, he had to pay back the dowry which came with his wife, plus £750 interest calculated as having accrued during the brief months of their marriage.

After the death of Eleanor, George Bowes threw himself into work. He became the MP for Durham in 1727 and held the seat until his death, although in the intervening 33 years he made only one recorded speech in the House. But most of his efforts went into the development of Gibside - works which were to turn the estate into one of the glories of Northern England. Work on the grand design began in 1725 but, if it were to be later praised as a fabulous creation it began with an act of destruction. The village of Gibside, then as big as neighbouring Whickham, stood in the way so the residents were evicted and the whole village razed to the ground to make way for the gardens which now stand on the site. George Bowes' great project now began to take shape - a project which preoccupied him for the last 35 years of his life. The gardens were landscaped and in 1733 work began on the great bath house of Gibside, followed by a walled garden, new carriage drives and the great octagon lake.

In June 1743, George Bowes married for the second time to Mary Gilbert, almost two decades after the death of Eleanor. His new marriage took his attention away from the great estate, but construction work resumed four years later. New stables were built, a remarkable ice house in which ice for the kitchens was stored underground and, most impressively of all, work began on the Grand Walk - the imposing mile-long avenue of trees which leads to the great house itself.

Six years after his marriage, just months short of his 50th birthday, George Bowes became a father for the first time. His wife gave birth to a daughter, Mary Eleanor, named after the two loves of his life - his present wife and the wife he had lost all those years earlier. The following year he began work on Gibside's crowning glory - the statue of Liberty which stands, master of all it surveys, from the top of its 146 foot tall column. The statue is ostensibly a monument to British Liberty as represented by the victory of the established order over the Jacobite Pretender Bonnie Prince Charlie five years earlier and the freedoms which allowed men of property to flourish. But more than that it is a monument to George Bowes himself. By now he could look back on 50 years in which he had overcome family tragedy, conquered the wilderness of the Derwent Valley and survived the vagaries of political and economic fortune. He had tamed them all. Having conquered one world, George Bowes began his preparations for the next and, with his health failing, he began work on the last of the great works in his palatial grounds - the chapel. He died the following year, in 1760, before his chapel was completed.

George Bowes left his daughter a £600,000 fortune built on coal and the most stately pleasure gardens in the North. But it was to prove a strange inheritance for the little countess. George was already an old man when Mary Eleanor was born and throughout her childhood the new arrival was treated as a little adult rather than a child. Left largely alone in the echoing halls of the great house, Mary Eleanor was just 10 years old when her father died. She was exceptionally bright and had a reputation for being bookish - a trait which signified an independent streak She was particularly well-read in her favourite subjects - botany and architecture - twin interests which she used to great effect in her new empire, adding splendid flower beds and gardens to the landscaping works of her father. Rare plant species from all over the world were collected and brought to Gibside.

This remarkable young woman soon began to attract the interest of a variety of suitors - although it has to be said as much for her estate as her undoubted free spirit and intelligence. She too attracted such interest at an uncomfortably young age. When she was just 13 she moved briefly to London with family friends to become part of Society. In October 1763, Mrs Montague, her chaperone, wrote from Gibside to her confidante Lord Bath that "a horrid plot to abduct Miss Bowes" had been uncovered. She confided that "a famous pimp" had been sent to Gibside carrying a £20,000 bribe - a substantial enough sum now but then a king's ransom - to convince one of the estate's trusted footmen to take part in the plot. The teenage heiress was to be abducted on behalf of an MP who hoped to marry her or, more precisely, marry her fortune. But the plot was thwarted when the footman revealed his intentions to his girlfriend, Mary Eleanor's maid, who remained steadfastly loyal to her employer and informed the family.

However, the free spirited Mary Eleanor was not to be abducted, nor married off to the highest bidder - she was determined to have a say in her own destiny. James Lyon, the famously handsome 9th Earl of Strathmore, emerged as the clear favourite to win her hand and offered a marriage to her family. It was to be an arranged marriage, brokered in the usual way with all the financial negotiations which went with it, but there was no question the heiress was also keen on the arrangement. Her family, however, were dead set against the idea mainly because her intended was Scottish. But Mary Eleanor had inherited her father's stubborn streak and would have her way regardless of family wishes. As the wedding approached, she appeared to have second thoughts, admitting the couple were separated by a gulf: "I found our tempers, dispositions and turns different. I wished to retract but my pride and sometimes my weakness would not let me." With cold feet, they were married on her 18th birthday - February 24th, 1767.

In April of the following year, she gave birth to a daughter, Maria. She was the first of the couple's five children and, along with their family, the estate prospered during their first years together. In 1770, Gibside played host to possibly the most elaborate party ever thrown in the county of Durham to celebrate Mary Eleanor's 21st birthday. The young couple were fantastically glamorous, the intelligent young heiress and her dashing new husband. And the ball they staged that February was unrivalled in the north country. A contemporary account observed: "A great entertainment was given at his lordship's seat, at Gibside, to a number of gentlemen in the two counties. An ox was roasted whole which, with some other victuals and some hogsheads of strong ale, were given to the populace, many hundreds having assembled there to celebrate the day. The house was open for 10 days to all persons who chose to repair thither to regale themselves."

But the babies and the great parties could not hide the growing cracks in the marriage. They were not, as Mary Eleanor had herself foreseen, ideally suited and those differences in temper and dispositions grew ever wider as time went by. He was easy going with company, an amiable man-about-town. She inherited her father's quick temper and ever changing moods. She had her prejudices - even among her own children where she unreasonably favoured her daughters while harbouring an unjustified dislike of her elder son. In many ways, the couple could not have been further apart. The earl's passions including rearing fighting cocks, going to the races with his friends and breeding partridges. If he was far from well-read, she immersed herself in books and learning and was the author of a five-act play The Siege of Jerusalem. She was one of the foremost experts in botany of her day and threw herself into the workings of the estate. In 1772, she had a greenhouse built which was stocked with specimens from around the world including one of the most famous orange groves in England and she also had an ornamental pond created. In 1810, Jesse Foot wrote of the couple: "The earl was not exactly calculated to make even a good learned woman a pleasing husband. Her judgment was weak, her prudence almost none and her prejudice unbounded."

The strains were not helped by the fact she was hated by her husband's family and his brother openly insulted her in public. Over the years, the couple grew ever more distant - and Mary Eleanor embarked on a number of liaisons. She had a flirtation with her husband's gamekeeper and, when that liaison ended, went on to have a long relationship with his brother. A close long-term friendship with a gentleman named George Grey developed into a full-blown affair. But fate intervened before matters could move much further. In 1776, her husband developed consumption and set sail for Portugal where he hoped to find a cure. He died en route to Lisbon, leaving Mary Eleanor a widow at the age of 27.

If the members of polite society expected Mary Eleanor to wear the mantle of grieving widow for the rest of her days, they could not have been more mistaken. Free of the restraint that duty to her husband brought, George Bowes' spoiled child indulged herself to an astonishing degree. Attractive, wealthy, intelligent and free - it proved a heady cocktail for a variety of suitors. And if her life to date had been adventurous - with attempted abduction, glamorous marriage and early widowhood - her future liasons were to prove positively scandalous. During her torrid affair with George Grey, Mary Eleanor fell pregnant. The couple were engaged before the pregnancy became common knowledge but, out of the blue, another suitor appeared on the scene. And if the sudden death of her husband had ended one mismatch and pulled her from the romantic frying pan, she quickly found herself in the fire with her new beau - the cad "Stoney Bowes".

Andrew Robinson Stoney was born in Ireland in 1745, the youngest son of a respectable family. He was described by Jesse Foot as follows: "The person of Bowes was rather in his favour and his address was, probably, when young, captivating. His speech was soft, his height more than five feet ten. His smile agreeable, his wit ready, but he was always the first to laugh at what he said, which forced others to laugh also. His conversation was shallow, his education was bare and his utterance was in a low tone and lisping."

This ruthlessly ambitious rogue joined the Army and became a lieutenant in the 4th Regiment of Foot, finding himself posted to Newcastle. At the age of 23, he found himself a catch - the young coal heiress Hannah Newton. Her family were the owners of Burnopfield House, built by her father William Newton in the 1720s. She was said to be short, dark, and not the most attractive of women, but when her father died in 1763, Hannah Newton inherited a fortune worth around £20,000 per year. The wealthy heiress became an obvious target for Andrew Robinson Stoney and after a whirlwind romance they were married at St Andrews in Newcastle on November 5th, 1768. The couple took up residence at Cold Pigg Hall near Lanchester, but almost immediately Stoney's cruelty showed its face. It was said the unfortunate Hannah suffered both mental and physical torture at the hands of her new husband.

During the brief months of their marriage, the cruelties escalated. On one occasion he is known to have thrown his wife headlong down a flight of stairs. He was in the habit of feeding her nothing more than an egg a day and several times locked her naked in a closet for

Gibside Chapel
(Picture courtesy of Durham County Record Office)

some perceived misdemeanour. Within weeks she was dead and buried in Tanfield Cemetery. Although there was no evidence to prove it, the widespread belief was she had been driven to her grave by her beastly husband. He, however, profited from the marriage and the widower retired from the Army - his career was about to take him down a very different path. His attentions were now turned towards Mary Eleanor Bowes.

In a matter of months after her husband's death, Mary Eleanor began to enjoy the life of a single woman. Almost as quickly, a series of anonymous letters began to appear in The Morning Post news paper querying her morals and highlighting her affairs. The author of these poisonous letters was none other than Andrew Robinson Stoney. However, the cad then wrote a series of florid letters defending her character against the very accusations he had written. These, he signed and quickly emerged as the public champion of Mary Eleanor against those who would blacken her character. The ruse appeared to work and the countess herself began corresponding with the dashing Army officer who defended her name.

Mary Eleanor Bowes - who earned the nickname The Unhappy Countess (Picture courtesy of the Bowes Museum)

But Stoney was not done there. He bribed mutual acquaintances to make sure his admiration for Mary Eleanor was dropped into casual conversation which would eventually find its way to her ears. He hired a conjurer to read her fortune, it prominently featured a handsome Irish army officer. He wrote letters to Mary Eleanor claiming to come from a fictitious Durham woman - a woman distraught that Stoney had called off their relationship because he was so in love with the countess. He leaked news that the Strathmore family favoured the suit of Mr Grey - a move calculated to enrage the feisty heiress against her interfering family.

Finally, Stoney's coup de grace came on January 13th, 1777 when he challenged the Rev Henry Bate, editor of The Morning Post, to a duel to defend her aggrieved honour. There have been suggestions that the dual was fixed - Stoney was a notorious coward and Bate was one of the foremost duellers in England - while other witnesses suggest that Stoney used a ruse to ensure he came to no real harm - the fight took place in pitch black in a tiny room above a London pub, Stoney having made sure the candles would be blown out the second the action started. Nevertheless, he suffered three sword wounds to his chest, lost a great deal of blood and was carried home to his bed. However, the entire episode appealed to Mary Eleanor's romantic sensibilities. Three days before the duel she had been making arrangements to marry George Grey, four days after it she was married to Stoney and for some time slept with the sword he had used to defend her honour under her pillow.

Almost immediately, Stoney began to show his true colours. Sensibly, the countess had drawn up a pre-nuptial arrangement and had put all the deeds to the Gibside estate in trust with herself as the sole beneficiary. However, the silver-tongued charmer launched into a successful campaign to have the terms changed and have the deeds put in joint names. The pair moved in at Gibside and the adventurer who had fallen on his feet showed a penchant for high office to go with the fine living. Within a month, he attempted to win the Parliamentary seat of Newcastle, but narrowly failed by just 95 votes. Stoney made wild and unsubstantiated allegations of vote-rigging and bribery to keep him from the seat which came to nothing. After spending a small fortune on lavish parties for the rich and powerful over the next three years, particularly the region's judges, he was appointed High Sheriff of Northumberland. But his ambition was bought at a price - both financial and personal. The lifestyle became ever more lavish, the gambling became ever more heavy and the cost of entertaining became ever more exorbitant. Within a year of the marriage, Stoney Bowes ordered the felling of trees for timber on the Gibside estate to raise cash, but for the most part they were left to rot where they fell. The new lord of the manor was intent on living up to his position, spending small fortunes on fine food and finer clothing and losing even larger fortunes at cock-fighting and horse-racing. By 1779, only two years after the wedding, Stoney Bowes sold off his wife's town house at Chelsea to pay for his gambling debts. Gibside - a byword in high society for hospitality and lavish entertainment - was closed to visitors as the great house became increasingly run down and the accounts ledgers mysteriously vanished.

At the same time, rumours began to emerge of ill-treatment in the home. Word seeped out through the servants of dark goings on at the house. It was said that Stoney subjected his wife to barbarous cruelty and refused to allow her clothes or servants. George Grey's daughter was born in August 1777 and the couple's own son was born five years later, but the births did nothing to stem the flow of scandal attached to the family. Nursery maid Dorothy Stephenson later swore she had witnessed the cruelty inflicted on Mary Eleanor, including: "many violent blows on her face, head and other parts of her body, he often kicked her and sometimes pinched her ears nearly through." On one occasion, Stoney threw a dish of hot potatoes at his unfortunate wife, then forced her to eat them from the floor until she was sick and poured wine over her to wash away the mess. The beatings and the humiliation became more and more public as the countess endured years of bitter unhappiness.

One account of their life together concluded: "While pretending great tenderness to his unhappy wife, it is easier to imagine than describe all the secret villainies and degradations by which such a tyrant can make every moment of a woman of feeling and refinement as bitter as death. In the first place, Bowes carried on the most licentious intercourse with women of all kinds. He seduced almost every maid servant and all the farmer's daughters that he could." Among the indignities he piled upon her, was forcing his wife to entertain his many mistresses and their families to dinner, where she would serve tea before he left with them. If he couldn't seduce his servants and tenants, it didn't stop his lusts. Farmers' daughters

ANDREW ROBINSON BOWES

Contemporary caricature of Stoney Bowes

reported him peering through their windows at night. He got the wet nurse Mrs Houghton pregnant and raped both the nursery maid Dorothy Stevenson and her replacement Elizabeth White.

After six years of marriage, the few remaining visitors to the house described Mary Eleanor as pale and dejected. She had developed a facial tick and asked permission of Stoney before she carried out even the most minor of tasks. The torments which had reduced her to this shadow of her former self emerged later in court. He forced his wife to lie down on the floor while he fastened her long hair in a chest and locked it until: "her will gave way to his diabolical wishes". To further force her to submit to his will, Bowes made his wife write "The Confessions Of The Countess Of Strathmore" - a completely fictitious and exceptionally graphic account of her supposedly scandalous life before the marriage. Bowes threatened to publish the salacious diary, which he kept under his pillow, as a means of blackmailing his wife and, every night, would read aloud some of the juicier excerpts for his own entertainment. As one account concluded: "Every mental and physical suffering that ingenuity could devise was inflicted upon her."

Late in January 1785, Mary Eleanor sent messages to a trusted former servant saying she feared for her life and wished to escape. Arrangements were made and, while the couple were staying in London, she waited until Stoney had gone out to dine one evening and escaped with her maid to a solicitor in Oxford Street. Mary Eleanor moved into a new home and began proceedings against him in the ecclesiastical courts. To keep the pressure up, Bowes took rented lodgings in the same street and shadowed her every move while using the estate's funds to buy the silence of all the maids he had seduced and all the children he had fathered.

It took about a year for the case to come to court. Evidence was presented that Stoney had regularly beaten her black and blue. He had refused her the use of her own carriage and had denied her permission to send or receive letters which effectively made her a prisoner in her own palatial home. The countess's loyal household servants were unceremoniously sacked and replaced by those appointed by Stoney, who acted as his eyes and ears around the estate. He ranted and raved constantly, swearing at her in front of the staff. Evidence was presented of "beating, scratching, biting, pinching, whipping, kicking, imprisoning, insulting, provoking, tormenting, mortifying, degrading, tyrannising, cajoling, deceiving, lying, starving, forcing, compelling and wringing of the heart." True to form, Stoney presented The Confessions Of The Countess Of Strathmore as evidence in his defence, he accused her of lustful affairs with a footman and a gardener and said she had behaved with: "the utmost insolent contempt and disobedience and with the greatest impropriety and indecency." But the court was unmoved and found in favour of Mary Eleanor. He was ordered to pay her interim alimony of £300 a year until larger matters could be settled. Proceedings were now underway towards a full divorce which, in line with the pre-nuptial arrangements set in place by the resourceful bride, would hand over full control of Gibside and its lucrative rents to her.

Having lost the first round of the legal battle to hold on to his new found wealth - and facing almost certain defeat in the latter stages - Stoney Bowes settled on a drastic plan of action. He returned to Gibside and hired two burly pitmen from the estates, named Pigg and Chapman, along with a young messenger boy and a business associate from Newcastle. This motley gang rented lodgings in London and for several weeks haunted Bloomsbury Square where Mary Eleanor was now living. Sometimes on foot, sometimes in carriages with the blinds drawn and sometimes in disguise, they spied on the every move of the countess. As Stoney had planned, she became aware of the stalking and when a constable named Mr Lucas offered to protect her, she hired him. Unbeknown to her, Lucas was in the pay of Stoney.

On November 10th, 1786, Mary Eleanor went shopping in Oxford Street taking her maid and Mr Farrer, her solicitor's brother. When she was in a shop, Chapman and Pigg turned up and the terrified woman locked herself in the back room while sending for help. Within minutes, Lucas arrived and escorted Lady Bowes and Mr Farrer to her waiting coach. With the lady safely in the coach, Lucas dismissed her servants and replaced them with his own armed attendants, including Chapman and Pigg, and a new coachman took over the reins.

They trotted off at sedate pace to Highgate Hill where, waiting in the road, stood the figure of Bowes. He politely asked Farrer to leave and climbed into the coach next to his terrified wife. The coach sped off at breakneck speed, leaving Farrer to rush to summon help from the court authorities. For the next 11 days, the terrified countess would be held captive and subjected to all manner of degradation.

Bowes plan was to abduct her, force her to drop the claim against him and take him back as her husband, then claim to the courts she had been deranged all along. During a desperate flight back to Durham, Bowes produced a piece of paper agreeing to put a stop to proceedings in the ecclesiastical court, which she refused to sign. According to the evidence later presented to court by Peter Orme, the messenger boy: "He then beat her on the face and body with his clenched fists, that when she attempted to cry out he thrust a handkerchief into her mouth; that, on the most trifling contradiction while on the road, he beat her with the chain and seals of his watch on the naked breast and that, at last, provoked by her firmness, presented a loaded pistol to her head and threatened her life if she did not immediately sign the paper."

After a breathless race northwards, they reached Streatlam - the ancestral home of the Bowes family. Ensconced in the castle, Bowes once more attempted to persuade Mary Eleanor to behave, as he saw it, as a dutiful wife and again the spirited woman refused. Twice he flew into a violent rage, pointed a loaded gun at her head and bid her say her final prayers but she was a woman who had already been pushed to the edge during years of abuse and she refused to surrender to him.

The court constables were on their way from London, Bowes was becoming ever more desperate and the enterprise became ever more absurd. As word spread, gangs of local pitmen gathered to surround the house and lit fires to ensure Stoney could not escape. Chapman and Pigg were appointed to act as Mary Eleanor's servants and carried her against her wishes to her bed. To put the authorities off the scent, Bowes had two of the castle's domestic staff dress up in finery and make regular appearances at Streatlam's windows imitating the couple, waving to the miners gathered outside. So convincing were they that the court sheriff served papers on the servants while Bowes made his escape, dragging his unfortunate wife behind him in the middle of the night to a nearby cottage on the estate. There, according to the evidence, "he behaved to her in a manner shocking to the delicacy of civilized life, by reiterating his threatenings and, finding threats in vain, throwing her on the bed and flogging her with rods."

190

In the morning, while it was still dark, they left the cottage. Chapman rode a horse with Mary Eleanor clinging on behind him on a seven-hour journey in pitch black over the moors through the worst the Durham winter could throw at them. Through a raging storm they rode to Appleby. The countess had by now lost one shoe and a stocking, was bitterly cold and was said to be in a most distressed state. For six days, the party crossed the moors backwards and forwards looking for a means of escape through snow drifts up to four feet deep. Meanwhile, the authorities were on the hunt for them: a wanted poster describing Bowes as "the greatest monster that ever disgraced society". Eventually, running out of ideas, Bowes headed for Darlington along a dismal and trackless course to an attorney's house. Here, Mary Eleanor was shut up in a dark room and, while a red-hot poker was held to her breast, she was threatened "with a mad doctor and strait waistcoat," if she did not agree to sign the papers.

Still she refused and by now, the court officials were hot on their trail. With the constables banging on the door of the lawyer's house, Bowes skulked out of the back and through the yard of a neighbouring pub before again escaping on horseback over hedges and ploughed fields with his pursuers now only yards behind. Bowes collared an old countryman in the fields and offered him cash to escort them over the River Tees but instead, he grabbed the bridle to hold onto the fugitive while the constables caught up. Bowes produced his pistol to threaten the old man but, before he could shoot, he was felled with a blow from Christopher Smith, the constable of Neasham, and a posse armed with sticks set upon Bowes to attempt his capture. Smith later gave evidence that: "While Bowes struggled with me, one of my pistol handles broke in my hand and by pulling them away the guard of the trigger cut a piece out of the foremost finger of my right hand. I threw the pistol away and with the other gave Bowes a blow upon the right side of his head, which knocked him from the horse. Fearing he had more pistols about him that he might shoot some of us I gave him another blow upon the back part of the head and cut it about two inches. Lady Strathmore asked if he was killed and desired we would not strike him again and several times bade us search his pockets for pistols and take care he did not shoot some of us."

Mary Eleanor had almost died of exhaustion and exposure during the escapade and could not stand for a month afterwards. Bowes, meanwhile, was taken back to Darlington and, after being treated for

A dishevelled Stoney Bowes is brought before the Court of the King's Bench in 1786 after the failure of his desperate plan to kidnap Mary Eleanor,
(Picture courtesy of the National Portrait Gallery, London)

his wounds, was escorted back to London by three Bow Street Runners sent north for the purpose. On November 27th, a mere 17 days after the mad episode had started, Bowes was brought before the magistrates. He was pale, with a week-old stubble on his chin, and wearing dirty boots, a drab greatcoat, blood-stained shirt and a red silk handkerchief covering the wound to his head. A contemporary account said: "He was supported by two men, yet nearly bent double with weakness in consequence of his wounds. He frequently appeared on the point of fainting and his appearance on the whole was the most squalid and emaciated that can possibly be imagined." He was jailed for three years for the enterprise, the time to be served in King's Bench prison, was fined £300 and was declared a bad debtor as his unpaid bills and gambling accounts finally caught up with him. His accomplice Lucas was sentenced to three years and a £50 fine.

So impoverished was he in the end that, from that point onwards, the phrase "Stoney broke" passed into the English language. He was to spend the rest of his life either in prison or under the supervision of the governor. Bowes served the next three years of his life in the state rooms of the prison - outside the walls but living under the rules of the jail. In 1789, the unfortunate Mary Eleanor finally got her divorce. So traumatic was her suffering at the hands of her husband she was said never to be the same again.

With the divorce and consequent loss of income, Bowes was moved from the comparative luxury of the state rooms to a cell inside the prison walls. But bars were not enough to keep the devious Stoney Bowes in check. During his imprisonment, he seduced the daughter of one of his fellow inmates - a formerly wealthy landowner who had lost his fortune. She went on to have five children by him even though she suffered treatment as bad as either of his previous wives - abuse she tolerated for the sake of her children. He grew insanely jealous of her and for more than two decades, Bowes locked her in the house all day until it was she who was the real prisoner as his behaviour grew ever more bizarre. An apartment outside the prison overlooked his home within the walls and Bowes became convinced that the young man who lived there was wooing his captive. On several occasions, Bowes dressed as a woman and attempted to flirt with his neighbour across the street to prove he was right before finally tearing off his dress to display himself, jeering at his shocked neighbour.

Bowes added heavy drinking to his lengthy list of vices. He refused to spend money he considered unnecessary and would not buy brooms for the house, insisting his two daughters gather dirt with their bare hands to keep the place clean. Meanwhile, he was involved in lengthy litigation in an attempt to win what he believed to be his rightful dues from the Bowes estates.

Mary Eleanor finally died in April 1800 and that same year, Stoney Bowes was released from prison after 11 years behind the walls. He remained under supervision of the governor and took a house in St George's Field, where he was obliged to live under the rules of the prison. He fleeced all manner of attorneys, borrowing money from them to fight the case which was never repaid. When the legal profession refused to advance him any more money, he turned his attention to his own family. Bowes insisted that he continued to own estates on Tyneside and borrowed money from his sisters' husbands, using the land as collateral. Faced with a difficult day in court, he would employ a succession of cunning devices to delay the inevitable. On at least one occasion, he administered himself a small dose of poison in prison so that he was violently sick in the coach on the way to court and the hearing had to be postponed. Once he swallowed a draft of calves' blood, then regurgitated it at an appropriate moment, claiming he had ruptured blood vessels in his stomach and, again, the moment of truth was put off.

One by one, the cases were lost and, one by one, his remaining friends deserted him. In the end, his only comfort lay in drink and he wallowed further and further into misery watched over by his long-suffering partner. By the Christmas of 1809, he was slipping slowly towards death - but even at the last Andrew Robinson Stoney Bowes had one last piece of wickedness up his sleeve. There was still a little money left in his kitty which would take care of his common-law wife and their five children but, on his death bed, he refused to leave it to her. After all the sufferings she had endured to protect her beloved children, she now faced the prospect of being widowed, penniless. Only at the very last did his surgeon, Jesse Foot, persuaded him to relent and leave her a pension of £100 a year - small recompense for the miseries she had endured.

Andrew Robinson Stoney Bowes finally slipped away on January 16, 1810, still under the rules of the prison far away from the Liberty which towered over his former home. His epitaph was written by Jesse Foot, who said of him at his death: "He was a villain to the backbone."

CHAPTER 20
FELONS, FAWS AND FIGHTERS

PROBABLY the most hideous crime ever committed in the Derwent Valley went entirely unpunished. In June 1789, a group of boys went fishing in Ebchester Burn and made a gruesome discovery - the body of a child, buried in the mud on the banks of the stream. For reasons which will never be known, a stake had been driven through the child's body fixing it into the earth. Very few details are known of this crime, but it was recorded that this was the third murdered child to be discovered in the area in the previous few months. Incredible as it may seem today, the possibility of a serial child killer living in the valley was never even investigated as there was no Commissioner of the Peace living within 12 miles of the neighbourhood at the time.

The forces of law and order were barely adequate anywhere in the Derwent Valley. At Tanfield, there was growing public unrest about the increase in crime which followed the opening up of coal mines in the area. While most were petty crimes, some were more serious. On New Year's Day 1796, the hemp winding rope at Tanfield Moor pit was cut, which would have meant the first person trying to descend the shaft would have plunged to their certain death. In response, a private police force was set up. The Tanfield Association For the Prosecution of Felons was established by a group of farmers, landowners and tradesmen at a meeting in one of the village's pubs on November 4th, 1799 and continued in existence for 50 years until the establishment of Durham Constabulary. A similar association was set up in Ryton during the 1740s onwards, where parishioners made regular contributions to pay for the investigation of crimes, and in the early 1840s, the Derwent Iron Company employed its own constables to keep law and order.

The rules of the Tanfield Association promised: "that we will use our utmost endeavours to apprehend and prosecute to conviction all and every person who shall commit burglaries, thefts, assaults or other misdemeanours, in or upon the persons, properties or cattle, and that ample rewards shall be offered to any person giving information against offenders stealing turnips, peas, potatoes, raiding gardens, stealing horses, cattle or sheep. Persons apprehended will be prosecuted to the utmost rigour of the law".

*Two tramps resting at Shotley Bridge in the 19th Century
(Photograph courtesy of Beamish Museum)*

But for the most part, the authorities appear to have been more concerned with dealing with paupers and beggars than with the spread of violent crime. During the 17th Century, every parish or township was responsible for paying for the relief of the poor and most were anxious to keep their taxpayers' bills down. Consequently, many paupers were forcibly removed back to their parish of origin to be cared for there. The records from Tanfield show the bills incurred while escorting the poor from the area: three shillings to take Ann Grey back to Newcastle, four shillings to take Ann Farthing to Ebchester, four shillings to take Mary Morton to Ryhope and seven shillings and sixpence for escorting an unnamed widow and her four children to Whickham.

Keeping the poor was an expensive business and the records show that while the Overseers of the Poor were happy to pay out relief when it was needed, they also kept a keen eye on the recipients. In 1820, Thomas Davison, a pauper child who had been sent out as an apprentice by the Tanfield board, was given 20s to set up as a shoemaker and the board agreed to pay for some clothes for Mary Campbell's 11-year-old daughter so she could be sent into service as soon as her mother saw fit. However, the board also decided to end payments to Hannah Wood "in consequence of being in the habit of harbouring a number of strolling people from time to time whose characters are suspicious." The fear of gypsies and hawkers was such that the Overseers were instructed to prevent them from lodging in the lanes and take them into custody if they refused to move on.

The board appeared to have a particular problem with one Francis Coxon who by 1822 had been in receipt of relief on and off for four years: "entirely through idleness and unwillingness to work." The overseers complained that Coxon had just been released from the House of Correction for the third time and had been offered work for up to 20s a week but continued to lead: "an idle and profligate life". Coxon and his wife were now back in the workhouse where: "their behaviour to the keeper of the house and to the overseer is extremely impertinent and wicked, quite inconsistent and unbecoming to their situation as dependents for relief and, knowing him to be strong and in good health, we think it nothing short of robbery to suffer them to continue in the house any longer." The board called on the magistrates to jail Coxon for a longer sentence the next time he came before them but it was a call which went unheeded - he was back at the workhouse the following year and was refused relief because: "he is a very idle person more inclined to poaching and to go bird catching."

But there were also more serious problems which required the attention of the magistrates. As events in Ebchester showed, crimes against children are not a new phenomenon. In an age without effective contraception, legal abortion or any semblance of social security, there were numerous instances of appalling cruelties inflicted on unwanted children. In 1748, Christian Gowther, the wife of a Morpeth tinker, was charged with murder.

She had been contracted by Jane Gattis to care for her illegitimate child, who was then just a few months old. Instead of discharging her duties, Gowther left the helpless child by the roadside somewhere in the wastes of North Durham. She stood trial at Durham, accused of "abandoning and exposing it in the parish of Lanchester," but was acquitted because, thankfully, the infant was found alive.

Not all cases ended so happily. In the summer of 1858, a 24-year-old domestic servant named Elizabeth Hall, from Winlaton, became involved in a romance with Gloster Smith, a teacher at the village school. Her family objected to the affair and eventually, after the couple had continued to see each other for nine months, she was sent away to an aunt's house in Darlington to find work. However, over the next few weeks, Elizabeth made several secret trips to Newcastle by train, the last of which took place on Saturday, January 29th 1859. An exhausted Elizabeth returned home at 6.30pm, complaining she was in a great deal of pain. By the following morning she was extremely ill, but refused medical help. Eventually, when her aunt insisted that a doctor be brought, Elizabeth confessed that during her visit to Newcastle she had in fact had a miscarriage and had thrown the foetus onto a fire.

Despite the attention of the doctors, she became gravely ill and, on Monday, February 7th, Elizabeth Hall died. A post mortem examination revealed that she had been poisoned, but the actual cause of death was the violence used to induce an abortion. Back in Winlaton, Elizabeth's mother had discovered an unsigned letter written to her daughter saying that their meetings had to stop, but that she should go to the place as instructed and all the expenses would be taken care of. Shortly afterwards, Gloster Smith was arrested on suspicion of procuring the abortion which had killed

Elizabeth Hall, but the inquest jury found that there was no evidence to link him directly to the death and he was released without charge.

There were also crimes against older children. On the morning of January 8th, 1750, Robert Hopes, a 10-year-old boy, was crossing the windswept Whickham Common on his way to school when he came across a man with a woman sitting on his knee. She asked him where he was going and he replied that he was going to school, at which point the man leapt to his feet and grabbed hold of the terrified youngster. The schoolboy was dragged into a nearby hollow and was stripped of his clothes with the exception of his breeches and shoes. His attacker kept telling him throughout not to cry out or he would cut his throat. During the struggle, young Robert somehow managed to escape and ran to the nearby fields where his father was working. Mr Hopes and a posse of neighbours ran up onto the common and captured James McFidum, who was handed over to the authorities and taken to Durham Gaol.

McFidum, who was also known as James McFarlane, was suspected of being a member of one of the gangs of fugitives and outlaws - known as faws - said to infest the lower reaches of the Derwent Valley. Throughout his trial he claimed to be dumb and therefore could not have been the man who attacked and threatened young Robert. The schoolboy however insisted McFidum was his attacker and he was convicted and executed in August of that year.

As the 18th Century drew to a close, this corner of the Derwent Valley became notorious as a hide-out for criminal gangs - pick-pockets, hawkers, footpads and rogues who could ply their trade in the bustling streets of Tyneside then make their escape into the wild moors. Most infamous of all was the Barlow Gang, who hid out in the tumbledown lodges on the fell above Winlaton from where they ventured out into the crowded maze of streets which made up Newcastle. This motley collection of thieves and shoplifters were also known to have hideouts on Gateshead Fell and venture as far south as Bishop Auckland.

In the last few days of December 1781, pickpocket Elizabeth Whitebread was captured in Newcastle. The authorities were determined to capture her fellow members of the Barlow Gang who they said: "have for some time past infested the markets in this town and generally resort to fairs in the country". Over the next month, the arrests piled up. In January 1782, three members of the gang were taken and were incarcerated in the House of Correction in Newcastle. Henry Cunningham, who was thought to be the gang leader was not a pretty picture. Then aged around 30, Cunningham had lost two fingers and a thumb from his right hand and boasted scars across his right jaw and under his left eye. A former pitman from Cumberland, he was said to have a dark, swarthy complexion, dull black eyes and long, black rough hair. When arrested, he was wearing an old, coarse slouched hat and dirty breeches made of doe skin, blue coat and waistcoat and a black silk neck cloth. Cunningham claimed to be an innocent tradesman who travelled the country selling pots and mugs in the summer and repairing lanterns in the winter. Arrested with him was his common-law wife of five years, Ann Hamilton, from Scotland. The fair-haired Hamilton was aged around 35 years and had a small round face and a squint in one eye, but was immaculately dressed when captured, wearing a short red cloak, a remarkable flowered chintz gown and a silk handkerchief. The third member of the gang was sailor's wife Mary Wilson, a fellow Scot aged 50 who was described as having star marks on her forehead, cheek and lip.

The gang, it would appear, included entire families. A matter of days later, another seven members were arrested. Thomas Douglas, his wife and 15-year-old son David were captured, along with Thomas' brother John and his wife Eleanor. Also brought in were Thomas Colpitts and his wife. They were all said to frequently change their names to confuse the authorities and would rendezvous at the Crown and Canon in Winlaton to plan their crimes. The gang were said to have two warehouses, one at Gateshead and one on the fells, where their stolen goods could be safely stored. The arrests appear to have done little to break up the gang. On October 12th, Thomas Ridley of Barlow was convicted of petty larceny at Newcastle Quarter Sessions and was sentenced to seven days hard labour at the House of Correction then to be whipped on Tyne Bridge.

Four years later, the Barlow Gang was still going about its business. In January, 1786 four members of the gang were spotted acting suspiciously outside several of Newcastle's linen drapery shops and were followed to an alehouse in Pipewellgate. All four were detained on suspicion of preparing to steal goods from the shops, although Walter Clarke escaped while he was being taken to the House of Correction. The three women with him were detained - Jane Clark, Eleanor Murray and the notorious Elizabeth Thompson, who had only been released from prison three days earlier.

Several members of the gang had military backgrounds. Abraham Smith, a 21-year-old tinker born in Leadgate, near Ryton was jailed alongside fellow gang member John Cooper in March 1786. Smith, who stood five foot five inches tall with long curly brown hair and a swarthy complexion, had just returned from America where he had fought for his country as a soldier in the War of Independence. Cooper was only 17 but had already spent several years at sea, although he had lately earned a living selling books and pamphlets. Both found a new home in the Barlow Gang and both ended up in the House of Correction.

At Newcastle Assizes in August 1786, several members of the gang were brought to trial. Jane Clark, whose husband Walter had escaped as the gang were brought back to prison, was sentenced to be whipped and then jailed for two years' hard labour in the House of Correction. Mary Brown was sentenced to a whipping and one year's hard labour. Elizabeth Smith received the same sentence for shoplifting. The court heard how Smith, under her real name of Ann Gregg, had broken out of Carlisle Gaol and made her way to Newcastle only days before the offence took place. Elizabeth Thompson also received a whipping and one year's hard labour. Most scorn was reserved for Frances Atkinson, who had brought her six-year-old illegitimate son George Wilson to do the stealing for her. While she distracted the shopkeeper, the boy stole 13 yards of printed calico.

The Newcastle Courant recorded: "she has taught him to be very dextrous with taking up and going off with goods, whilst she is engaging the attention of the shopkeeper another way." Atkinson was also sent to prison for a year's hard labour. The Newcastle Courant crowed: "These five female convicts are part of a certain notorious gang of thieves, many of whom are now pretty well known among the people of trade in this town, particularly the Linen-drapers; and such discoveries have lately been made, as we hope cannot fail of soon exterpating the whole gang."

It would appear it did nothing of the sort. In July 1789, two years after being released from prison, Frances Atkinson was again arrested for stealing a pair of shoes from a shop in Newcastle's Castle Stairs. She was sent back behind bars and ordered to be whipped for her crime. Finally, having served two terms of imprisonment, she was taken to Berwick from where she was transported to the colonies.

However, Frances Atkinson escaped lightly. By now, the Clarke family were among the most notorious criminals in the North-East. Jane Clarke had been released from prison and was reunited with her husband Walter and their two daughters, Jane and Eleanor. Both the Clarke children were aged around 20 and lived, for the most part, on Hedley Fell, between Ryton and Winlaton. That summer, the family and the other members of the Barlow Gang were to be embroiled in grisly murder.

In August 1791, an elderly shopkeeper named Margaret Crozier was brutally murdered in her own bed in the Northumberland village of Elsdon. Burglars had forced the door of her home and, although the deep knife wounds to her hands made it clear she had fought desperately for her life, she had been overpowered, her throat slit and a handkerchief tied tightly around her face to suffocate her. The motive was clearly robbery - Margaret Crozier's home doubled as the village drapery and much of her stock was found to be missing. The killers left a trail of evidence - a blood-stained knife had been abandoned beside her body and prints from a pair of hobnailed boots were found outside the door.

Farmer's boy Robert Hindmarsh - then aged just 10 - told the magistrates he had seen a man and two women in the area the day before the murder. The man was eating mutton using a knife similar to that found next to the victim and he was also wearing distinctive hobnailed boots. Other witnesses said they had seen the three leaving the area with a fully-laden donkey the following day. Constables caught up with the suspects and arrested William Winter, a member of the gang who had been released from prison earlier that year. His shirt was found to be caked in blood. Shortly afterwards, Jane Clarke was arrested with her two daughters, who were found with a nightcap and apron belonging to the deceased.

They were all held in solitary confinement in the notorious Morpeth Jail before being brought to trial in Newcastle in August

1792. When the court had heard the evidence of Robert Hindmarsh, William Winter confessed to the robbery and gave evidence against his accomplices. The trial heard that in July of the previous year, only a month before the murder, the elder Jane Clarke had visited Margaret Crozier's shop and was seen behaving suspiciously, paying close attention to the stock and the lay out. She was said to have persuaded her young daughters to commit the robbery, despite the possible sentence of execution, telling them: "what's five minutes hanging to a year's pleasure." Winter told the court that the old woman had been alive when he left the house, but the two women had gone back to make sure the victim remained quiet.

Jane Clarke was acquitted, but her two daughters and Winter were found guilty of murder and sentenced to be executed. On the morning of Friday, August 10th, 1792, all three were taken outside the city walls to a spot near the Waterloo Inn where a raucous crowd of thousands had gathered in high spirits to watch the spectacle of a triple hanging. Winter apparently accepted his fate with resignation, but Jane and Eleanor proclaimed their innocence to the last. The hangman was William Gardner, a man who had recently been convicted of stealing sheep and sentenced to death. By agreeing to hang Winter and the Clarke sisters, he escaped the gallows and had his punishment commuted to transportation for life.

After the execution, the bodies of the Clarke sisters were handed over to the anatomists for dissection, while Winter's body was gibbeted near the scene of the crime until it rotted. Robert Hindmarsh, the boy whose evidence sent all three to the gallows, was thought to be in danger at the hands of the surviving gang members and was taken into the protection of Rev Johnson of Bywell, near Stocksfield. Almost a year to the day after his daughters were hanged, Walter Clarke met his end the same way - publicly executed at Morpeth for a burglary at Corbridge.

Justice in the 18th and 19th Century was severe. In 1800, there were 200 separate offences for which criminals could be hanged, including stealing from a shipwreck, shoplifting of goods worth more than 5 shillings or impersonating a Chelsea Pensioner. The vast majority of people taken to the gallows were burglars and highway robbers, not the dashing highwaymen of legend but common footpads. The stocks were still a punishment available to the courts, as was flogging, transportation to the colonies or being sent to one of the stinking, rat-infested prisons where one in four prisoners died every year of disease. But the severity of the sentences appears to have done nothing to deter crime, serious or otherwise, even in days when it was possible to be hanged for stealing bread.

In some cases, the crimes were spur of the moment. In March 1759, a William Moffat of Swalwell was caught by the Press Gang, the band of armed men who roamed the streets of the nation's ports looking for likely candidates to be kidnapped from their homes and forced into service with the navy. Unsurprisingly, Moffat resisted and during the struggle one William Bell was stabbed five times and later died of his wounds. A reward was placed on Moffat's head and he was eventually tracked down in Cumberland and put on trial for his life, but was acquitted of all charges.

Other crimes which attracted the death penalty were pre-meditated, despite the terrible sentence which could result. In July 1818, a house at the hamlet of Stargate, between Winlaton and Blaydon, was burgled by a man named Parker. The owner, pitman Thomas Snowdon, was out for the day with his wife Jane. The couple had visited friends at Greenside for the annual hoppings and did not return home until midnight when they discovered the burglary. All their clothes, their bedding and their valuable silver spoons had been taken but, worst of all, their dog was dead beneath a pile of stones. The burglar had stoned the unfortunate animal to death to stop it barking. Parker was eventually arrested and pleaded guilty at Durham Assizes, for which he was sentenced to death, though there is no record of the execution ever being carried out.

As well as crime, the lower reaches of the Derwent Valley had also developed something of a reputation for wild living - particularly in the fields of gambling and poaching. The practise of bull-baiting continued well into the 19th Century. Certainly in 1700, Ambrose Crowley had course to complain about one of his workmen who was asking for sick pay, yet had on an earlier occasion been found at a bull-baiting event in Winlaton when he had been claiming to be too ill to work. After1828, when Winlaton Church was built on the site, the gamblers moved to a new venue further up the valley on Barlow Fell where it is thought to have thrived until the 1850s. Cock-fighting was also immensely popular among the factory workers and their miner neighbours and there were cockpits in Winlaton, Winlaton Mill and again on Barlow Fell which were among the most celebrated in the region and where the prize money could reach as high as £20.

The Derwent Valley would prove hard work for those preachers who tried to turn the residents away from such things. In November 1742, John Wesley came to the village of Tanfield to preach to the locals: "Here a large company were gathered together from all the country round about, to whom I expounded the former part of the fifth chapter to the Romans," he recorded in his diary. "But so dead senseless unaffected a congregation have I scarce seen, except at Whickham. Whether the Gospel or law, English or Greek, seemed all one to them". On his return, shortly after Christmas that year, he wrote: "More than once I was nearly blown off my horse. I met the society in a large upper room which rocked to and fro with the violence of the gale, but all was calm within as we rejoiced together in hope of a kingdom that cannot be moved."

The preachers may have been fighting a losing battle. When it came to poaching, complained the gamekeepers of the neighbouring Bowes estate, the men of Winlaton and Winlaton Mill were second to none. The most notorious of all was William Renwick who, according to local legend, led a gang of Winlaton men in a successful poaching expedition to Alston in 1839 after which they were cornered in a local pub by a posse of gamekeepers. Realising they were surrounded, Renwick led the charge to escape felling several with the butt of his gun in the rush. One of the gamekeepers was so badly injured in the melee he later died of his injuries, although no charges were ever laid against the ringleader.

Renwick also excelled at one of the other great past-times of the day - bare-knuckle prize fighting. In the days before the Queensbury Rules were introduced, there were few regulations to govern the conduct of these savage fights and no limit to the length a bout could go on. In October 1837, Renwick was matched in an epic battle against the black fighter Young Molyneux in a contest held in Northumberland. The fight went on and on into the night until eventually the Winlaton man lost in the 87th round when he was unable to stand after being head-butted. So impressed were the spectators that a rematch was arranged. This fight took place in Shap in June 1839 for a £100 purse to the winner, which Young Molyneux again collected.

Dancing bear entertains children in Leadgate (Photograph courtesy of Beamish Museum)

Despite the two bruising beatings, Renwick's career continued and on Hedley Fell in 1850 he fought and lost once more, this time at the hands of Coffee Johnny, a six foot six inch tall Winlaton blacksmith who would later achieve fame in the song The Blaydon Races. John Oliver earned his nickname through his habit of keeping visitors waiting while he finished drinking his coffee and, although only 22 years old at the time of his fight with William Renwick, was already well on the way to becoming one of the Derwent Valley's most famous figures of the 19th Century. The fight with Renwick took 36 rounds and lasted more than an hour, by which time the ageing fighter had to be brought home in a cart and required lengthy medical attention. Coffee Johnny, however, went on to take part in a series of bouts, including one at Tanfield where he is reputed to have won a bruising battle then went on to fight the promoter, a local landlord, who tried to withhold the purse. Two years after his epic fight with Renwick, he married a local girl, 15-year-old Elizabeth Greener and the couple went on to have eight children. For the next 25 years, his fame spread, as a blacksmith and a fighter. A distinctive figure in his trademark tall white hat, Coffee Johnny followed the local hunts and was seen at horse racing meetings around the North. He finally died of pneumonia at his daughter's home in Blyth in 1900, aged 71. Such was his fame that when his coffin was returned to Blaydon railway station on the way to his funeral, a crowd of thousands thronged the streets and a band was said to have played "When Johnny Comes Marching Home Again" as the funeral procession made its way to his final resting place.

But if fighters like Coffee Johnny could achieve fame for their prowess in the ring, the prize fights they took part in were famed for their brutality. An anonymous account survives of one such bout, fought on Barlow Fell on Monday, October 25th, 1824 between Winlaton butcher Thomas Dunn and Newcastle bricklayer Jem Wallace. A crowd of 2,000 people gathered to watch the pair do battle for the princely sum of 40 sovereigns. The anonymous broadsheet writer set the scene in the florid style of the time: "The road to the mill on Monday morning seemed all alive, the weather promised to be fine, loads of toddlers jogging over the ground bid fair to make a strong muster. On arriving at the ground we were somewhat disappointed at finding so few carriages - the rough commoners, yokels and men of metal from Winlaton mustered strong. Much time was lost in making a ring and the rain fell for quarter of an hour. It cleared up and at 10 minutes after 1pm Wallace shewed, but the ring, by the rush, was immediately broke in, the ropes and stakes were trod underfoot and such a scene of confusion occurred."

So great was the crush to get a view of the fight that one elderly spectator fell beneath Dunn's carriage and suffered two broken legs, dying of his injuries a few days later. It appeared unlikely that the fight would go ahead but eventually men on horseback managed to clear a space for the ring to be repaired and they patrolled the perimeter, keeping the spectators at bay so the fight could go ahead. Finally, after almost an hour of chaos, the boxers emerged and stripped for the fight. "On peeling," the writer observed, "the difference between them was great. Tom looked the heaviest but his flesh was loose and fat, he seemed to be all the worse for the training he had got while Wallace had the advantage in height, length of arm and was in tip top condition."

The first round went to Dunn, the Winlaton man landing a punch which left Wallace's cheek so red many in the crowd thought first blood had been drawn. But from the second round, the tide turned decisively - Dunn was cut and in the third "Tom received a snorter on the smeller which brought the claret in streams." By the fourth round, Dunn was incapable of defending himself and being

Fist fight at Muggleswick (Photograph courtesy of Beamish Museum)

pummelled by his opponent, roared on by a bloodthirsty crowd: "It was evident Tom was nearly done up; one peeper had taken its departure and the other was fast going the same road - he was quite confused from the effects of the last round - in fact he was too blind to see his man." At the end of the fifth round, his seconds resorted to pouring brandy into their man and in the seventh, as he grappled with his opponent in a vain attempt to keep him at bay, the Winlaton man fell to the ground and Wallace crashed down on top of him, leaving Dunn vomiting blood in the centre of the ring. In the eighth round, after taking several more sickening blows, Dunn's corner threw in the towel.

The crowd were said to have left hugely disappointed that the fight had lasted a mere eight rounds, a jubilant Wallace was carried triumphant from the ring with barely a mark on him. Dunn, however, was a sorry sight. "Tom presented a most terrific appearance," according to the broadsheet, "the blood streaming from his head in several places and literally washing him; his face scarce bore a trace of humanity, both eyes being cut severely and the left jaw a little splintered, his right hand had also gone. We do not remember a man so terribly punished in such a short time."

Other fighters fared even worse. In 1835, prize-fighter John Brown suffered a savage mauling in a bout at the hamlet of Leadgate, near Chopwell. Friends carried him to the nearby Three Horse Shoes pub where he died of his injuries and his opponent Robert Forbister was later found guilty of manslaughter.

Not all gambling centred on violence. Boat races between the keel men of Stella and Derwenthaugh were commonplace, with up to £60 resting on the outcome and much more in side bets. Even more bizarre competitions and entertainments were to be found at the hoppings, the annual fairs held in several villages around the North-East to celebrate the date when labourers were traditionally hired for a year's work, either in the pits or the farms. Blaydon, Swalwell, Barlow, Greenside and Winlaton all had an annual hoppings along with countless other villages around the region where, as well as entertainment, there was a chance to compete for prizes. An advertisement for Swalwell Hoppings of May 1758 proudly boasted that, along with more conventional running races,

Carousel at Winlaton Hoppings
(Photograph courtesy of Beamish Museum)

Thomas Prudhoe, Winlaton chain maker, outside his Hood Square forge in 1890. This may well be the Thomas Prudhoe whose son died in a tragic accident on the opening day of Blaydon Races (Photograph courtesy of Gateshead Libraries Service)

there would be dancing competitions to win ribbons, grinning competitions to win tobacco, ass racing and "a man eating a cock alive, feathers, entrails etc". Horse racing was the most important sport of them all. At one stage, almost every village had its occasional horse races, including a famous race meeting at the annual Winlaton Hoppings. But the most celebrated of all were, of course, the Blaydon Races.

Horse racing was first held at Blaydon in 1811, but the meeting was abandoned and not revived for 50 years. It was staged again in 1861 on a mile-long oval course known as Blaydon Island, which has long since disappeared. The opening day of the meeting was marred by tragedy when a 14-year-old boy, the son of Winlaton chain maker Thomas Prudhoe, was killed as he tried to dash across the course during a race. Nevertheless, the races were judged a success and were staged again in June the following year. The day of the races dawned bright and warm which drew crowds so great that extra trains and omnibuses were laid on and were immortalised in the

Geordie Ridley song written on the afternoon and first performed that very night. Blaydon races proved popular through into the early years of the 20th Century, but were abandoned on the outbreak of the First World War. In September 1916, the Ministry of Munitions gave special permission for the races to be staged once more to boost civilian morale. Around 4,000 punters turned up, but the day turned into a full-blooded riot after the heavily-backed winner of the opening race, Anxious Moments, was disqualified after a stewards' inquiry and the crowd tore apart the offices of the course. It was to be the last time the famous old races would be held.

CHAPTER 21
LEAD AND WHISKEY

IN August 1892, the widow Snowden made her butter as she did every week. For the last 24 years, her family had lived in a farmhouse converted from the old workshops of the Silver Tongues lead mine on the banks of the Derwent near Allensford. The mine had a long and illustrious history dating back to the 17th Century when it was valued more for the silver mined there as the lead. In 1624, King Charles I had granted the mine to George Villiers, the Duke of Buckingham, as part "of the mines of silver or of lead mixed with silver in or near Muggleswick, alias Mugglesley, in the County Palatinate of the Bishopric of Durham and within the compass of 10 miles of Muggleswick for 21 years". Chief among these mines was Silver Tongues, which produced 30 ounces of silver for every tonne of lead ore. Buckingham did not enjoy the wealth generated by Silver Tongues mine for long. One of the most notoriously corrupt figures of the 17th Century, he was murdered three years after being awarded the Muggleswick mines, stabbed to death by a sailor in a Portsmouth pub.

The mine finally closed in 1876, leaving only the Snowden family to earn a living on the site of one of the richest mines ever worked in the Derwent Valley. On that fine summer's day, as she always did, Mrs Snowden sent her eldest son into the mouth of the mine to fetch water to cool her freshly-made butter. When he failed to return, she went to the mine and found him lying dead - overcome by the toxic fumes which seeped from the old workings as he collected water. The grief-stricken woman rushed to her son's side and tried to revive him but, within seconds, she too lay dead in the mouth of the mine. After the tragedy, her remaining children, one daughter and three sons, moved to Castleside as the family became the final victims of the lead-mining industry in the Derwent Valley.

Lead shaped the Derwent Valley long before its younger cousin steel. It seems likely that some mines date back at least to the 12th Century and that they in fact began life as silver mines. Lead ore is rich in silver and large quantities of the precious metal have been mined from deep beneath the valley over the years. It is thought that the monks of Blanchland mined for lead and silver almost from the moment the abbey was founded - at the time the Bishop of Durham operated a mint in the city which required a ready source of the precious metal. At the end of the 19th Century, the owners of Healeyfield mine, near Castleside, claimed the mine had been in operation for no less than 800 years which, if true, would date it from around the same time.

Certainly, Shildon mine, which lies a mile or so to the north of Blanchland, was in existence by 1468. In that year, King Edward IV granted to George Willaby the rights to work a number of lead mines, including Shyldeyn mine, in exchange for one-twelfth of the silver. Within 100 years, it appears there were several silver mines being worked in the valley. Records from 1545 show mines in the area of Muggleswick being leased to the Duke of Suffolk.

Although a handful of lead mines had been worked for many years, it was events at the end of the 17th Century which were to truly transform the face of the Derwent Valley. In 1687, a meeting took place of the Society of Mines Royal - the body which oversaw all mining activities in the realm on behalf of the king. It reported that "a great quantity of silver ore" was being mined from Muggleswick where 54 ounces of pure silver had been recovered. This report provoked something of a silver rush in the Derwent Valley over the next few years as land was leased and mines sunk in a bid to exploit the reserves beneath. Five years after the society's report, the London Lead Company was formed in the Half Moon Tavern in London's Cheapside. Sometimes known as the Quaker Company, because many of the senior figures in the company were followers of that religion. It was this company which opened up the lead reserves of the Derwent Valley over the next 100 years.

Several mines were opened in quick succession, most notably Jeffrey's mine and Ramshaw mine, where the imprints of children's clogs thought to date back to the 17th Century have been found. These mines, which lie a couple of miles south of Blanchland near the hamlets of Ramshaw and Hunstanworth, fed the new smelt mills which refined the ore into metal. In 1702, two agents of the London Lead Company were sent to the valley to buy up mines and they are known to have visited mills at Acton and Feldon, which lie close to Edmundbyers.

At first, lead ore was mined and transported down the valley by pack horse to Ryton, where The Ryton Company, which had perfected the complex process of refining silver from the ore, operated a mill. But it was a long and laborious journey. Several of the mines in the Derwent Valley were on land owned by the Earl of Derwentwater, including Healeyfield mine. Others were held by Tom Forster, including Shildon and Jeffrey's. When both lost their lands as a result of their part in the ill-fated rising of 1715, much of their property was given by the Crown to Greenwich Hospital, which sent a surveyor north to report on the condition of its new lands. He wrote back asking for his report to be postponed because of the problems he was encountering - winter starts early and continues late, he bemoaned, and snow lies on the highest peaks for five months a year. "In the first place, it is such a part of the world that they are seldome without rains" and described the whole place as "mountainous and rotten." The roads in the area were so bad that no cart could use them and everything had to be brought in and out of the valley by packhorse - even well into the 19th Century. In 1823, the noted road-builder John McAdam was sent north by Greenwich Hospital to improve communications. He reported back on the state of the roads: "They are altogether the worst that have yet come to my knowledge" and added that those roads which did exist were built in a "slovenly, careless manner."

With roads, where they existed at all, impassable, the only option was to take the ore to market by pack horse. Teams of a dozen horses, all strung together, carried the ore north out of the valley in huge packs tied across their backs. They crossed over Burntshieldhaugh Fell and past Slaley and Hedley-on-the-Hill, then down to the mill at Ryton or the wharfs of Stella on the Tyne. The journey, even by 1750, took days to complete, with the horses resting by the side of the road on the way.

The opening of smelt mills close to the mines was an obvious move, it was cheaper and easier to move finished metal rather than bulky ore. By 1704, the London Lead Company had acquired Ryton Mill and four years later, the ore from Blanchland was being processed at nearby Acton Mill. Within another year, the company had opened Whiteheaps mine close to Ramshaw mine and the Derwent Mill was opened to serve the two. Reeding mine to the north was opened in 1720 as the explosion of mining activity continued. By June 1721, Shildon mine, the oldest and, at that stage, the most famous of those operating in the area, was producing something in the order of 1,600 cwt of refined lead a year and around 1,600 ounces of fine silver. The mines appeared to be a licence to print money. By 1725, the company had finally got its hands on Feldon Mill and had sunk deeper shafts at Shildon and Jeffrey's mines, where a petrified prehistoric forest was found underground with trunks six feet wide and leaves still on the branches. Other test digs were carried out across the valley which was soon riddled with shafts and bore holes. Great waterwheels up to 50ft in diameter were installed to power Ramshaw and Whiteheaps mines and powerful ore crushing machines were built at Jeffrey's and Acton Mill.

For more than 50 years, the London Lead Company made good profits from the Derwent Valley - but towards the end of the 18th Century, the industry began to suffer hard times. The amount of lead won from the mines dwindled, the price offered on the market was falling and the company decided that the mines were just about at the point of exhaustion. No new veins were opened and the amount spent on maintenance declined. By the turn of the century, many mines were in a state of semi-dereliction, several were flooded, particularly at the lowest levels, and the shafts were in a dangerous state of disrepair. Teesdale seemed to offer better prospects and much of the company's energy was exerted there. It was a state of affairs which would provoke a long-running battle for control of the valley's lead.

The history of the Derwent Valley's lead mines is extremely complicated. The land on which the mines stood has had several different owners over the last 300 years. The Dean and Chapter of Durham was the most important landlord, but several other families also had holdings in the area, the Clavering family of Greencroft and Axwell Park, the Silvertop family of Minsteracres, the Bakers, the Ords, the Cappers and, not least, the trust established by Lord Crewe. Each of these landlords could lease the rights to all or part of their land to a company to carry out mining, for a period of usually 10, 20 or 30 years, or alternatively set up a mining company themselves. After the lease was up, it may have been renewed or another company may have been invited to tender for the rights. Consequently, at any one time there could be half a dozen mining companies working the lead veins and over the last three centuries dozens of different companies operated in the valley.

Over the years, there have been at least 14 major mines - although not all at the same time as different sites became exhausted. Broadly speaking, there were four areas in which mining took place: a group of mines to the north of Blanchland which included the original Shildon mine as well as Beldon Shield mine; a group of five mines further south around the villages of Ramshaw and Hunstanworth; three smaller mines which stood a mile or two south of Edmundbyers and finally a group much further to the east which included Healeyfield mine and Silver Tongues mine, which stands near The Sneep, a mile or so upriver from Allensford. Smelting took place at four sites, which broadly correspond with each group of mines: there was a smelt mill at Healeyfield; another at Feldon which served the Edmundbyers mines, two mills at Jeffrey's mine in the Hunstanworth group and another two mills at Acton, which is north of Blanchland and not far away from the mines there. In addition, there were countless test pits and smaller mine workings scattered across the area.

In the early days of the 19th Century, a challenge arose to the London Lead Company's dominance of the area. The company seemed intent on abandoning the area and several mining agents attempted to persuade them to go. In 1800, the Easterby Hall Company was set up, made up of businessmen from Tyneside and the Yorkshire Dales, with the intention of winning several of the leases then operated by the London Company. Gradually, as these leases came up for grabs, the new company took them on - and then usually found itself involved in protracted legal disputes with the former owners over the state of dereliction they found in the mines they had acquired.

The leading light in the new company was Frederick Hall, who built Ruffside Hall, which now stands on the banks of the Derwent Reservoir, as the headquarters for his mining business. It was Hall who led the legal actions against the London Lead Company and its agent in the region Thomas Dodd. The pair regularly found themselves on opposite sides of a courtroom. Easterby Hall felt that the London Company had simply let the area go to waste and that all the mines left in the valley had winnable reserves - Dodd was convinced they were not economically viable and therefore expending large amounts of money propping them up was a waste.

Frederick Hall however was convinced that there were workable reserves and spent fortunes of his company's money opening a new mine at Beldon, sinking deeper and deeper shafts, repairing the damage done by years of London Lead Company neglect and introducing new technology and manpower to the mines. By 1811, Hall had brought in six steam engines to the Derwent mines to replace the earlier water wheels for crushing - the engines also pumped floodwater out of the levels, work which had previously been done by boys with buckets. It took four years of work to restore Jeffrey's mine to its former state - and all the time costs mounted without any lead coming out of the ground to pay for it.

The tension appeared to be getting to Hall. So determined was he to succeed that, even with lead prices at rock bottom and a depression in the industry which saw hundreds of miners laid off around the region, he employed anyone who would work in his pits. Dodd wrote in 1811: "The mining countries are getting into great distress and the people are flying in all directions for employment and none to assist them, but Frederick Hall who employs all that go into Derwent."

It could not go on and that same year the business collapsed with debts of £460,000. But it was only a temporary setback for Hall. Within months he was back at the head of another company - the Arkendale and Derwent Mining Company. The new company stopped the repair work at Jeffrey's and moved the men to Shildon mine, where there was workable ore. Once some profits started to roll in again, the work recommenced at Jeffrey's and eventually it too started to produce workable ore. But still Dodd was convinced his old legal enemy Hall was in trouble. In January 1813, he wrote, with barely disguised glee, that the directors of the new company: "had seen their errors and are now economizing on some of the tremendous expenses 'til now outlaid and they are controlling the actions of Frederick Hall, which up to the present time have been most unaccountable. He is almost mad, raving and swearing like a madman and tells them to smash the equipment to pieces in his fits of rage."

Hall's company continued to run the mines, with some success, until 1832, when most of its interests were taken over by the Derwent Mining Company. By this point, the lead industry had recovered and the new company was behind another great wave of expansion. By 1858, the Derwent Mining Company employed somewhere in the region of 400 men, of whom 265 were pickmen working underground - the high point of lead mining in the valley.

Initially, few of these men came from the area. In 1801, the parish of Hunstanworth had a population of 215 people, most of whom were farmers or farm labourers - at that point only a handful of people were working in the London Lead Company's derelict mines. In 1842, the chief agent of the Derwent Mines gave evidence to a Government commission that although some of the company's miners lived locally, the vast majority came from Stanhope or Allenheads. Every week, regardless of the season or the weather, these men would walk the 10 miles to work over the moors before descending to the bottom of the mine. During the week, they would stay in one of the lodging houses near the mine, then would return to their homes at the weekend. "Around the mines, the fell is altogether uninhabited," he told the commission.

Compared to coal miners, the lead miners had comparatively good conditions. They worked an eight-hour day, five days a week. The lead mines worked on a system of bargains. Every month or so, depending on the custom at the time, the owners would negotiate a new deal with the miners. An individual or group of workers would agree to work a certain part of the mine in exchange for a percentage of the value of the ore which was won - whoever offered to work for the smallest percentage was hired. Often a miner would negotiate a bargain for a section of the mine which would then be worked by his entire family and children as young as 11 would work alongside their father. The miners were paid what was owed to them twice a year - although they also received a subsistence wage, which in 1864 stood at seven shillings a week. Industrial relations appear to have been quite good. In neighbouring Weardale, a succession of strikes took place in 1795, 1816 and again during the1870s and 1880s. Similarly, the rest of the orefield was the scene of rioting during the periodic depressions in the industry. There are recorded riots in Allenheads in 1760, Rookhope in 1795 and Alston Moor in 1797, but the Derwent Valley remained peaceful.

The ore was removed with pickaxes and, where the vein reached a wall of stone, gunpowder was used to blow a way through - although in the poorly ventilated shafts the smoke could linger for hours afterwards and make work impossible. The lead mines had their casualties - but the safety record was much better than in the neighbouring coal mines. In August 1826, 15-year-old George Craft died in a fall of stone at Jeffrey's mine, but such incidents were rare. Between 1855 and 1862, the most serious incident in all the Derwent mines combined was an accident in which one miner lost an eye. In comparison, over the same seven years, five coal miners died in Hedleyhope pit, another three at Iveston and two in Delves.

The lead miners also had better living conditions on the whole than their counterparts in coal. Most lead miners' houses had one bedroom yet they could be home to a family of 12, making it desperately overcrowded. The lodging houses where most lived during the week were even worse. On average, 14 men would sleep in a dormitory - one room which also served as living quarters, washroom and kitchen. They were expected to sleep two to a bed and the bed linen was washed twice a year, when it would be taken home by one of the miners and brought back on Monday morning. Squalid as it appears, conditions did have some advantages over the coal miners - for the most part the lead miners' homes were up in the dales and therefore there was fresh air and fresh water, compared to the slums of the Durham coalfield. Most lead miners also had smallholdings attached to their homes, where they grew vegetables or raised some livestock and therefore, even in the worst of times, managed a better diet than other miners.

Where the lead miners fared worse than the coal miners was when it came to the dust. It was not roof falls or mine explosions which killed them, it was constant exposure to the choking dust which ate into their lungs almost from the very second they went down the mine. The lead miners died in droves of the disease now known as silicosis. Within a year or two of starting work as teenagers, the miners would notice a blue-ish phlegm which grew thicker and thicker as the years went by. They would cough up dry dust and then it would begin to affect appetite, miners often complained that their breakfast would be vomited back up during the walk to work. By the time they reached the age of 30, almost all were short of breath which affected their ability to work and gave them a hacking cough. In 1864, the average age of workers down the Derwent mines was 28 - this was largely because by the time they reached the age of 40 no-one was fit for such work.

The silicosis made the miners all the more susceptible to chest diseases such as tuberculosis, which spread like wildfire in the overcrowded lodging houses. Hundreds of miners, weakened by years of disease, died from it - the average lifespan of a 19th Century lead miner was 51 years of age. Twice the Government set up a commission to look into the health of lead miners, in 1842 and again in 1864, but little was done. Indeed, the Derwent Mines Company persuaded two of its miners to attend the second of these commissions and give evidence that they were unaware of any miners having died under the age of 50 - despite the record books being full of them.

At first, the mines and the lodging shops were pretty much all there was in the upper Derwent valley. There were no friendly societies, few shops and few chapels. The influence of Methodism was one of the factors in ensuring there were few pubs. John Wesley first preached in Blanchland on March 24th 1747 - when he referred to the village as "a heap of ruins". He was invited to return the following year and this time preached in the house owned by the London Lead Company as the miners gathered for their six-monthly pay. The founder of Methodism also preached at Dene Howl, near Healeyfield in 1772. In the earliest days, the miners were given drink to celebrate the completion of a difficult job but the practice was phased out as the temperance movement spread throughout the valley. By the 1840s, drunkenness was grounds for instant dismissal.

The influence of Methodism was also important in ensuring that serious crime was rare - but not unheard of. Perhaps the most famous incident came on November 28th, 1808 when William Richardson, Easterby Hall and Company's agent in the area, was travelling from the firm's Yorkshire headquarters to Blanchland with six months worth of wages for the firm's men, more than £930 in five-guinea and £1 notes. Close to Wolsingham, Richardson claimed he was accosted by two highwaymen, one armed with a pistol. The gunman seized his bridle and pointed the barrel of the gun at him, while his accomplice cut the straps of the saddle bags and the pair made good their escape with the cash. A reward of £50 was offered for the arrest of the two men and although several suspects were questioned, all were released for lack of evidence. Eventually, Richardson himself was arrested and spent some time in Durham Jail before he too was proven to be innocent, although he remained dogged by the scandal afterwards. No-one was ever convicted of the crime and from that point onwards a troop of dragoons accompanied the pay waggon, which in later years contained several thousand pounds.

Like their counterparts downstream at Winlaton and Swalwell, the lawless elements of the Upper Derwent Valley thrived on many trades as well as simple robbery. Gambling was one occupation which attracted the miners and was carried out at several secret venues. Among them was Govan Gill, a natural amphitheatre just to the north of Edmundbyers. During the 19th Century, it was used for regular cockfights - gamblers kept the area's reputation for witchcraft alive by spreading the rumour it was the site of a coven to keep away prying eyes. Poaching was another illegal activity which thrived. In May 1788, an exasperated William Routledge wrote to the steward Arthur Murray about the never-ending problem of poaching and fence-breaking at Burntshieldhaugh, just north of Blanchland. The ringleader was a local man, he said, George Beck: "who brought all the blackguards from Allenheads and Rookhope with him to hunt and he will not be stopped." The miners were also a ready market for illegally distilled or smuggled whiskey. With duty on spirits higher in England than Scotland, a thriving cross border trade in smuggled spirits grew up. Illegal distilleries are known to have existed at Tow Law, Satley, Rowley and Cornsay and there were probably many more hidden away in the secret gullies of the valley.

But the lead mining areas were now turning more into settled communities than just work places for miners scattered across the fells. During the early 1860s, a new village was built at Hunstanworth with houses to replace the lodging shops. There was also an influx of miners from Wales and Cornwall and by 1861, the population of the parish stood at 778 - more than treble the number of 60 years earlier. At its height, Hunstanworth sent 35,000 lead ingots a year to the Tyne for export and, as it grew in economic importance, more facilities opened up in the area. The first school had opened in Blanchland in 1750, paid for by the Lord Crewe charity and taking the children of local miners. It does not appear to have been a particularly impressive place of learning and in 1778 parents drew up a petition claiming that the present teacher was incapable and added: "children who went for many years to that school were not able to read or write fit for business". The Lord Crewe charity opened a second school at Newbiggen in 1799, where a grant of £11 a year paid for a teacher and fuel. A school for 120 pupils was opened in Hunstanworth in 1862 and at around the same

Sheep shearing at Nookton Farm near Blanchland, possibly from 1890 (Photograph courtesy of Beamish Museum)

time, new pubs opened at Bay Bridge and Ramshaw, a grocery store was opened at Jeffrey's mine and a reading room which doubled as a chapel on Sundays was opened as well.

But it appears that here, as elsewhere, there was a certain tension between recent immigrants and the established community. In the early 1860s, a group of 32 Cornish miners were brought to the Derwent Valley to work in the mines and they seem to have been immediately at odds with the locals.

This simmering tension boiled over on November 17th, 1866 when a group of 27 Cornishmen gathered outside the newly-opened Miners Arms pub in Bay Bridge. The Cornishmen felt that landlord George Mawson favoured locals over them and at 6pm that night gathered, as the court charge sheet said: "to vent wrath upon the landlord." The mob pelted the pub with stones and did considerable damage: two local men were injured after being struck on the head, George Wilkinson, a smelter from Ramshaw and Joseph Murray, a

Lead miners at Whiteheaps mine in 1930
(Photograph courtesy of Beamish Museum)

miner at Jeffrey's. Despite their wounds, both managed to escape to Blanchland to raise reinforcements. Order was restored when PC Beattie of Blanchland led a baton charge against the crowd, which left two Cornishmen injured among the piles of stones they had collected as ammunition. Eight men were eventually charged at Hexham Police Court with riotous assembly for their part in the incident.

By 1870, lead mining was in serious decline. The coal mines, particularly those operated only a few miles away by Consett Iron Company, were offering better wages and miners deserted the industry in droves for the nearby towns. Increasingly, bargains went unworked as the mines struggled to find anyone willing to take them. In 1872, the Derwent Mining Company was wound up with debts of £1,700. A new company took over and the industry limped on into the 20th Century, but it was a shadow of its former glory. Between 1871 and 1891, the population of the Derwent's lead district halved - mines went unworked, mills fell into disuse and cottages stood empty. Although the last of the Derwent Valley's lead mines did not close until the 1980s, the damage was done in the previous century. By 1901, the population of Hunstanworth had fallen by 500 back down to 220 - only a handful more than it had been 100 years earlier before the great lead rush began.

CHAPTER 22
THE BLACK

DEEP beneath the ground, the black began to move. Somewhere among the labyrinth of pitch black passageways which made up Stargate Pit, dirt began to trickle from between the stones, then the roof collapsed in a huge fall of rock which sent echoes rumbling up the deserted tunnels. Finally, the dust settled and the tunnels fell silent once more.

No-one heard the fall. It was the weekend and the mine was empty. The only people working were the surface men who fed the furnace - the furnace which sent a draught of air through the mine workings, channelled by an elaborate system of partitions to disperse the gas. But down in the Brockwell Seam - 150 metres below the earth - methane gas seeped gently out of the workings and collected behind a wall of newly-fallen stone where the ventilation could not reach. In the villages and hamlets surrounding the pit, 50 men and boys of the foreshift slept soundly in their beds.

Stargate Pit lay near the road from Ryton to Winlaton and was, in some ways, the most modern of its day. It opened in 1803, having taken three years to dig down to the Brockwell Seam - the deepest in the coalfield - which lay almost 500ft below the surface. A steam engine brought men and coal to and from the surface - a rope was hung down the shaft with loops at regular intervals to which wicker baskets called corves were attached. These baskets held either coal or men and were hauled to the surface by steam power.

Most of the miners lived in the hamlets around the pit - Greenside, Woodside, Stella and Dog Leap - and, as elsewhere, several entire families worked together at the pit. Children as young as six years old worked as trap boys, opening the trapdoors to let the loaded tubs pass through. Shortly before 3 o'clock on the morning of May 30th, 1826 they began to gather at the pit head where the steam engine was already in motion for the start of the early shift. Fifty men and boys went down the mine that day. Among those rubbing sleep from their eyes were trap boys John Hall of Woodside and Thomas Waugh of Folly, both just 10-years-old and facing a long shift in the darkness of the mine. One by one, they lit their candles, sat in a corve for the

Stargate Colliery pithead in 1900
(Photograph courtesy of Beamish Museum)

descent or simply grabbed hold of a loop in the line and disappeared into The Black.

As they reached the level of the Brockwell Seam, the first arrivals began to make their way to the coalface while others were still on the rope descending the shaft. Strung out in a long line of ones and twos through the mine workings, their way lit by candlelight, they stood no chance. The explosion ripped through the mine destroying everything in its path. Bodies were torn limb from limb, burned beyond recognition, crushed beneath falling rock. It roared up the shaft where several miners were still descending and spilled out of the mouth of the pit. So great was the force that 23-year-old John Grey, who had just reached the bottom of the shaft, was blown to the surface. Thomas Stokoe, 48, had been half way down alongside his 15-year-old son Matthew - both were found dead back at the pit head. Miraculously, two other miners had been in the shaft when the explosion took place and had also been thrown back to the surface, but had somehow survived.

As the roar of the explosion reverberated around the valley, families and fellow miners rushed to the scene. The carnage on the surface, where the remains of pit ponies mixed with the charred debris blown up from the mine, was as nothing compared to the horrors below. One eye-witness from Winlaton recorded: "This was such a sight as was never seen in the neighbourhood, the clouds as it were, stood still, the very earth was said to wonder to hear the cries of the people."

In the pit, the handful of survivors now faced renewed dangers - the roof collapsed in several places burying miners alive, while gas seeped from the disturbed workings to poison those who could not escape. John Browell and his brother William were at the bottom of the shaft but luckily had been sheltered from the full force of the blast and both had been knocked unconscious. There seemed no escape up the main shaft and instead the brothers went deeper into the mine, crawling over the mangled bodies of their dead colleagues, the blackened carcasses of the animals and the smouldering remains of the tubs. Finally, after a hellish journey of about a mile, they escaped through a narrow drainage tunnel which led out into a nearby stream. Horse-keeper William Roddam was dragged unconscious from the wreckage by the first rescuers to reach the scene and went on to make a full recovery.

But the survivors were few and far between. During the course of the day, the rescue turned into the grim task of retrieving the bodies. Among the dead were John Hall and Thomas Waugh, the 10-year-old trap boys. Other families faced unspeakable grief that day. Leonard Dowsey, a 38-year-old miner from Woodside, was killed alongside his 12-year-old son John and his 28-year-old brother Rodney. Teenage brothers Joseph and Thomas Howden, also from Woodside were killed. The Robson family of Greenside suffered particularly badly with three young brothers killed alongside each other, John Robson, 21, Robert Robson, 17 and 15-year-old James.

The death toll was creeping ever higher. In the end, 28 men and 10 boys were found to have died in the Stargate explosion and around a dozen were seriously injured. It was the area's worst pit disaster to date and left the Derwent Valley in mourning. Most of the dead were buried at Ryton Churchyard and a committee was set up to relieve the suffering of the bereaved, which included 19 widows and more than 60 children. Landowner George Silvertop, of Minsteracres, donated £100, as did the owners of the mine. But the mourning did not last for long and within a matter of weeks the pit was working once more.

Two years later, on the night of December 1st, 1828, a storm blew up. William Roddam, the horse-keeper who had been dragged unconscious from the wreckage of the explosion, was working alone in the lower levels of the mine. The swollen waters of the Tyne rose to such an extent that they flooded the old mine workings and rushed through the tunnels into the Five-Quarter seam. Around a dozen miners working at the higher levels escaped the rising waters but Roddam and 14 of his horses were swept away to their deaths. His body was not found until the seam was drained in October 1880 - 52 years after Stargate Pit finally claimed his life.

Popular images of the mines focus on the industry's Victorian heyday, but the history of coal mining in the area in fact stretches much further back in time. For hundreds of years, coal was the foundation on which English prosperity was built - indeed one of the most potent symbols of the British establishment is built on coal from the Derwent Valley. When Windsor Castle underwent huge structural alterations in 1357, Henry de Strother, the then Sheriff of Northumberland, was engaged to ship 600 tons of coal from the manor of Winlaton down south for use in reducing the lime needed for the massive construction project. On behalf of King Edward III, de Strother paid £47, 19s and 8d for the coal which was transported by pack horse down to the Tyne at Stella where a team of 170 men were waiting to load it into 33 keel boats which were rowed to ships waiting at Newcastle. In all, it took 54 days to load the coal, by hand, into the waiting ships before they began the arduous journey down the coast to London then across land to Windsor.

Most Medieval mining took place close to the Tyne where the coal lay only several feet down and in some places, including the lower reaches of the Derwent Valley, actually burst through to the surface. The earliest reference to coal mining in the area comes from 1356, when Bishop Hatfield granted to Sir Thomas Gray and John Pulhore, the then rector of Whickham, a 12-year lease on five mines near Whickham. These mines are thought to have been some of the most lucrative in the whole region at the time, although they would soon be surpassed by those at Winlaton. By 1425, it is known that there were at least two pits being worked at Winlaton and by the era of Elizabeth I, the manor was producing a phenomenal 25,000 tons of coal a year. At nearby Ryton, the industry was certainly established by 1409 when mineral rights for the manor were licensed by the bishop to John Carnis and William Tyndale.

In the industry's earliest days, the most common form of mine was the bell pit. A narrow shaft was dug down so miners could reach the coal seam, a couple of miners descended by rope and then dug out the coal they found there. Once the pit had been worked, it took on the appearance of the cross section of a bell - narrow at the shaft and widening out to a broad base where the coal had been removed. The coal was hauled back to the surface by buckets with rope and pulley and then transported down to the staithes at Derwenthaugh or Stella on horseback. Here it was loaded into keel boats, small rowing boats built specially for the purpose, and ferried downriver to Newcastle where it was loaded into collier ships bound for the south. Although each individual shaft produced only a small quantity of coal before the ground became unstable, there were so many pits working in the area thousands of tonnes of coal a year were being shipped out of the Tyne in the Middle Ages. Already, Newcastle was known as the coal mining capital of the world and the banks of the Tyne were piled high with black gold awaiting transportation.

However, if the most important mines lay near the Tyne, there were several already in operation further up the valley. It is thought that mining has taken place at Collierley, present-day Dipton, from the middle of the 14th Century and Bishop Hatfield's survey of 1350 refers to the existence of coal pits near Lanchester. By 1440, the records of Bishop Neville show one Robert Hall paying rent for a mine at Iveston and negotiating payment for another which was about to be sunk. Those same records also mention that former coal mines were now lying waste at Benfieldside and Consett.

These early mines may have been simple, but they came complete with all the dangers for which the industry would soon be notorious. In 1610, one Thomas Carnaby, described as a coal workman of Winlaton, was buried at Ryton following an accident at work - the first recorded casualty in the valley's pits. In fact, the earliest records of mining activity in a particular area can often be found in the parish burial registers. It is known there was a coal mining industry at Blaydon in the early 17th Century because on August 22nd 1628, the churchyard witnessed a double burial, of "Thomas Proctor slaine in a kolepyt at Blaydon and John, son of Thomas Jobson of Winlaton, slaine in the same kole pyt." In Ryton churchyard, there is a memorial to John, son of William Sherbourn, who, in 1717, "Fell down a shaft by the breaking of a chain".

By the late 17th Century the increasing demand for coal, which was by then replacing wood as the main source of domestic fuel, and the exhaustion of the shallow seams on the banks of the Tyne, was beginning to force the miners further inland. The great coal owning families opened pits further and further into the valley. Here the coal seams lay far beneath the surface and mines took on more modern characteristics - deep shafts which were descended first by ladder and then by wheel and cage, sprawling networks of tunnels where hundreds of miners could work at once and underground waggonways where the coal was moved in tubs, either pushed by men or hauled by ponies.

Above ground, new waggonways - precursors of the railways in which tubs laden with coal were pulled along wooden tracks by horses - were built to haul the coal the increasing distance from the inland collieries to the staithes on the Tyne. By 1630, small scale waggonways existed at Whickham and Ryton to transport the coal down to the river - but as more pits were opened up further and further inland, it became necessary to construct more and more waggonways. By 1680, The Main Way had been constructed which stretched from Derwenthaugh right up to the pits at Pontop Pike. Coal poured down this route to the staithes which stretched from Dunston to Stella and blackened the banks of the river.

These waggonways proved to be the spark by which the rivalries between the great coal barons of the Derwent Valley - most notably the Bowes, Clavering and Cotesworth families - escalated into a state of all-out war in the early years of the 18th Century. In many cases, connecting the pits to the staithes meant running waggonways over a neighbour's land and great prices were demanded for permission to do so. This network of waggonways - and the complicated financial arrangements which went with them - led to open conflict between the great families of the North.

The war between the three families appears to have started in 1712. Sir John Clavering, of Axwell Park, was attempting to exploit lucrative inland coal reserves further up the valley, especially in the area around Tanfield, Pontop and Greencroft. To do so demanded waggonways to bring the coal to the Tyne. However, Lady Bowes, who held the Gibside estates, realised she could effectively hold her neighbour to ransom if she refused to allow the waggonways to cross her land and persuade others to do likewise. William Cotesworth, who had by then emerged from obscurity to become the acknowledged head of the cartel of local coal owners, was persuaded: "at the pressing insistence of Lady Bowes" to destroy a waggonway laid over Whickham Fell by Sir John, to force him into a deal for the Derwent Valley line. Having talked Cotesworth into the dispute with her powerful neighbour, Lady Bowes then retreated from the fray and left Cotesworth to pick up the legal bill when Clavering sued over the destruction of his line. The incident would spark a feud between Cotesworth and the Bowes family which would last a generation.

Clavering not only sued Cotesworth over the destruction of the Fawdonfield waggonway, he resorted to strong arm tactics himself. In June 1713, a gang of roughs, led by Sir John and a constable named John Armstrong, turned up at a Whickham Fell quarry owned by Cotesworth and brought work to a halt. According to eye witnesses, the mob included "a number of foul-mouthed women" who were joined by Sir John in hurling abuse and threats at the workmen while constable Armstrong prevented any work taking place. The anger soon spilled over into a violent confrontation, with picks and shovels used as weapons and one of Cotesworth's workmen suffered a broken arm.

But Cotesworth was not to be intimidated and he brought rival legal proceedings against the Clavering estate. The landowner eventually earned the unending hatred of the Clavering family when he almost succeeded in having Lady Clavering - by then the head of one of the North's most respectable landed families - thrown into London's notorious debtors' prison The Fleet. Having lost the legal dispute with Cotesworth, Lady Clavering was staggered when court bailiffs arrived at her door in the middle of the night in April 1716, threatening to put her behind bars. She wrote: "A messenger sent down with a warrant from the Lord Chancellor to arrest me and carry me up to The Fleet, he entered my house with several more to assist him with such violence and treated me with such indignity as if I had been a publick Malefactor by pulling me out of my chamber and pressing me against the door he's bruised all my arm and nothing would serve him but he would force me out of my house at near 11 o'clock at night, though I gave myself into his custody as his prisoner and offered him the keys of my house. Never gentlewoman was soe used as I have been."

If the Bowes family had been able to stay out of this war until now, they were dragged into it when Cotesworth revealed his intention to run a waggonway across the Gibside estates. The fiery George Bowes, now the head of the family, made it abundantly clear that he would tear up any line which Cotesworth attempted to run across his lands and told his neighbour in no uncertain terms. So violent were his threats that on July 5, 1721, Cotesworth wrote to Lady Bowes about her son: "he seems to threaten to take away my life by unlawful means with many repeated abuses and affronts."

There may have been a degree of snobbery at work in the dispute between Bowes and Cotesworth. William Cotesworth had been born of humble stock, described as the son of a yeoman, who had amassed a fortune through trading as a merchant in, among many other things, the swords produced at Shotley Bridge. He claimed to earn £30,000 a year, a monumental sum in those days, and had risen to become High Sheriff of Northumberland mayor of Gateshead and also owned swathes of land in Gateshead and Whickham. Bowes let it be known that Cotesworth had once been a menial servant employed at Gibside - a deeply personal insult in days when social standing was all important.

But the young George Bowes was not afraid to insult people he felt had wronged him. It was a rashness which almost cost him his life at the hands of the family's other great enemy. In 1726, the endless arguments over waggonways culminated in a pistol duel with Captain James Clavering, the experienced military man who had led the hunt for the earl of Derwentwater during the Jacobite rebellion 11 years earlier. Clavering was twice his age and a crack shot, but it didn't stop the 25-year-old agreeing to the contest which ended in the young George being wounded in the arm.

It was Bowes himself who finally put an end to the war between the great families, shortly after his narrow escape at the hands of Captain Clavering. Some months earlier, the courts had found in favour of Cotesworth and he was forced to accept the waggonways would cross Gibside land. In the wake of these two decisions, Bowes persuaded the families to bury their respective hatchets and form a cartel of coal owners, known as the Grand Allies, to regulate the coal trade, its disputes and its wage rates in the north - and to take on the power of the London merchants in the south.

The Grand Allies supervised the opening up of the inland coalfield, Tanfield Moor Pit opened in 1742, Greencroft in 1745 and Bankfoot in 1794. By that year, the staithes at Derwenthaugh, which served the coal mines of the Derwent Valley, employed 600 men and boys and 400 horses in the loading of the coal and 200 keel men in transporting it down river.

But the great impetus to open up the coalfields of Durham came after the 1820s. The development of steam engines to sink the shafts, work the ventilation and haul the coals meant mines could go ever deeper. The invention of the railway opened up the hinterland and the development of safety equipment such as lamps meant the miners could work ever further beneath the earth. When the Derwent Iron Company was founded in 1840, it required a massive supply of coal to feed its furnaces. Within a matter of months, the Iron Company owned pits at Blackhill, Consett, Delves Lane, Leadgate and Dipton and over the coming years opened more at Medomsley, Chopwell, Garesfield, Langley Park and Westwood. By 1870, coal mining was the dominant industry in the Derwent Valley.

But if the industry was now among the most modern of its day, some of its practices were unchanged since Medieval times. Miners were bonded labourers - every 12 months they signed an agreement which effectively sold themselves into slavery for the coming year. The miners agreed to work for one master at a set rate for the year and it was a criminal offence, which resulted in up to three months in prison, if they failed to turn up for work or looked for work at another mine. Even when the contract was up, the miners were not allowed to work elsewhere unless they could produce a leaving cer-tificate from their previous employer - which meant the coal owner could effectively insist the miner stay at his pit. It was common for fugitive miners to be declared runaways and pursued by the authori-ties.

One of the oldest surviving binding agreements dates back to November 1766 and was drawn up by George Silvertop, the coal owner who lived at Minsteracres, and the miners of Bushblades Pit, near Dipton. The document includes a series of clauses, spelling out what the miners were expected to do and their rates of pay, one shilling and eight pence for every tub of clean coals and eight pence for every yard hewed. The contract also outlined the system of fines which would apply if they failed to deliver: one shilling for every tub of coal not filled to the brim, one shilling for coming up from the mine before the day's work was finished. The agreement also included the clause: "The said George Silvertop from time to time in the payment of their wages shall have liberty to deduct one shilling for every day any one of them refuseth to work or disturbeth the work or puts any other person to do so or insists on more wages than what is hereafter covenanted." Other such agreements explicitly outlawed joining a union or striking.

Despite these legal restraints, repeated attempts were made to form trade unions among the miners and on several occasions there were strikes - but in many cases the ringleaders were dismissed, evicted and blacklisted. One of those who kept the spark of trade unionism alive was Tommy Ramsey, the Blaydon-born miner, who travelled the coalfield summoning workmen to attend meetings with a wooden rattle. He too was blacklisted for his pains and found it impossible to find work in the North-East. But in 1869, Ramsey was one of the founding members of the Durham Miners' Association - the pitmen's first true trade union. In 1872, just a year before Tommy Ramsey's death, the coal owners were finally forced to recognise the union and the system of bonded labour was ended.

Until 1842 women and children as young as six were still working in the coal mines - even after that date older children were allowed to work in the pits and there are stories of boys as young as ten being carried to work by their father while still asleep. They worked as trap boys, sitting alone in the dark to open the trap doors to let the coal tubs pass, they worked the ventilation or helped tend the pit ponies. The hewers at the coal face, who used picks and brute force to cut the coal, worked a six-hour shift for between three and five shillings a day, but many of the surface workers were still working 11 hours a day. Tubs of coal which were deemed to have too high a stone content would be laid out - and the hewer was paid nothing for them.

Miners underground at Axwell Park Colliery in 1930
(Photograph courtesy of Beamish Museum)

Most miners lived in tied cottages - houses owned by the pit. For the most part, they were squalid and overcrowded homes, built on unpaved streets with one stand pipe serving as many as 50 families. Often there were just two rooms per family and at Leadgate, the outside ash midden was shared by a dozen houses and the privy between three. Disease spread quickly among these tightly packed and unsanitary slums and there were regular outbreaks of serious illnesses, such as the smallpox which raged through Dipton in the early 1870s, claiming at least 17 lives.

But basic as these homes may have been, they were at risk if the miner lost his job or went on strike. Two of the most famous songs written by Tommy Armstrong, the legendary Pitman Poet born in Shotley Bridge in 1848, concern the eviction of striking miners. South Medomsley Strike and Oakey's Strike Evictions describe local families being thrown out of their homes by the coal owners. The miners' greatest wrath was reserved for the candymen - rag and bone men who earned their nickname by giving sweets to children in exchange for rags. It was these candymen, guarded by police, who did the dirty work of throwing families out into the street and inspired Armstrong to write the lines: "What would I dee if ah had

*Striking miners picking coal at Chopwell in 1926
(Photograph courtesy of Beamish Museum)*

the power mesel? Ah wid hang the twenty candymen and Johnny that carried the bell."

The dispute which led to the evictions at South Medomsley began in November 1885 when the colliery's miners, who already earned 10 per cent less pay than the county average, refused to accept a further 10 per cent pay cut. All were given 14 days' notice that their employment was to be terminated. On December 5th, the miners went out on a strike which would last for three long months through one of the bitterest winters in living memory. The dispute quickly became as bitter as the winter chill - according to the records of Dipton parish, colliery manager Wilfrid Tyszack "in consequence of threats called in the police" and on New Year's Eve the family of every striking miner was given notice to leave their colliery-owned home. Over the next two months, as the strike dragged on, several families found themselves new lodgings or moved in to already over-crowded homes with family and neighbours. But there were 11 families who could find nowhere to go.

On Monday, March 1st, a blizzard blew up, remarked upon as severe even by North Durham's standards, which deposited several inches of snow across the valley. It was still blowing the following

The streets of Leadgate (Photograph courtesy of Beamish Museum)

day, which had been set aside for the evictions of the final families. Despite the howling gale and driving snow, Superintendent James Oliver and 72 policemen turned up to escort the candymen brought in from Consett to do their work. All 11 families, including women and children already malnourished after two months of the strike and with nowhere to go, were thrown out of their homes.

Nine days after the evictions, lawyer's clerk Samuel Longstaffe wrote a letter to the Newcastle Daily Chronicle condemning those responsible for evicting families in a snowstorm and attacking Tyszack for employing police and candymen: "to commit cruelties on humble sons of toil, who had been unable to rent other houses and were stricken with poverty and defenceless women and babes, unparalleled in this country and of which even an autocratic despot like the Czar of Russia would be ashamed." Tyszack, claiming he was not responsible for the evictions and objecting to the description, sued the paper's publisher Joseph Cowen for libel at Leeds Assizes two months later and won the then astonishing sum of £1,200.

It is therefore unsurprising that feelings ran high among the miners and occasionally spilled over into violence during industrial action. In 1844, during the first great county-wide strike, a meeting of 20,000 miners took place at Tantobie as the strike reached its 10th week. The first evictions of the strike were taking place at nearby Tanfield, a calculated move according to the owners' later evidence to Parliament, having selected: "an outside and thinly populated portion of the colliery district for the purpose of awing and intimidating the orderly and well disposed portion." So concerned were the local magistrates that violence might break out at Tantobie that Robert Surtees, the magistrate, historian and writer, brought a troop of dragoons and another of infantry to the field to ensure the meeting dispersed peacefully. Tensions did, at times, explode - on at least one occasion, literally. During 1849, a local pay dispute at Hobson Colliery led to a number of striking miners and their families being evicted. The action only served to spread the dispute further and escalate tensions. On January 19th, 1850 a gang of armed men marched into Hobson Colliery and ordered the men who were operating the furnace to leave. They then threw damp coals on the furnace to make it smoulder and then threw a keg of gunpowder on top. The resulting explosion destroyed the boilers and put the pit out of action. A reward of £50 was offered to catch the culprits, but they were never found.

Twice during the closing years of the 19th Century there were county-wide strikes in Durham sparked by an attempt by the Durham Coal Owners' Association to cut the miners' wages. The strike of 1879 lasted six weeks and closed down Consett Iron Works for a month. The management at Consett learned their lesson and set about building up a three-month stockpile of coal in case of any repeat. When the second strike broke out in 1892, large numbers of pickets tried to stop the company moving the coal from the stockpile to the furnaces and Consett had the worst levels of violence in the county as a large contingent of police were drafted in to keep the coal moving. William Jenkins, the hard-line general manager of Consett Iron Works, wrote to chairman David Dale: "The police are completely inadequate to cope with the present emergency and it would seem to me that at places similar to Consett where legitimate stocks of coal are held for consumption by peaceable men who have nothing to do with the strike, the proper plan would be to get the strongest possible legal force, either a troop of dragoons or of infantry, to check this barbarous progress. It is monstrous that while we have stocks of coal on our own premises here ready to be transported into mills we are debarred by a lot of men like barbarians pelting stones from doing this."

The miners worked in terrible conditions. Many of the seams were so shallow the miner would work in a tunnel only inches high. Some mines were so wet the hewers would be lying in water for the entire shift, while others were so dusty the miners would spit dry dust - almost all developed the trademark hacking cough which was the first sign of the onset of miner's lung. But it was the constant threat to life and limb hanging over the pits which marked the industry out from any other. Roof falls and crushing, flooding or suffocation, fire or explosion - the mine had dozens of ways in which to claim lives.

Accident records from County Durham's pits are woefully inadequate - but painstaking research by the Durham Mining Museum gives an indication of the extent of the dangers found in the mines. The museum details the stories of more than 500 men killed in the Derwent Valley's mines between 1850 and the outbreak of the First World War - not in great explosions or collapses, but in individual accidents in individual pits. This litany of tragedy does not include the daily accidents, the broken bones and the blindings, which left miners unable to work in an age without social security, nor is it thought to represent a complete picture of the deaths which occurred at the coalface. The stark figures do not reflect the human tragedy suffered by the miners' families, where stories of bereaved widows being evicted from their tied cottages within weeks of a miner's death are commonplace.

Judged solely by numbers, Blaydon Burn pit was the most dangerous in the area, with 39 men and boys killed during the period, closely followed by The Bute pit at Tanfield Lea with 35 - although this may be down to better recording of accidents. Certainly, there was plenty of competition for this dubious honour. A total of 27 men and boys died in The Derwent pit at Medomsley, 26 at The Towneley at Ryton, 25 in Chopwell, 23 at East Tanfield pit, 21 each at The Anne pit in Burnopfield and Hamsterley, and 20 each at Garesfield and Iveston.

A brief look at a typical mine, the inappropriately-named Delight pit at Dipton, shows the daily horrors faced by the miners and their

Derwent Street in Chopwell in 1900
(Photograph courtesy of Beamish Museum)

families. Although coal had been worked in drift mines around Dipton for centuries, the first deep mine was sunk in the village in 1842. Work began on The Delight pit in 1854 and it opened in April the following year. By 1902, by which time many of the highest seams had almost been exhausted, The Delight Pit provided work for 293 people, 242 of whom worked below ground and 51 of whom worked on the surface, although by the outbreak of the First World War more than 500 miners earned their living at the pit.

By the close of the century, The Delight was one of three collieries working in the parish of Dipton. Miners worked three separate seams of coal: The Busty seam lay 380ft below the surface and was almost five feet thick, which made it comparatively easy to work; The Main Coal seam lay another 40ft down into the earth and was only three feet thick, while the lowest seam, The Hutton, lay 680ft down below the surface and was six-and-a-half feet thick.

Within days of opening, The Delight had claimed its first victim - 11-year-old William Elliott was found dead at the bottom of the shaft on April 8th, a local boy who had strayed too close to the workings. The first recorded death of someone working in The Delight was 12-year-old John Young, crushed to death in November 1867 beneath two tubs fully loaded with coal which he was driving to the surface. Although his death is the first to be recorded in the pit, it seems unlikely to have really been the first fatality, given that the pit had then been open for 12 years. But little John Young would be followed by many more.

In April of the following year, a miner named Fairless was killed as he stood at the bottom of the shaft, hit by falling stone dislodged somewhere above him. In March 1870, Anthony Ridley, a 16-year-old waggonman, was run over by a set of wagons. William Storey, a 25-year-old mason, died in September 1873 when he inexplicably stepped out of the cage as he descended the shaft and fell to his death. In August of the following year, 21-year-old Thomas Young, died as he rigged up a charge of gunpowder to blow a hole in the rock and the explosive went off prematurely.

Some of the deaths were as a result of inexperience. Richard Jackson was killed in November 1877 as he hewed coal from the face. The boy was just 16-years-old and doing a job normally reserved for more experienced men. Twice he was warned by his workmates that the place he was working was unsafe, but he continued until killed by a fall of stone. Others were simply down to being in the wrong place at the wrong time - such as 33-year-old labourer James McGee who was one of the few to die on the surface, run over by a line of tubs.

One of the most dangerous occupations was that of stoneman - the men who used gunpowder to blast away the rock and expose the coal - a job normally reserved for more experienced hands. But that was no guarantee of safety. In October 1883, 41-year-old Joseph Graham was suffocated when blasting rock. He had fired one shot of gunpowder then returned to the scene to prepare a second shot, unaware that the explosion had blown down a door which regulated the ventilation and was overcome by the fumes. There were other obvious dangers: 32-year-old Joseph Maudlin died in December 1886 and 55-year-old John Robinson died in May 1890 when the explosions they had set off caused the roof to collapse and they were crushed. Their colleague Christopher Bates, 23, died in March 1889 when the gunpowder he was using set off an explosion of firedamp.

By the 1880s, the first rudimentary health and safety legislation was beginning to impact on the mines, which meant at least that there was a full inquiry into the death of each miner. Hewer James Walker died on New Year's Eve 1893 when he was crushed under a five-inch thick flat stone and an inquiry. It concluded that 25 yesr old had failed to put adequate props in place to support the roof and had continued hewing coal five feet beyond the nearest safe support.

In May 1903, Reuben Wymer was loading a cart with eight-foot long steel bars, each weighing more than one hundredweight, which had been brought to the pit in a railway truck. He had successfully managed to load three of them into the cart when his horse moved forwards. The 36-year-old fell backward onto the ground and the three steel bars tumbled out of the cart onto his stomach. He died the following day of his injuries.

Early on New Year's Eve 1904, Oliver Taylor was working on the pit railway when several trucks skidded on the frost-covered rail. The 55-year-old leapt down to put a chock in the way but fell beneath a waggon, which passed over his legs. He died of shock and loss of blood. The Delight's only multiple death accident occurred on December 4th, 1911 when hewers John William Greener, 45, and William Walker, 32, were crushed beneath a fall of coal. Their deaths took the total to 16 men and boys by the outbreak of the First World War, but The Delight would claim many more lives before it finally closed in November 1940.

Nor did the danger to life and limb end at the pit head - it spread out into the communities which huddled around the mines, intersected by the railways and surrounded by the shafts. In 1728, John Wild of The Spen, near Winlaton, died when he and his horse plummeted down a disused mine shaft as they rode near their home. In November 1764, a servant girl had a remarkable escape as she walked near Gibside and fell the best part of 200 feet into a disused mine. She found herself up to her arm pits in water but thankfully found a length of floating timber and clambered on board, thereby saving herself from hypothermia or drowning. She lay there for two days and two nights until she was discovered and brought to safety. Others were not so lucky. Peter Nowell, a nail-maker by trade who had recently lost his job, was killed in May 1817 as he tried to dig coal from an outcrop at Whickham to keep himself and his parents warm - his efforts dislodged a one-tonne rock which crushed him to

Coal miners at Kiln Pit Hill
(Photograph courtesy of Beamish Museum)

death. Three months later, keelman John Simpson of Swalwell, suffered a fit while at work and fell from his boat into the Tyne where he drowned. In October 1879, David Tweddle was killed and Sarah Hunter lamed when a rope used to haul coal wagons up Cookgate Bank at Burnopfield snagged, then suddenly whipped free. But each of these tragedies would pale into insignificance next to the greatest disaster of them all at West Stanley in 1909.

On the afternoon of February 16th, Stanley went about its business in pale sunshine. A charity concert in the Irish Institute to raise money for the building of St Joseph's Church was just coming to an end, those miners who were not working were gathered on the ends of street corners. All stopped at 3.45pm when they heard the first muffled bang and, exactly 50 seconds later, the deafening roar as an explosion ripped through the Burns Pit.

Within minutes, a crowd of hundreds had gathered at the pithead. When the tongues of flame appeared above the pit wheel and the roar subsided it was clear that this was a disaster on an unprecedented scale. The explosion had ripped through all four seams and there was barely a house in the town which had not lost a loved one. Some survivors made it to the surface - including 26 men trapped together in the Tilley Seam 800ft down - but, despite the heroic efforts of the rescue teams, there were few who made it out of the mine.

The disaster at West Stanley pit was the worst in the history of the Durham coalfield. In all, 168 men and boys lost their lives that day, 59 of them under the age of 20. For most death was instantaneous, for some it was anything but. The disaster left an entire town in mourning and a coalfield in shock. Henry Street - a terraced row of 12 houses - had lost 17 miners. Among the dead was Tom Riley - who left a wife to care for their 11 children; four members of the Hodgson family and a miner named McGeary, who that morning had brought his young son down the pit to see the place where he would start work the following week. One by one the bodies were brought to the surface and claimed by the relatives waiting there - some looked as if they had fallen asleep, some came out in bags.

Within 24 hours, the tiny telegraph office at Stanley had received 600 messages of sympathy including one from the King. On the day of the funerals, Stanley was brought to a standstill by a crowd of 200,000 mourners from across the country. The Burns Pit Disaster was the defining moment in the history of the North Durham coalfield and one which demonstrated that, almost 100 years since the disaster at Stargate, the coal mines were as dangerous a place as ever.

CHAPTER 23
THE HALLY WELL

WELLS and natural springs have, throughout the ages, been accredited with magical or healing powers. From Medieval times, pilgrims would travel miles to visit acclaimed springs and, in an age of superstition, they grew very popular - particularly if miraculous powers were claimed for them. One of the earliest is thought to have been at Blanchland. There are no records of where the Ladywell stood, although almost certainly it was associated with the abbey and may well have been close by. The name suggests the well may have been associated with the Virgin Mary, in whose honour the abbey was dedicated, and may have been a destination for the many travellers who made the pilgrimage to Blanchland in the early part of the last Millennium.

But it was the well at Shotley Bridge which was to have the most dramatic, if short-lived, impact on the Derwent Valley. In the early Victorian era, the health properties of spring water were once more becoming prized and visitors flocked to the spa towns of Harrogate, Bath and Chester where the waters were taken as a tonic for a variety of maladies. The Victorians, possibly with some justification in an age when cholera and typhoid thrived in the industrial slums, turned in increasing numbers to spring water and fresh air as the solution to many of their illnesses. The spas thrived and, as the health of their visitors prospered, so did the economic fortunes of those towns which could lay claim to healing waters.

Into this medical boom came the extraordinary character of Jonathan Richardson - a man who was to have more profound an effect on the history of the Derwent Valley than probably any other. Richardson, who lived in Shotley Bridge at Snows Green, was a director of the Northumberland and Durham District Bank and an entrepreneur who appears to have been always on the look out for a money-making scheme. He found one in the waters of Shotley Bridge.

For centuries, the old spring at Shotley had bubbled from underground and formed in a natural basin surrounded by hillocks of moss and grass, from where it drained into the river. Records show

Shotley Spa (Photograph courtesy of Beamish Museum)

that as late as 1806, the spring could still be found and people would travel miles to collect the supposedly healing waters. Shortly afterwards, the site was drained. However, Richardson heard the story and during 1837, with the help of locals who remembered the old spring, traced its source. Having found the original spring, Richardson set about tracing a second source of the waters and by December of that year work had started on creating the spa itself. Now that he had his water and work on the grounds was underway, Richardson dreamed of building a spa town on the banks of the Derwent to rival Harrogate.

Shotley Bridge was then a small, but not insignificant village with a parish population of around 500 people, scattered along the banks of the Derwent. The bridge itself dated back certainly as far as the 14th Century and several important industrial sites had grown up in the immediate vicinity. The sword mill on which Shotley had built its name was a shadow of its former self, by then producing more plough shares than swords and teetering towards it eventual closure three years later. But there was a thriving flour mill at Shotley Bridge which had already stood for around 100 years and would survive until the middle of the 20th Century.

The most important industry in Shotley Bridge at the time was the making of paper. On April Fool's Day, 1799 the Annandale family - who had previously been involved in the industry in Scotland - opened their first paper mill on the Derwent. In 1812, the family acquired the site of two existing mills at Shotley Grove, including the old Ealands corn mill which dated back to Medieval times but which was then owned by Thomas Johnson and producing brown paper. Finally, in 1842 the enterprise took over a third mill at Lintzford, which was first recorded as a corn mill in 1694 when it was let by Cambridge student Christopher Hunter to Newcastle businessman John Sandford, the financier behind the Shotley swordmakers. By 1703 it was making paper and continued to do so until 1924 when it converted to an ink works.

By the middle of the 19th Century, the Annandale family's three mills employed around 300 people, half of them girls who picked through the rags to extract the fibres which were turned into paper. Originally, the paper was made manually, sheet by hand-pressed sheet, but gradually technology intervened and by 1860 the water wheels had been replaced with steam power. Paper produced at Shotley Bridge found its way almost everywhere, from the pages of Bibles to bags holding sugar, it supplied Her Majesty's Stationery Office and the card to stuff shirt fronts. Before the mills closed in 1905, the Annandale family had paid for the building of a school which opened on Cutlers Hall Road in 1841 where 157 pupils - the children of the paper mill workers - were educated. The family also made donations to build a Baptist chapel in Shotley Bridge.

However, even by the standards of Victorian England, the conditions found in the Annandale paper mills were appalling. At around the time that Shotley Spa was being opened, the Annandale mill at Shotley Grove provided work for 19 women, eight men, 10 girls and five boys. During the 1840s, a Parliamentary Commission set up to investigate the conditions of work in the paper-making industry examined the mills at Shotley and the everyday working routine of the children who shredded the rags. The children worked almost 12 hours a day, starting at 6.30am and finishing at 6pm, for six days a week with only one formal holiday a year, Christmas Day. One boy gave evidence to the commission that he had worked one shift from 5am one day until noon the next, a 31-hour shift for

*Workers at Shotley Flour Mill at the turn of the century
(Photograph courtesy of Beamish Museum)*

which he was paid a flat rate of three farthings an hour. And throughout this shift, the children would stay in the rag room - so thick with choking dust that they could barely see, dust which worked into their lungs and covered the food which they ate as they worked causing many to retch it straight back up. Others developed coughs and shortness of breath from the noxious fumes used to turn the fibres to pristine paper sheets. One man gave evidence of his childhood at the mill, saying: "The rags were not thoroughly boiled then, bleach and vitriol doing most of the job. As a lad I had to empty chests by myself with a hand hook. My fingers would often bleed and my lungs often felt as though they were bursting with the fumes and the effort."

The contrast between life in the paper mills and the genteel spa being created on their doorstep could not have been greater. The bog created by the seeping water was drained and the spring was diverted via a pipe to a rustic shelter which was at the heart of the spa grounds. The water ran down the pipe which went through a heavy

Shotley paper mill 1910
(Photograph courtesy of Beamish Museum)

vertical stone and flowed out of a spout into an iron-stained stone basin. To reach this font, the visitor first had to ascend a series of three circular stone steps before partaking of the health-giving waters. The font was enclosed within an elaborate trellis work which supported a thatched roof. Nearby, two cottages were built. The first contained a saloon or meeting place where the water was served to visitors. The second contained two bathrooms with a heated shower bath and dressing room, each lined with white tiles and mahogany, where visitors could immerse themselves completely. Ornamental gardens with footpaths and a broad carriage drive were laid out in the grounds - all leading to the spring itself.

Almost immediately, several miraculous cures were claimed for the restorative waters of Shotley Spa. One man had what was described as "a chin-titter" which disappeared overnight after a visit to Shotley. Another man said to be so weak that he could only speak in whispers was remarkably revived after drinking the waters. In July 1838, an old man emaciated through "constant vomiting, water brash and heartburn" was discharged from Newcastle Infirmary and taken to Shotley barely able to walk. He stayed for three weeks and left "in better health than he had enjoyed in three years." One woman received relief from a complaint of severe haemorrhaging , several stomach and intestinal disorders were said to have been cured after taking the waters at Shotley and countless skin complaints and nervous twitches were completely cured by its healing powers. The well enjoyed a particular reputation for helping sufferers of tuberculosis - a common and potentially deadly complaint. A ditty composed at the time claimed:

"No scurvy in your skin can dwell
"If you only drink the Hally Well."

The reputation of Shotley and its healing powers was spreading. A series of experiments was carried out on the water to test its composition and it certainly does appear to have had unusual properties. During the early 1840s, a Dr Glanville visited Shotley as part of his tour of the nation's spa towns and examined the water. He noted that the water changed in a peculiar way when left in a glass. "At first it is perfectly clear and transparent, in an hour or two it turns slightly opalescent," he wrote. "This appearance becomes gradually more intense and assumes at the same time a brownish tinge while the inner side of the glass and bottom is covered by a myriad of air bubbles." The doctor declared the spa at Shotley to be on a par with its famous counterpart at Bad Ems in Germany and recommended Shotley water for the treatment of all manner of ills: circulation problems; glandular problems; dyspepsia; blood impurities; skin diseases; scurvy and, when heated in a warm bath, for the relief of rheumatism. He added: "Properly attended to, the water, which differs in composition from all the others, may be made instrumental in the recovery of many disorders which no other water in the country can cure."

Other eminent doctors agreed. A succession of physicians declared themselves amazed by the healing properties of Shotley waters and they were joined at the spa by chemists such as Mr West of Leeds, who found large amounts of chlorides of sodium and calcium, carbonate of soda and traces of chloride of magnesium, carbonate of iron, silica, bromine, iodine and potash in the residues left by the spa water.

The remarkable powers of Shotley Spa made it famous. The entry fee to the spa was modest, which attracted more and more visitors.

At its height, 60,000 people a year came to the village to take the waters. Charles Dickens visited Shotley at the age of 27 as a guest of his friend Robert Smith Surtees, the noted writer who lived nearby at Hamsterley Hall. Such celebrity visitors merely served to enhance the spa's name. To house the growing flow of tourists, Jonathan Richardson built the elaborate Springfield Hotel - long since demolished - close to Snows Green Road. Other visitors took lodgings with local families for the duration of their stay. In 1842, Richardson also built Shotley Park as his own private mansion opposite the entrance to his spa and with a road leading directly into the grounds. The opening of another more important road added to the success of the spa. In its earliest days, visitors' only means of reaching the spa was by stagecoach along the rutted cart tracks which led from Gateshead to Medomsley and then down the hillside into Shotley and on to Blanchland. In 1832, a consortium of local businessmen led by the Annandale family had commissioned a survey to open a road from Shotley to the newly-built Scotswood Bridge at Newcastle. The Low Road was

The venture stagecoach passes through Shotley Bridge
(Photograph courtesy of Beamish Museum)

finally completed in 1843 giving direct access from Tyneside to the spa and increasing the flow of visitors ever further. Richardson, the successful entrepreneur who had made all this happen, was held to be something of a local hero and in June 1850, when he returned from his grand wedding tour with his new wife, he was met by 100 horsemen, carriages and countless footmen to escort them along Snows Green to their new home.

But the future of the Derwent Valley was not to be as a spa resort. The demise of Shotley Spa came quickly and the seeds of its destruction lay in the very minerals which gave the water its distinctive taste. Within two years of Shotley spa opening, geologists had found ironstone at the Blue Heaps near Consett and reported it to Jonathan Richardson. Within a year, work would begin on the great ironworks at Consett, financed by Richardson. But his new vision of creating the largest ironworks in England ended the dream of creating a second Harrogate at Shotley. The great industrial edifice at Berry Edge was not in keeping with the genteel world of Shotley spa and, as the outposts of the great ironworks crept ever closer, the numbers of visitors dwindled and eventually dried up.

But if the spa failed to prosper, the same could not be said of Jonathan Richardson. Although his bank collapsed amid financial scandal in 1857 having loaned too much money to the new ironworks at Consett, he continued to live in his mansion at Shotley Park with his wife. Jonathan Richardson died at home on Christmas Day 1871, surrounded by his 40 children and grandchildren. And although his spa failed to live beyond the turn of the century, his legacy to the Derwent Valley proved far more enduring.

CHAPTER 24

THE MUD AND THE BLOOD AND THE BEER

FROM the moment ironstone was discovered at Consett during the autumn of 1839, the face of the Derwent Valley changed forever. A quiet rural backwater was transformed almost overnight into a powerhouse of the industrial revolution - home to one of the largest ironworks in Europe where thousands of migrant workers huddled around the chimneys, furnaces, mills and coal mines which made up The Company. By the 1860s, the beginnings of a settled community had grown up at Consett - but for the first 20 years of its existence, the town was one of the wildest, most lawless and most violent corners of the Kingdom.

Berry Edge, as it was known in the 1830s, amounted to little more than a cluster of farmhouses clinging to a windswept hillside. There were reckoned to be around 30 simple cottages in 1831, scattered across the bleak hill top and home to 150 souls - as well as the more substantial properties Carr House, Barr House and Delves House. These stood on the roads, described as little better than sheep tracks, which criss-crossed the open moor and provided the only link with the outside world. The stage coach from Catterick to Edinburgh passed nearby, crossing the Derwent at Allensford, while Shotley Bridge could be reached by stage coach from Gateshead, a journey which went on up to Blanchland. During the 1830s, the first rail lines were built across the moor to link Stanhope with the Tyne, a line which also served the pits at Medomsley. A railway station was built at Rowley and up until the 1850s passengers from Berry Edge had to take a pony and trap ride up to the station, paying a sixpence toll to do so. But, for the most part, the original inhabitants of Berry Edge eked out an isolated existence high on the wild moor with little contact with the outside world.

All that changed with the coming of the ironmasters. In 1840, the Derwent Iron Company was founded by a partnership of North-East entrepreneurs to exploit the iron ore reserves found at Consett. Jonathan Richardson, the entrepreneur behind Shotley Spa, bought up a great deal of land in the area and leased back the rights to work the minerals on it to the iron company. He was also the managing director of the Northumberland and Durham District Bank which forwarded increasingly large loans to finance the huge investment needed to found an ironworks. Work started immediately on an enterprise which within five years would become the second largest ironworks in England. To attract new workers to this outpost of civilisation, The Company offered high wages by the standards of the time and workers poured in from Ireland, Wales and the Midlands to build the works, mine the coal and feed the furnaces. Soon, the great chimneys were going up, the shafts were being sunk, the railway sleepers were being laid and an entire town was being built to house the workforce. Labourers and their families poured into Berry Edge in their thousands as a rural way of life disappeared under a blanket of smoke which belched from the furnaces.

For a few months at least, Consett clung on to the remnants of its rural past. A brief look at the Census of 1841 - compiled in June of that year, a matter of months after The Company had been founded - shows how little life appeared to have changed. The population of Benfieldside Parish had doubled over the previous decade from around 500 to around 1,000, but a significant part of this increase could probably be put down to the growth of Shotley Bridge, where the spa had opened three years earlier. There were a few dozen labourers, some of them Irish immigrants, but for the most part the Census records servants, farm workers, papermakers, tradesmen and professionals. In neighbouring Conside and Knitsley, the picture is the same. There were only four families living in Delves, including 30-year-old blacksmith Thomas Little who lived with his wife and four children. Among his nearest neighbours would have been Robert Hardy, who farmed at Knitsley with his six children, and their near neighbour Thomas Reed, a 45-year-old farmer who lived with his wife, two children and three servants.

The 1841 Census is a last snapshot of a world about to be turned upside down. Even as Robert Hardy and Thomas Reed were bringing their horses up from Knitsley to be shoed by Thomas Little that summer, the agents of the newly-formed Derwent Iron Company were buying up and leasing land on the hillside. By the end of the year, there would be two blast furnaces underway at Consett. The Census itself contained the first signs that things were changing: at Stanfordham there were four nameless Irish labourers and platelayer Richard Jopling, two craftsmen gave their address as the Derwent Ironworks while another six labourers were to be found at Consett. The first of many immigrants had begun to arrive.

*Haymaking in Shotley Bridge - although the rural way of life
continued at places like Shotley, as this photograph from the early
20ᵗʰ Century shows, it disappeared overnight at Berry Edge
(Photograph courtesy of Beamish Museum)*

Within a year, this trickle had become a flood. Over the next few
years, according to a Parliamentary Report of 1847, The Company
built 14 blast furnaces; two mills for puddling, hammering and
rolling 900 tons of bar iron a week, 12 refineries, 22 steam engines
to turn the machinery and 35 coal and ironstone pits. As the great
enterprise grew and grew, more and more workmen poured into the
area. One of the early arrivals was Joseph Nicholson of Swalwell,
who later recalled: "Lodging was difficult to get. Few houses were
built and many a family went into one before either windows or
doors were put on." Such was the urgency to bring in workers that
many of the houses were said to be occupied before even the roof
was in place and the Census of 1841 shows three people in Blackhill
were living in tents.

The population statistics tell the story. Consett itself - a scattered
rural community of 150 people before the arrival of The

*Possibly the earliest surviving image of the new ironworks at
Consett. This engraving, which may date back to the late 1840s,
shows the works continued at full pace through the night
(Photograph courtesy of Durham University Library)*

Company - was home to 2,700 people by 1851 and almost 5,000 by
1861. The same was true of the surrounding villages. The population
of Benfieldside parish, which stood at 500 in 1831, had reached
4,000 by 1861 and the population of Iveston parish, which included
Leadgate and Crookhall grew from 450 in 1841 to 2,500 just ten
years later. Taken as a whole, the population of the district stood at
around 1,000 before the discovery of ironstone, most of whom lived
at Shotley Bridge, but by 1851 it has passed 8,000 and by 1861 there
were around 13,000 people living on the hillside.

This great wave of immigrants, desperate to make a new life for
themselves, found a tough life waiting at Berry Edge. In the early
days, the town amounted to little more than a work camp. The
Company built houses for its workmen to live in and by the 1880s it
owned 2,700 homes which were huddled together around the
ironworks in terraced streets known as The Company Rows. Not
only did the population owe their livelihood to The Company, it was
also their landlord and enforced rules of expected behaviour on its

employees and their families both at work and at home. The Company, founded on principles of Victorian paternalism, won widespread praise for the way it provided for its workmen. A Parliamentary Report of 1850 entitled The State Of The Population In The Mining Districts highlighted the houses, roads, drains, police and schools which were funded by The Company. In the earliest days, it ran its own store and some of the workmen's wages were paid in vouchers which could only be redeemed in the shop for groceries, until the Co-Operative movement established a presence in the area. In later years, the Company would open its own infirmary. The report concluded: "even if no sense of moral responsibility toward these 15,000 people had actuated the gentlemen who embarked on this great commercial enterprise, the lowest motives of calculation would have induced them as men of business not to expose such a vast capital without taking some security, as far as was possible, against the ignorance or misconduct of their work people."

But despite the Parliamentary praise, the town which was created at Consett offered only the most basic of comforts. The houses that these work people found themselves in have long since been demolished. They offered little in the way of comfort and, as the enterprise grew at bewildering speed around them, some people actually found themselves living inside the works. The houses were tiny, often made up of just two rooms, one on the ground floor and one upstairs, reached by a ladder. They were also hopelessly overcrowded. On average, there were six people living in each of these two-room homes and often there were many more. It was common to find anything up to half a dozen children sharing the same bed and, on occasion, two families would share the same house to save money, with a curtain across the room providing the only privacy. The houses were cold and draughty, there was no running water and the toilet facilities were an outside ash midden shared by several families.

Even by the end of the 19th Century, these homes were considered to be unfit. In his annual report of 1896, Consett's medical officer of health praised the company for building new houses to replace those built 50 years earlier. The report said: "The older houses are of miserable construction and are quite out of date." The report went on: "The system for excrement disposal is the objectionable midden privy. These erections are too close to the

*A view of Derwent Street, in Blackhill, at the turn of the century
showing children playing in the road
(Photograph courtesy of Beamish Museum)*

dwellings, are large, open, often below the level of the ground and do not provide for a proper admixture of excreta and ashes. There are also about 400 water closets in the town, but in many instances they are filthy, very much neglected and very often rendered useless by the wanton destruction of the tenants. It would offer a salutary lesson if a few of these offenders were prosecuted and made examples of."

The town which those first arrivals encountered was basic, as this extract from The Consett Story shows: "In the early days, the Consett market square was one huge clay hole for odds and ends. The old Tin Mill pit was a quaint rickety looking place. Nearby was a causeway or bridge, whose footway consisted of traverse pieces of wood which were, like the hand railings, constantly getting out of place. No sooner had the traveller run the gauntlet of these trap holes than he had to step over an open sewer or gutter." There were two stores in the centre of town which served the growing population and the rest of what is now Middle Street was made up of low cottages. The town was, at first, solely geared to feeding the works - railway lines criss-crossed the centre of town to bring coal and ore to feed the foundries and take the iron to market.

Consett was a wild frontier town. Despite the presence of thousands of labourers from all parts of the country, there was no police force to speak of. Two officers stationed at Durham were detailed to protect law and order in Consett and it is said that when they reached the town, they were pelted with stones and other missiles by a mob of navvies determined to keep them out. So bad was the situation in the early days that The Company appointed its own private police force made up of a handful of constables. It was not until 1856 that the first police station was set up in the area, at Shotley Bridge, and it was 1877 before a police station was opened in Consett itself - more than 30 years after the ironworks opened. Not surprisingly, Consett was a lawless place with a fearsome reputation for violence and regular outbreaks of rioting which were only quelled with the deployment of soldiers. Animosity between English and Irish workmen, fuelled by religious bigotry, racial hatred and a plentiful supply of beer, boiled over into open warfare at regular intervals.

John Calvert, the town's pawnbroker, wrote in his diary of 1844: "In passing the Highgate public house I witnessed a sight which was not uncommon in those days. In the lower rooms of the public house there was not a table or chair but had its legs broken off, and these a number of mad drunken fellows were wielding to some purpose on each others heads. The landlord, Mr Moore, was in his shirt sleeves and his arms from his hands to his elbows were just as though they had been dipped in a blood-kit. I have stood in my doorway and counted a dozen fights all going on at the same time. The road in front of my house was, in winter, knee-deep in mud and in many places a horse was in danger of disappearing altogether."

On occasions, the rioting reached such intensity that lives were lost. On February 8th, 1846 a full-scale riot between heavily-armed gangs of English and Irish labourers broke out at The Highgate pub and spilled over into the surrounding streets. The pitched battle lasted for several hours, with many innocent bystanders caught up in the fighting. A contemporary account of the riot records: "This evening, an alarming disturbance took place at Black Hill between the English and Irish workmen employed at Derwent Iron Works. It appeared that during the evening, several of the workmen were drinking in a public house kept by Mr Moore and a fight took place in which one of the combatants, an Irishman, was severely beaten. This so excited his companions that they immediately collected

Children outside the Miners Arms in Blackhill, scene of much of the
rioting of the 1840s
(Photograph courtesy of Beamish Museum)

together a numerous body of their countrymen, some armed with sticks, others with pokers, shovels and similar weapons and they forthwith made an indiscriminate attack upon all in the village. The first person they met was a man named George Patterson who was immediately felled to the ground. Another man named Gilroy was so maltreated as scarcely to be recognised. The rioters then attacked the public house and in a short time every pane of glass was broken, the inmates making a precipitate retreat by the back part of the premises. By this time, the whole place was in a state of the utmost alarm and excitement and the English workmen in order to defend themselves were obliged to give battle to the assailants. The consequences may be imagined. The parties attacked each other with loud yells and in the most fierce manner and it was not until two o'clock in the morning that the riot had expended itself." The riot ended when Superintendent Hall, based at Whickham, arrived with a large body of police to restore order. When the rioters finally withdrew, six Irishmen lay unconscious and bleeding on the ground, 40 of their countrymen were seriously injured along with a similar number of Englishmen. Three of the wounded Irishmen subsequently died of their injuries.

Resident John Mewes, writing in 1847, gave another eye-witness account of the violence which marked the early days of Consett's history. He wrote: "I have not seen much excitement, but I shall not forget the Berry Edge riot, though it occurred a canny bit ago. I well remember the day on which it broke out. It was, I believe, a Sunday and I was out with another tradesman when he suggested we should go into a public house for a slight refresher. However, we had not been long there when we heard an angry and excited clamour of voices. Immediately afterwards, a gang of men rushed into the place and we hurried out of it as sharply as we could. When I reached home, I found the shutters up, the windows barred and the doors securely fastened. I tapped at the shutters and fortunately for me my wife guessed who it was and at once admitted me. But I was glad to get into safer quarters, for the men outside were swearing terrible vengeance. The soldiers were brought over and they remained till the riot was quelled. I am certain the riot lasted three days and I believe four. Some people actually went into the country to their friends."

A further riot occurred in 1847 when rumours spread that English workmen were about to attack the Catholic chapel in Blackhill. The threat was averted when a large detachment of the county police were despatched to the area but tensions remained high amid rumours that armed Englishmen were planning to fire on the congregation. Violence finally broke out on November 14th, which the Newcastle Journal reported was: "aggravated by large numbers of the unemployed parties having come there from other places in the expectation of getting work in which they were disappointed. There had been previously a quarrel between the parties and some skirmishing in which the English were victors and on Sunday the Irish mustered strong with the intention of revenging their past injuries. The tumult at one time rose to a great height, stones were thrown and in one case a knife was drawn, but happily the manager of the works with great firmness and energy, interfered and expostulated with the men on the impropriety of their conduct with such good effect that order was eventually restored, but not until severe injuries had been inflicted on both sides."

Three months later, 12 men were hauled before Durham Assizes for their part in the November riot: Henry Jackson, Heron Lowe, Henry Smiles, Thomas Kearton, Hugh McCoglin, Smith Pearson, John Davison, Joseph Milburn, James Murphy, Patrick Lawson, John Fitzpatrick and John McAvay were all treated leniently, bound over for the sum of £20 to keep the peace. In the aftermath, calls went out for a greater police presence and that winter, Durham's chief constable Major James Wemyss wrote in his annual report: "At Shotley Bridge ironworks, a population not of the most orderly habits amounting to 18,000 has sprung up within a few years and an increase in the police force in this district is imperatively called for, there being at present only two officers stationed in that vicinity. The necessity of additional protection there has been manifested by the rioting which has recently occurred as well as on former occasions and by the fact of the Company keeping three or four private policemen at their own expense."

But the most famous of all was the Battle of the Blue Heaps, which took place in 1858. As was the case with many of the encounters which marked the early days of life in Consett, the Battle of the Blue Heaps was born of the deep-seated animosity between the rival factions inside the ironworks. The Irish immigrants who arrived in Consett during the 1840s were fleeing starvation in their native country caused by the potato famine which had claimed the lives of one and half million of their countrymen. These new arrivals, destitute and often illiterate, were prepared to undercut the wages of English labourers or break strikes in order to get work to support their families, which in turn caused resentment among the native population. It took only the smallest spark for it to spill over into open violence.

Late in 1857, a crisis blew up at the ironworks which threatened the livelihood of everyone who worked there. Since its founding, the business had grown at remarkable speed. In the first five years of its existence, the Derwent Iron Company borrowed £500,000 from the Northumberland and Durham District Bank to pay for the enormous costs of building the ironworks and town - loans later described by the Bank Of England as being of "a most unsuitable nature." The Company sunk its own coal pits, leased several others and invested in a huge network of railways linking the iron ore deposits of Cleveland with the limestone deposits at Stanhope and the markets at the Tyne. By 1857, the company's debt had reached £750,000, much more than the small bank could sustain and much more than the iron company itself was worth. In November, the Northumberland and Durham District Bank was forced to close amid financial scandal - it had so much money tied up in the iron company that it had simply run out of cash.

The City of London wanted the works to be broken up and sold off to settle the debts - a course of action which would have thrown thousands out of work in an age when unemployment meant the threat of starvation and risked civil unrest. Smaller investors and the management at Consett wanted to try to salvage the ironworks and a seven-year battle for control ensued which eventually led, in March 1864, to the formation of the Consett Iron Company. But amid all this uncertainty, simmering tensions boiled over on the streets of Consett in the first days of April 1858. The Irish labourers, fearing they would bear the brunt if the Company was forced to lay off workers, rioted. On the night of Saturday, April 3 a young Englishman named Sanderson was attacked by a group of three Irishmen in Blackhill and beaten "in so savage and ferocious a manner that for some days his life was despaired of." As was now customary, his friends retaliated, but order was restored when two of the Irishmen were arrested and brought before the magistrates in Shotley Bridge two days later. One of them, Peter Kelly, was fined 10s for his part in the attack.

But the matter did not end there. The following week, the English sought their revenge on the others they suspected of assaulting Sanderson. A mob besieged the house of John Howett of Derwent Hall where they attacked the occupants with sticks before finally being driven off by the police. The town was by now on a knife-edge. On the Monday, the day after the attack on Howett's house, 700 Irishmen gathered in a field at Number One and marched down to Blackhill. The mob reached The Commercial Inn and demanded the landlord Joseph Curry hand over two of his customers to face an almost certain lynching. Curry refused and held the mob at bay with a loaded pistol while he barricaded the doors to protect his family. An anonymous witness describes the gun battle that followed: "The signal to fall to was then given to the mob who commenced to break down the doors, destroy the window frames and glass by means of stones brickbats and other missiles. Curry, considering his life in danger and desiring to intimidate the infuriated mob, fired two shots from a gun which took effect on two or three persons. The fire, however, was speedily replied to. Five shots were fired in rapid succession through the window and, as the people had very nearly succeeded in effecting an entrance through the broken windows and doors below, Curry, his wife and family and those who were in the house, deemed it expedient to beat a retreat by a back door carrying some money which was in the house. Scarcely had the occupants of

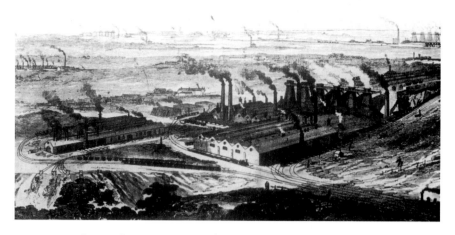

An early engraving of Derwent Iron Works 1857
(Picture courtesy of Beamish Museum)

the house made their escape than the Irish came pouring in and, discovering that the birds had flown, they commenced the work of pillage and demolition. The house was ransacked, all the furniture was destroyed."

Having wrecked Curry's house, the mob was finally persuaded to disperse by the Reverend Hannigan. The following morning, the Irish gathered in even greater numbers at Number One, but committed no further acts of violence. Then in the afternoon, one of the ringleaders of the Commercial Inn riot, also named Kelly, was arrested in David Brannegan's pub in Blackhill. He resisted arrest but when finally captured was discovered to be carrying a handgun. As word of his arrest spread like wildfire a crowd of 2,000 Irishmen assembled at the Blue Heaps, "the majority of them armed with guns, sickles, scythes, bludgeons and other weapons". The police, fearing that the mob was about to storm the police station and free Kelly, had him spirited away to Gateshead - then went to face down the rioters, bringing with them three pieces of ceremonial canon which were aimed at the ranks of the Irish. At that point, a small army of English labourers - many of whom were also carrying pistols - arrived on the scene and took up positions facing the Irish. The two sides advanced to within 300 yards of each other and a bloody battle appeared inevitable, despite the best efforts of priests and police to mediate a truce. However, before the first shot could be fired, a 200-strong detachment of the Nottingham Militia armed with rifles arrived from Newcastle and forced the crowds to disperse. The army was then stationed in Blackhill for some time to ensure the warring parties stayed apart. In the end, 37 people were brought to court for their part in the riot.

Beer and boredom probably played as much a part in the violence as bigotry and it is no surprise that most of the riots appear to centre on one of the numerous pubs which were springing up. In Consett's earliest days there was no theatre, no park, no library, no newspaper, no sporting clubs - in short no distraction from the endless slog of hard physical labour other than the pub. By 1851 there appears to have been six pubs in Consett and a further four in Blackhill. In 1842, just two years after work started at The Company, Consett's first temperance hall opened for business - but it would seem that they were fighting a losing battle. With no licensing laws and a shift system that meant there was always a gang of labourers ready to slake their thirst after a day's work at the furnaces, the pubs - such as The Puddlers' Arms - were packed 24 hours a day. John Calvert recorded in 1860: "There is more beer than water in Berry Edge. Charles Allen (brewer of Annfield Plain) told me that during the twelve months that John Robson was his tenant, he sold more than 15,000 half barrels of beer. Robson's was the only beerhouse in the place at that time. It was besieged at five o'clock in the morning by the night-shift men, and by the day shift men at night, so that Robson had little or no rest."

A further example of the drinking habits of the day comes from further down the valley in Winlaton. In February 1873, Robert Brown, the landlord of the Red Lion, was taken to court for assaulting his wife Mary. The court was told that the day before the assault Brown had downed 50 pints in one drinking spree, ending his session with a remarkable 10 pints in just 30 minutes. Brown was sent to the cells at Gateshead where he suffered such severe bouts of alcohol withdrawal that he became violent and was eventually confined to the lunatic asylum at Sedgefield.

For the first 20 years of Consett's existence, the conditions in which its residents lived and worked were squalid in the extreme. Even the most basic of human needs went unmet. There was no water supply for the thousands of workmen and their families other than the wells which had existed before the days of The Company.

The banker John Gledstone, who with John Calvert would become directors of the Consett Water Company, wrote in his diary of the appalling state of the water supply in 1859: "The condition of the place is most deplorable. The best well is rented at more than £50 per year and only supplies eight or ten barrelsful per day. The barrel is often filled at water courses or any other place where water can be had. The demand for water is so keen that numbers of women race quarter of a mile to be first at the cart and of course many of them return with empty cans. After working hard all day, the men have to wait for supper till at last the necessary water is borrowed of a neighbour who is able to spare it. Cattle have access to a dam, which is the main supply, and besides being contaminated by them, the cart-man has several times bathed in the dam before filling the water cart. At Leadgate, the women have to wait so long for their turn for water, that they take their knitting with them."

Mr Gledstone and Mr Calvert set about trying to introduce clean water to the town. Calvert's diary records in 1860: "We are looking for a supply of water. There is none except which is drawn from the old shaft. The women are there by three or four o' clock in the morning. There is many a fight among them. The cartmen get water out of a dub in Knitsley Burn while the lads are bathing in it. Water is pumped from Boggle Hole into a pond, which is a receptacle for dead dogs and cats; but the people have no choice. Three or four in a family have to wash in one water."

The newly established Consett Water Company applied for an Act of Parliament to allow them to supply water to the town and were successful, despite 11 petitions being lodged against them. In the end, Calvert was forced to pay £300 through his solicitor to the Dean and Chapter of Durham in order that the church would not oppose the scheme when it went before the House of Lords.

Unsurprisingly, given the appalling sanitary conditions and the overcrowding which existed, disease spread like wildfire among the workmen and their families. The chief medical officer's report of 1896 highlighted outbreaks in the previous 12 months alone of measles, whooping cough, scarlet fever, enteric fever, puerperal fever, diphtheria, influenza and typhoid. Such diseases could have terrible consequences in a population often undernourished and overcrowded. In 1880, an outbreak of scarlet fever claimed 25 lives in Consett and as late as 1901 there were 19 cases of typhoid in the town. Life expectancy was low and child mortality reached dreadful levels - in 1886, the village of Leadgate saw the deaths of 43 children under the age of five in just 12 months.

Nor was there any respite at work. In the early days, a typical labourer's shift at The Company amounted to 12 hours of backbreaking work amid the noise, the searing heat and the dirt. But in addition to the toil, they faced the daily dangers present in the ironworks. With little health and safety legislation, records from the early days of the works show a catalogue of fatal accidents. The worst occurred on April 17th, 1847 at Crookhall foundry, when two travelling entertainers, an old man and his daughter, turned up at the works. The pair started singing ballads to entertain the workers in the hope of a few spare coppers. During the entertainment, the boiler burst with a tremendous explosion in which, according to a contemporary report: "The boiler was torn to pieces and portions of it were blown an immense distance." When the dust settled, six lay dead - both entertainers, father and daughter, were killed instantly, along with two labourers, the fireman and a stranger who happened to be passing by.

Many more were killed at the main works in Consett. In May 1854, two were killed when a boiler exploded inside the ironworks. The following year there were at least three fatal accidents: in March a Michael Meehan was killed when he fell into a furnace, in November one man was killed when a boiler exploded and six days later another boiler exploded killing John Eltringham of Burnopfield. On August 23rd, 1861 two men died in the Derwent Foundry at Blackhill. Robert Stirling and Robert Birtley had been fixing trestles beneath a huge mould made of brick and iron when the supports gave way and the two-tonne structure fell on top of them. Stirling was killed on the spot, but Birtley clung on to life for several hours before he too succumbed to his terrible injuries. Countless more were blinded or maimed as they tried to earn a living.

By the 1860s the workers had begun to form trade unions to demand better wages and conditions. According to one expert, Consett ironworks was plagued with industrial unrest after the financial collapse of 1857 and the early 1860s were described as a war of attrition culminating in the great puddlers' strike of 1866. On July 14th of that year, with iron prices depressed, The Company closed its mills saying it could not continue producing iron unless the

Medomsley Road in 1910
(Photograph courtesy of Beamish Museum)

puddlers accepted a wage cut. The men refused to accept the demand and so began a strike which was to last two months and close down the ironworks completely.

During the first six weeks of the strike, the ironworkers received little strike pay and nothing at all from the end of August. By the end of September, it appeared that the men were about to be starved back to work - news The Consett Guardian greeted with relief: "We confess that we have for some time trembled for the consequences to our workmen if cholera should make its appearance amongst us," read its editorial of September 29th. "They are quite unprepared for such a calamity and the state to which most of them and their families have been reduced by want of sufficient food would have, no doubt, rendered them ready victims to this dreadful disease which is now prevalent in many places no great distance from us. We're glad therefore that there is a probability of our neighbours getting to work and by having a sufficiency of food, render the possibilities of fatalities less amongst them."

The end of the strike was a great victory for the Consett Iron Company and two further pay cuts were pushed through in the coming months, while the leader of the ironworkers' union was

Ironworkers at Consett during the late 19th Century
(Photograph courtesy of Beamish Museum)

almost lynched at a meeting in the town that autumn. But the strike was to be a watershed in the history of Consett. The newly-formed Iron Company, which was led by several influential Quakers, reached a deal with the trade unions to agree a form of arbitration to settle future disputes and although there were strikes in years to come they were few and far between.

By the 1860s, civilisation was finally beginning to reach Consett. After 20 years of lawlessness, a rudimentary police force had put an end to the worst of the rioting, clean water was replacing the contaminated wells and the first signs of normal society were emerging. Within a generation, Consett had its own churches, newspaper, theatre, reading rooms, park, hospital, sports and social clubs, paved roads and street lighting. The newly-established Consett Iron Company, which inherited none of the debts of its predecessor, thrived where the Derwent Iron Company had failed so spectacularly. By the turn of the century, the town was gradually becoming a settled community rather than a frontier town filled with, as the official guide book put it, "more or less migratory adventurers". The works, its chimneys and its slag heaps, would dominate the valley for the next 140 years until they too came to an end.

CHAPTER 25
CAIN AND ABEL

DOCTOR Robert Stirling caused quite a stir in Burnopfield. The young physician was just 26 years old and proved an immediate hit with his new patients. He was confident, some even described him as headstrong, but had, by all accounts, a pleasant bedside manner with it. The red-headed physician was tall, handsome and charming. He arrived from his home in Dumbarton on October 20th, 1855 to take up a position as assistant to Dr Henry William Watson, the 34-year-old village doctor who lived with his wife Mary in Burnopfield House. New arrivals in the village were few and far between, which made the Scottish doctor an object of much curiosity. And, with such a pleasant character, good looks and a seemingly bright future ahead of him, he was also considered quite a potential catch for the young women of the area.

The morning of November 1st, dawned cool and crisp, much like any other late autumn day in the Derwent Valley. It was bright, but the first bite of winter was definitely in the air. The doctor, now into his second week in the village, was still finding his feet but was confident enough to do his rounds alone. However, with many of his possessions still en route from Scotland, he was obliged to borrow a silver pocket watch from Dr Watson before setting off to visit his patients in Burnopfield. After the first stage of his rounds, he took the road to Low Spen for several more house calls, which he completed just before midday and set off for the short journey along Smailes Lane back to meet Dr Watson. He would never be seen alive again.

When Doctor Stirling did not return by mid afternoon, his colleagues became a little concerned - concern which deepened as the afternoon turned to night. Although he was new to the area, it was a straight enough road from Spen to Burnopfield and it appeared unlikely he could have got lost. A search party was raised to look for him and the following day, word was sent to the doctor's family in Scotland. His father Charles and his brother Andrew travelled south to join the hunt. The doctor had such a reputation for impetuousness that the searchers considered the possibility he had left for The Crimea. Stirling was awaiting his call up papers to go to the famous hospital at Scutari and tend the wounded from Britain's war in

*Dr Henry Watson (seated) with his family in the grounds of
Burnopfield House in 1880, 25 years after the murder of his
colleague Dr Robert Stirling (Photograph courtesy John Uren)*

Russia. Two men, one of whom matched Stirling's description, had
been seen heading towards Newcastle by pony and trap and some
thought that the young doctor had gone to war.

It was five days before his blood-soaked body was found. The
leader of the search party, Thomas Holmes, discovered him lying at
the bottom of the hill concealed by bushes and to pile misery on
misery, Dr Stirling's father was alongside him when the discovery
was made. His son had been hideously murdered and mutilated. The
inquest would later confirm that Dr Stirling had been shot in the
groin, his throat slit and his face had been frightfully and repeatedly
injured with the butt of a gun. He had then been robbed and his body
dragged through the gorse bushes then rolled down the hill towards
the river where it had lain for five days. The handsome young doctor was unrecognisable and his father's grief was inconsolable. The
motive, a shocked village later learned, was almost certainly robbery.
His ring, 18 shillings and the silver pocket watch he had borrowed
that very morning were missing.

A £500 reward for information leading to the arrest of his killer was posted, but suspicion had already fallen on Jack Cain - or Whiskey Jack as he was known throughout the Derwent Valley. Cain was the biggest smuggler and distiller of illegal whiskey in the North of Durham. Originally, from Norfolk, he was the son of a gardener who, as well as tending the land, was involved in a more lucrative trade - smuggling. Cain's father would conceal the contraband once it was landed, using the cover of his gardening to bury smuggled goods until they could be moved in safety. Jack learned well from his father and, after drifting through Lancashire and Scotland during his early years, settled in Blaydon. Cain set up a series of stills throughout the Derwent Valley, hidden among the dozens of secret gullies on the moors where the burns would provide a ready water supply away from the prying eyes of excise men. He worked at night so the smoke from his flues couldn't be seen and sold the whiskey to farmers and miners. Trade was good and several legends grew up about Cain among his customers, who at first saw him as a Robin Hood figure constantly staying one step ahead of the law. The exact number of stills he owned was never known, although some found later at Shotley Bridge and Berry Edge were attributed to him. It was said that on one occasion he was caught red-handed when one of the excise men tracked him down to his still near Edmundbyers. A fight ensued during which Cain gained the upper hand, knocked the excise man to the ground and tied him up. The smuggler left the scene, taking his still with him to set up in a different part of the dale, then returned. He loosened his captive's ropes and threw him into the burn before this time making good his escape.

According to other contemporary stories, Cain was something of a Raffles figure, a well-educated businessman who could read and write and lived as a gentleman in Blaydon, riding out at night to take care of his stills then returning to respectability by daylight. The truth was far removed and when the battered body of Dr Stirling was discovered the authorities had one suspect - Jack Cain, who as well as being known to the police as a violent criminal, was known to have kept a still near the murder scene on Smailes Lane. He was arrested shortly after the murder by Superintendent Jabez Squires and a search of Cain's house uncovered a blood-stained knife which, he claimed, he used for skinning rabbits. One of his known accomplices, Richard Raine, a blacksmith from nearby Winlaton, was also arrested, along with a third man who was later released.

Cain and Raine went on trial for their life at Durham on July 25th, 1856 before Justice Willis in a two-day hearing. The prime witness against the pair was Ralph Stobart - thought to be the last man other than the killers to see Dr Stirling alive. Stobart was a sheep drover from Cumberland who had been visiting his sister and had set out on the road home. On the day in question, his sister had escorted him as far as the bridge over the Derwent at Rowlands Gill. As he made his way along the road, he saw two men approaching, one carrying both a stick and a gun. Deciding they looked menacing, Stobart hurried along his way, passing by on the other side of the road. A little further along the way, he bumped into Dr Stirling, heading back to Burnopfield in the same direction as the two ruffians. The drover and doctor briefly passed the time of day, before Stobart pressed on to take the Shotley road back over the moors on his long journey home. Minutes later, Stobart heard a single shot - almost certainly the shot which fatally wounded the young doctor. However, pressed by counsel for the defence, Stobart was forced to admit that while he believed the two prisoners were the same men he had seen that day on Smailes Lane he could not swear to it beyond doubt.

Labourers in nearby fields told the court they had heard clapping and shouting from the spot where the murder took place - and it was conjectured that the noise had been made by the murderers to imitate the sound of gamekeepers and drown out the victim's anguished cries for help. Police told the trial they had discovered a distinctive glass button with a copper shank at the scene of the crime and, when they had raided Cain's house, discovered a waistcoat which sported three of the same distinctive buttons, although a fourth was missing.

Evidence was given that someone resembling Richard Raine had visited Durham several days after the crime and had offered a pawnbroker in the city a silver watch. Jack Cain was said to have been seen in the city on the same day. When the pawnbroker refused to take the watch, despite Raine having offered to drop the price considerably, several witnesses reported seeing the angry blacksmith throw it into the River Wear. However, the pawnbroker was unable to categorically state that it had been Raine and there were several other witnesses - including the famous prize-fighter Coffee Johnny - prepared to say the blacksmith had been elsewhere on that day. Another witness reported being asked by Cain to wash his shirt which, he had said, had been soaked in blood when he skinned a rabbit.

Other evidence was presented to the trial of a more extraordinary nature. The victim's mother, who had travelled down from Scotland to attend the trial, was able to pick Cain out of an identity parade held in Durham Jail after seeing her son's murder in a dream. Meanwhile, further evidence was produced with regard to the motive for the murder. The first of the month was always rent day on the Gibside estates which surrounded Burnopfield. John Errington, a farmer and innkeeper who ran the Bute Arms at High Spen was due to take his normal route down Smailes Lane at noon on November 1st carrying rent to the Bowes family and it may have been that he was the intended victim of the robbery. It was said he never recovered from the shock of his narrow escape and died at a comparatively early age.

The evidence against Cain and Raine was fanciful in parts, circumstantial in others. Another witness said he had seen the pair walking on the road from Shield Row towards Durham at the time of the murder and they could not have committed it. It took the jury just two and a half hours to find both not guilty. No-one was ever convicted of the murder of Dr Robert Stirling. He was laid to rest in Tanfield churchyard and the story passed into local legend. It is said that the doctor's ghost still haunts the lonely country road - now known as Stirling Lane - and can be seen at the bend in the road where he met his gruesome end.

Cain was to live out the rest of his days in freedom - of sorts. His reputation as a harmless rogue was shattered and there was an attempt by his angry neighbours to drive him out of the valley. Stories grew up that the jury in his trial had been bribed, another that 11 of the jurors were ready to convict him and only the obstinacy of the 12th, a committed Quaker, saved him from the noose. But Cain found one man who believed in his innocence, Joseph Cowen the radical owner of several Newcastle newspapers who had earlier lost a libel action for his paper's stance against the South Medomsley strike evictions. Cowen gave him work as a gardener at Stella Hall, his Blaydon residence which was once home to the Jacobite rebel Lord Widdrington. Cain abandoned bootlegging and for 13 years he faithfully tended the land for Mr Cowen, rubbing shoulders with distinguished guests such as the Italian nationalist Garibaldi and Hungarian revolutionary Kossuth, before rheumatism finally forced him to hang up his trowel in 1868. Believing a sea voyage and warmer climes would aid his crippling condition, he set sail for Australia where he lived for several years. However, the homesick

Cain eventually returned to Blaydon. He lived until the age of 82 and, despite his long and successful career as a smuggler, died a pauper in Hexham workhouse in 1879.

Almost exactly five years after the murder, on Bonfire Night 1860, a roofer named Thomas John Batey met his death in Winlaton. Batey, a married father of three from Cuthbert Street in Blaydon, had been gambling at a pub named The New Inn. He was wearing a new suit and was seen to be carrying a substantial amount of money, said to be as much as £3 in gold. Afterwards, he went on to the Crown and Cannon pub in Winlaton with around a dozen friends. Shortly after midnight, landlady Jane Parker refused to serve the raucous crowd any more after they asked for a gallon of ale and they stumbled out into the street and made their respective ways home.

About 4am the following day, blacksmith George Nixon discovered Batey's body face down under a hedge on Blaydon Bank. Suspicion quickly fell on a notorious poacher Thomas "Lanky" Smith, who had been staying in Winlaton. Smith, whose face still bore the scars of a gunpowder explosion at the mine some years earlier, was a well-known figure. Despite his ironic nickname, Thomas Smith was uncommonly short but was powerfully built and had worked as a miner at several pits near Burnopfield and Pontop over the years. Lanky Smith had apparently confessed to a friend that he had knocked Batey over with a club with the intention of robbing him, but did not realise he had killed him until the following day. He had taken Batey's suit and hid his own shabby clothes in a nearby hedge, where they were found by police along with the club.

Once the body was discovered, Smith took to his heels. A week later he was arrested while working in an ironstone mine at Whitby, recognised by a fellow miner from the description of the dead man's clothes which the culprit was still wearing. Smith immediately made a full confession to the killing of John Batey, was sentenced to death by trial judge Justice Keating and was executed on December 28th, 1860.

Five years earlier, Thomas "Lanky" Smith, the famous poacher who knew the woods around Smailes Lane like the back of his hand and was no stranger to violent robbery, had been working in the Derwent Valley as a farm labourer. It was said that within hours of the disappearance of Dr Stirling, he had left the area without bothering to collect his meagre wages. Perhaps justice did in the end catch up with the murderer of Dr Robert Stirling.

ON New Year's Day, 1880, Robert Snowball went out to visit friends. The 26-year-old farmer's son lived with his ageing father at Belmont Farm, a homestead two miles south of Blanchland in the Burnhope Burn valley. Having spent the morning with friends, Robert returned briefly to the farm on the afternoon but announced he was setting out again to visit other neighbours and continue the celebrations. Life as a farmer on the edge of the Northumberland moors was arduous and did not give Robert much opportunity to mix with his friends from the village, which was a four-mile round trip. A lot of his spare time was spent working with wood, whittling and making small ornaments and pieces for the farmhouse. So talented was he, that he had set aside the upstairs part of the cow byre as a simple workshop and would often work into the night.

But, when he had not returned home by midnight, Robert's father began to worry. After a day spent celebrating and drinking with friends, his son would have to find his way home across darkened moorland paths to the remote farm. But it was late for the old man and so he asked the young housekeeper Jane Baron to wait up for Robert's return while he retired to bed. By morning, the old man was beside himself with worry. Jane said she had waited for a further three hours, but still the young man had not returned.

The old farmer went out to the cow byre yards from his backdoor to see if Robert had slept there. Blood was dripping through the upstairs floor boards onto the straw below. In a panic, the old man rushed up the stairs, fearing the worst and there found the body of his son, his skull crushed by a mighty blow and a blood-stained hammer still lying next to the body.

Dr Montgomery was brought in from Blanchland to examine the body. As well as the devastating single wound to the head, the doctor discovered bruising to the deceased's chest and a fractured jaw. He confirmed the large hammer, the sort used to break stones for road making, had been the murder weapon. The doctor deduced that the fatal blow had been struck to the back of the victim's head as he knelt at his tool cupboard. Quite literally, Robert Snowball had not known what hit him. The doctor returned to Blanchland and sent a telegram to the police in Stanhope informing them of what he had found.

An inquest was opened on Monday, January 5th in the house of PC Ferguson at Ramshaw before coroner Graham. The inquest was adjourned until January 21st to allow the funeral to take place and on Tuesday, January 6th, Robert was buried before a huge crowd of mourners at Blanchland Churchyard. Within a matter of hours of the funeral, superintendent Thubron turned up at Belmont Farm and arrested Jane Baron. The housekeeper was taken back to the house in Ramshaw and questioned at length, but the suspicion of a romantic liaison between her and Robert was never proven. The police suspected some sort of affair which had gone murderously wrong, or that she had defended herself against a drunken advance, but they had little evidence to back their case. Early the following morning, Jane Baron was taken to Consett Court and appeared before the magistrate Valentine Rippon JP where she was charged with murder.

The accused was remanded in custody and was taken to prison in Durham. Meanwhile, the inquest resumed at Ramshaw where, after three days of evidence and deliberations, the 13-man jury returned a verdict of wilful murder. But, curiously, the foreman of the jury, The Reverend Jones, vicar of Hunstanworth refused to sign the verdict with the other jurors. The Rev Jones was priest to both Jane Baron and Robert Snowball. Whether, as their priest, he knew something about the case which his vows forced him to keep secret will never be known. Jane Baron appeared before Durham Assizes for trial before Justice Stephen on Saturday. April 17th, facing the gallows. Throughout her trial, the housekeeper refused to speak a single word. The only evidence against her was circumstantial and only innuendo pointed at a relationship between her and Robert. In the end, there was only one course of action available to the jury - Jane Baron was acquitted of murder.

But it was also clear she could not return to Blanchland. The murder was one of the most infamous killings of the Victorian age. Tommy Armstrong, the pitman poet, wrote a song The Blanchland Murder which became one of the most popular of its day and pointed the finger of suspicion squarely at Jane. An object of local hostility and gossip, Jane moved to Hartlepool to begin a new life. She married a local man, but it was short-lived and her new husband died within a matter of years. Finally, she came home and took up residence in a miner's cottage at Blackhall Mill, once more living on the banks of the Derwent.

It was here that she took her own life. She kept her silence to the last and took her secret to the grave, but it seems likely she remained haunted by that fateful night at Belmont Farm to the very end. Whether she murdered her lover, defended herself against a drunken attacker or was an innocent woman hounded by gossip and suspicion will never be known. But in the end, she was the second victim of the murder at Belmont Farm. As the constable cut down the swaying body of Jane Baron from the creaking rope with which she hanged herself, all hope of solving the mystery of the Belmont Farm murder died with her.

ON the 16th of March 1865, convicted killer Matthew Atkinson was led from his cell in Durham Prison for the last time. His was to be a special place in criminal history - the last public execution to be held in Durham.

Matthew Atkinson was a brutal man - a drunken bully who had terrorised his unfortunate wife Ellen over many years. His neighbours reported that sounds of violence coming from their home were commonplace. Ellen was herself known to the police and officers would later give evidence of her intemperate behaviour. The pair had for some time lived in Cuthbert Street in Blaydon, which would appear to be one of the most notorious addresses in England - in 1860, their lodger had been Lanky Smith, who in that same year murdered their neighbour Thomas Batey while another neighbour had been none other than Whiskey Jack Cain. By December of 1864, the 43-year-old Matthew had found work as a miner at Garesfield Colliery and the couple had taken a pit house at The Spen, near Winlaton - a home they shared with their nephew Matthew Swinburne.

Eight days before Christmas, Atkinson and his nephew had gone on an all-day drinking session at the Hobson then returned home late at night. He arrived to find Ellen alone with another man, one Thomas Leyburn who, unsurprisingly, made a hasty exit. Sounds of a struggle could soon be clearly heard and Ellen ran screaming into the street, pursued by her husband who dragged her back into the house and bolted the door. Inside, Matthew Atkinson was laying into his wife with a poker - beating her repeatedly about the head and body. Her screams attracted the attention of the neighbours who threatened to break down the door to help her. But Atkinson made it plain he would shoot dead the first person who walked through the door - it was enough to ensure no-one dared.

So wild was his frenzy, so violent the attack, that after some moments Atkinson emerged from the house to get some fresh air and regain his strength. For something like 15 minutes, he prowled around the outside of the house before announcing his intention to return and finish her off. He then returned to the house and began to pummel Ellen's body ever more until, finally, it was lifeless. Three hours after he had started beating his wife, Atkinson invited his neighbours into the house to see what was left of her. They told the court that the unfortunate Ellen Atkinson was barely recognisable as a human being.

The investigation and trial were swift. It took the jury less than an hour to dismiss Atkinson's defence that his wife's behaviour had provoked him to kill. The only talking point was the anger directed against the residents of the village for refusing to come to Ellen's aid. The trial judge expressed his astonishment, while The Times newspaper issued a scathing editorial: "We verily believe there is but one place in England where this event would happen and that no other population but that of a colliery district would have allowed a fellow creature to be murdered almost before their eyes."

Now, having made his final peace with God, Atkinson began the solemn procession to the scaffold which had been built in front of Durham's courtroom. The convict, flanked by the priest and warders, made his way towards the noose where hangman Thomas Askern was waiting. Before the crowds, Atkinson was blindfolded, Askern tied the noose around his head and pulled the lever. Atkinson plunged downwards through the trapdoor, there was an almighty crack and he fell 15 feet in a crumpled heap on the floor. The rope had snapped and a bewildered Atkinson was extracted from beneath the scaffold very much alive.

A cheer went up among the crowd, in the deluded belief that this would be taken as an act of God and his life would be spared. As it became clear that Atkinson was to be hanged again, a wave of anger and revulsion swept through the throng and they surged forward towards the steps of the scaffold. The authorities feared a riot was about to break out and struggled to maintain order while rumours spread through the crowd. It was said that the prison had stopped buying rope and, to save money, substandard nooses were being made by the prisoners themselves. As the warders searched the prison for a suitable rope, Atkinson's life was prolonged for 30 agonising minutes and tensions threatened to boil over. When the condemned man was finally brought to the gallows for the second time, Askern was booed by the crowd which surged forward again. Unnerved by the situation, the hangman and his assistants handled Atkinson roughly, which inflamed tempers further. Finally, he was dragged to the trapdoor and the lever was pulled once more. But amid the confusion, the hanging was bungled - instead of breaking his neck, Atkinson was slowly strangled in front of a horrified crowd. The outrage caused by the death of Matthew Atkinson - including several thundering newspaper editorials - ensured the end of public hangings in County Durham. Instead, they would be conducted behind closed doors.

LAMB Shields Farm stands in a lonely corner of Muggleswick Common. In 1843, it was home to bachelor farmer William Lawson and his housekeeper Elizabeth Patterson of Rookhope. William's brother, Thomas, was a regular visitor to the farmstead, although there seems to have been little love lost between the two. On the morning of Saturday, May 6th, Elizabeth went home to Rookhope, as she did every weekend, leaving her employer alone. Early the following morning, sometime before 7am, Thomas Lawson visited his brother. He would later tell his family that he found the old man in good spirits. The reality was far more bloody.

Within minutes of his arrival, the two brothers launched into a quarrel over money. Thomas had just received a letter from an attorney demanding immediate payment of 11 shillings he owed Harry Ritson. Unable to pay, he went to his brother to ask him to return some money owed to him - a little over £2 paid for a flock of sheep the pair had jointly sold. William had held onto the money for the sheep and some money left to the brothers by their mother. Thomas had a wife and two children to support, William had only himself to look after - and the fact that he was keeping the money was already a source of some irritation to Thomas.

The argument spilled out of the house and into the cow byre. Thomas would later say: "I asked him for the money and he refused to do so. This vexed me and, as he was beginning to milk, I took him by the neck and we had a struggle. I thought I had done so much for him and he nothing for me." During the struggle, William kicked his brother in the left thigh and they both lost their balance, tumbling to the ground in the hay, Thomas on top face-to-face with his brother. In his fury, Thomas reached out and picked up a stone lying nearby and smashed it into his brother's head four times, knocking William unconscious.

"After he kicked me I got worse and that made me do it," said Thomas. "I thought he would not be so bad, so I didn't tell anyone." Bleeding heavily from his head wounds, William hauled himself to his feet. Meanwhile, in a blind panic, Thomas fled, running first onto the fells where he saw to his flocks of sheep before returning to his home. Doubtless, he thought his brother would recover and, at first, he did. William came round and went to get help. But after a few faltering steps, he fell to the ground weakened by the loss of blood and began to crawl on hands and knees looking for someone to save him.

Later that day, two of William's farming friends came to call, John Bainbridge of Pedom's Oak and William Ritson of Calf Close. The pair intended spending the evening with their friend at his farm but, finding the place deserted, assumed he had gone to spend the night in Edmundbyers and left. Hours later, Thomas Lawson's children visited the farm, unaware of the argument earlier that day and hoping to spend several hours with their uncle. When they couldn't get an answer at the farmhouse, they returned home to tell their father and he too went to visit Lamb Shields farm. It was a miserable night and pouring with rain. After searching the farm for his brother without success, Thomas returned home for a fitful night's sleep.

On Monday morning, John Bainbridge returned to the farm, this time making his way through a nearby slate quarry where he found William Lawson unconscious, but still breathing. The injured farmer had crawled 300 yards from his door for help before finally collapsing in the quarry and had spent 24 hours lying exposed in a downpour. It was clear the attack had left him near death's door and Bainbridge left to get help. William was brought inside to be cared for, before Bainbridge rode to Shotley Bridge to bring the police.

Officer Leybourne Wilson was the first on the scene. He went to Edmundbyers and arrested an itinerant Irish labourer who was working in the area. The suspect was questioned at length by the police but was eventually released without charge. Now the finger of suspicion was pointed at Thomas. Under questioning, he said he had been out all night at Waskerley looking for his brother, in case he had been lost on the fells. But the observant officer examined Thomas' boots and found them bone dry, despite the heavy rain. His suspicions aroused, the policeman then asked to see his shirt and found it spattered with his brother's blood.

Thomas Lawson was arrested and taken to Shotley Bridge. There was a lock-up in the upper rooms above the Bridge End Hotel, now known as the King's Head pub, where he was held and questioned further by police, though he steadfastly maintained his innocence. On Wednesday, May 10th, William Lawson died of his injuries. When told of his brother's death in the cell, Thomas Lawson said: "It's all up with me now," and confessed to the deadly assault. A police officer held up a stick which had been recovered from the cow byre and asked if it was the murder weapon, but Thomas told them he had killed his brother with a stone which he had picked up from the ground. An inquest was held at The Punch Bowl pub in Edmundbyers where, under oath, Thomas Lawson admitted to his part in his brother's death and at Durham Assizes he was convicted of manslaughter. Thomas Lawson was sentenced to be transported to Australia for life, far away from his beloved valley. But he never made it to the penal colony - he died two years later in the desperate squalor of an overcrowded prison ship waiting to set sail.

ON a beautiful August day in 1872, Isabella Young left her Blackhill home with her two young children for an afternoon stroll. All three were dressed in their finest clothes and, as mother and daughter walked through the village pushing the pram containing Isabella's new-born baby, they presented a picture of a contented Victorian family. The attractive Isabella was the wife of a papermaker, well-to-do, outwardly healthy and with everything to live for.

Shortly after 3pm that Monday afternoon, they reached the woods at Bridgehill. Isabella applied the brake to the pram and left it by the side of the road while she led her little girl into the dark woods.

The tragic death of Isabella Young, as reported in Illustrated Police News in August 1872 (Picture courtesy of Wicked Publications)

Without warning, the respectable wife and mother produced a dinner knife from her own cutlery set and slashed her daughter's throat. Terrified, the little girl fought for her life against her deranged mother, slipped her clutches and rushed home to call for help, her clothes saturated in blood from the wounds to her neck. But Isabella was too quick. She returned to the pram at the edge of the woods where she had left her baby, picked up the infant and took her into the trees. There she stabbed the trembling child through the stomach, then turned the knife on herself, slitting her own throat from ear to ear.

Miraculously, the two children survived the murderous attack and the baby's cries alerted two passing gentlemen who rushed to the blood-soaked scene. As the sun lit up the wooded glade, Isabella lay dead on the ground, her clothes stained crimson, while her baby fought for life next to her. Both children made full recoveries. A coroner's inquest later heard Isabella described as: "a great sufferer and this caused a morbid state of mind. She had a good home, was well provided for and lived upon the happiest terms with her husband." The jury returned a verdict that "the deceased had cut her throat while in an unsound state of mind."

TWICE in little over a year, the Victorian colliery village of Dipton was witness to brutal murder. The first case was the killing of Jane Johnson - a young woman who seems to have been extraordinarily unlucky in love. The daughter of an Annfield Plain miner, Jane had married Henry Atchison of Greencroft and, though she had a child, the marriage was miserable and they soon separated. Jane quickly fell in love again with one William Thompson of Felling and, though she was not yet divorced and aged just 20 years old, she married for the second time in February 1872. Jane's family disapproved of the marriage, believing it to be bigamous, and refused to speak to her. But her second marriage quickly turned sour and her father, now living at Pontop, agreed to take her back in.

During the summer, Thompson tried to patch things up with his wife and eventually his father-in-law allowed him to move into the family home. All went well for a little over a month until Saturday, October 6th 1873 when all three went for a day out in Newcastle. While they were eating in a pub, Jane bumped into some old friends and went off with them for a lengthy chat leaving Thompson brooding on his own. He later told police that he had felt humiliated being forced to sit on his own like a child and the couple had words on the way home. When they reached Annfield Plain, the argument boiled over. Thompson slapped his wife across the face and told her: "Wait until we get home. It will be either you or me for it." Jane hit him back, then began to cry. Witnesses heard her say: "You are not going to murder me. You always start to abuse me when my father goes out."

When they reached home, Jane started to make supper and asked her father to go down to the pub to fetch some beer. Minutes later, Mary Ann Parker, who lived two doors away, heard a fearful scream. There was a moment's silence then Jane stumbled out of the house and collapsed in the street bleeding from a horrific wound to her neck. A pathologist later gave evidence that her throat had been slit so deeply that her head had almost been severed. She died minutes later.

Nine-year-old Elizabeth Parker was playing in the street outside her house when she saw William Thompson running away. He was arrested within minutes at his brother's house in Dipton. Thompson claimed his wife had produced a razor during their argument and had killed herself. It did not take the jury long to convict him. He was hanged on January 5th, 1874.

Ten months after the hanging, Dipton was beginning to get over the shock when another drink-fuelled murder took place. Hugh Daley, an Irish miner with a fierce temper and a dour expression, lived at High Bushblades - a hamlet made up of a handful of houses near Dipton. One of his neighbours was Phillip Burdy, another Irish-born miner who lived with his family and brother Simon. Burdy was also known to like a drink, although he was generally well thought of by his neighbours and workmates, including Hugh Daley.

On Saturday November 7th, 1874, Daley rolled home from the pub and found Phillip Burdy lying helpless on his floor. Burdy was so drunk he couldn't stand, let alone leave, when Daley told him to. The drunken Daley was so enraged by Burdy's refusal to get up, he picked up the fireside poker and dealt him a savage blow to the head. Neighbour Ann Smith helped the stricken 40-year-old out of harm's way and into her house, where she tended his wounds, then joined Daley's wife in helping her husband to bed. It could have ended there but for the fact that Burdy, in his stupor, decided to return to the Daley house shortly afterwards to retrieve his cap which had been lost in the melee. On seeing him, Daley leapt from his bed and again cornered his neighbour, but this time Burdy did not escape so lightly. Blow after blow after blow from the poker fell on Burdy's head. The victim tried to escape outside, but Daley followed and continued to batter him. So great was Daley's rage that the three men who witnessed the attack were frozen with fear and did nothing to protect Burdy. They did however, call the police and PC Forster hurried towards High Bushblades. The officer later told the court that long before he arrived on the scene he could hear the sickening sound of the blows landing on Burdy's undefended head.

PC Forster was confronted with an appalling scene. Somehow, Burdy was still alive, but had suffered horrific injuries in the sustained attack. PC Forster ordered Daley to put the poker down, but the drunken attacker threatened to kill the officer. At that crucial moment, Daley slipped and fell. Within seconds he was in handcuffs while Burdy was brought back into the house for treatment. But it proved futile - Phillip Burdy breathed his last moments later.

The inquest took place at the Prince of Wales pub in Flint Hill and the trial started within the month. There seemed little argument and justice was swift. Hugh Daley hanged three days after Christmas, 1874.

IN the days leading up to Christmas 1908, there was only one subject of conversation throughout the Derwent Valley - the search for the missing 10-year-old Mary Donnelly. More than 100 police officers were looking for the little girl and the man last seen with her, Jeremiah O'Connor.

The 55-year-old Irishman, a former soldier with the Royal Irish Fusiliers, had recently moved to West Stanley from Haswell, where his wife and three children still lived. O'Connor had got a job at West Stanley pit and had moved into crowded lodgings in Pool Street. There were only two bedrooms in the house for the six people who lived there - Thomas Donnelly and his wife had one room, the Donnelly children, a boy and girl, shared their bedroom with the two lodgers, O'Connor and another man named Michael Brown.

O'Connor, it was said, had formed a close friendship with little Mary Donnelly. On Monday, December 14th, the miner returned from a drinking binge and invited the little girl to go for an evening walk in the country. She was never seen alive again. Neither returned that night and the following day search parties began to look for them. Four days later, a man called at a house at Gibside, his hands trembling, his shirt soaked in blood, his arms covered in cuts. The stranger told the owner, a Mrs Boyd, that he had been attacked by a navvy who stole his money and took his little girl away. When the owner of the cottage said she was going to tell the police of his story, the mysterious visitor ran off. He fitted the description of Jeremiah O'Connor and the police manhunt now turned its attention Gibside.

O'Connor was eventually spotted in fields near Tanfield on the Saturday morning - and was promptly arrested by Inspector Stark. The fugitive collapsed when told there was a warrant out for his arrest and he was taken to a nearby farm to recover. Feelings in

Stanley were running so high as the hunt for the missing girl continued, that O'Connor was taken to Consett by pony and trap to be held at the police station. There, the prisoner protested his innocence and stuck to his story - Mary had been stolen away by a passing navvy and the injuries to O'Connor's arm were inflicted during the fight to protect the girl.

The following day - just five days before Christmas - Mary's mutilated body was found under a hedge at Pea Farm, near Beamish. She had been brutally sexually assaulted and then killed in a savage and sustained knife attack. So prolonged and violent was the attack on the little girl, said Dr Benson who carried out the post mortem examination, she had almost been disembowelled. It appeared that she had died on the night she disappeared.

O'Connor maintained his story throughout the trial but, once convicted, he did not appeal. During his time awaiting execution, he received only one visit - from two of his children. Exactly one week before Jeremiah O'Connor was due to hang, as he sat alone in his condemned cell in Durham Jail, an explosion ripped through the colliery where he should have been working and killed 168 men and boys. Little attention was given to the execution when it eventually happened - West Stanley now had other problems. As he went to the gallows, Jeremiah O'Connor did not say a single word.

TODAY, the Derwent Walk, which stretches from Blackhill to Swalwell, is a tranquil if somewhat lonely walkway. But for almost 90 years from its opening in 1867 to eventual closure in 1954, the trains of the Derwent Valley branch railway line thundered down the tracks taking passengers from Consett to Newcastle. The line had passenger stations at Blackhill, Shotley Bridge, Ebchester and Rowlands Gill and also at Lintz Green.

On the night of Saturday, October 7th, 1911, the staff who manned Lintz Green station were waiting for the last train of the day. The station was probably the most isolated on the line, but during the day was reasonably busy with passengers from nearby Burnopfield, Lintzford and Friarside. By that time of night, however, all was quiet. Stationmaster George Wilson stood on the platform with booking clerk Fred White and porter John Routledge waiting for the 10.42pm train from Consett to Newcastle. Only four passengers got off, local men Samuel Elliott, Robert Wailes, Thomas Middleton and Charles Swinburne. The first three set off immediately on the mile-long walk to their homes at Low Friarside while Swinburne waited for his friend Fred White to finish work before they would make their way home along the footpath to Lintzford. As the rear lights on the steam train disappeared into the distance and silence descended on the platform once more, stationmaster Wilson and booking clerk White said their goodbyes at the end of a long day's work.

White went to lock up the offices while Wilson walked the short distance to the stationmaster's house only 50 yards away. But as White turned the key in the door, the silence was shattered by a gunshot. White raced towards the direction of the sound along with Charles Swinburne. The three men walking to Low Friarside heard it too and turned round to run to the station. Wilson's daughter Bertha also heard the shot and ran out of the house. The first to the scene was Thomas Middleton, who stumbled across the body of George Wilson lying at his own gate, covered in blood and unable to speak but still alive. Middleton and Samuel Elliott carried the stricken Wilson inside the house where they administered brandy and asked the wounded man to tell them who had committed the crime. He tried to breathe an answer, but it was impossible to hear and several minutes later he died.

Dr Wynne Boland was called to the stationmaster's house along with the police. The next morning the fatal bullet was found, along with a gag made of a linen cloth and sand. Almost certainly, George Wilson had been the victim of a botched robbery. Normally, Wilson would carry the day's takings from the station to his home after the last train had left for Newcastle. On the night of the shooting, he had for once changed his routine and had taken the money home an hour earlier after the last train to Consett had passed through the station.

The inquest was held two days after the murder in the first class waiting room of the station. So great was the public outrage at the murder that Wilson's funeral procession was filmed and was shown at local cinemas. The 60-year-old man was a devoted Methodist and was said to have led a blameless life. Soon, more than 200 police officers were involved in the hunt for his killer.

Eventually, there was a breakthrough. Police officers turned up at the Byker home of Samuel Atkinson, the 25-year-old relief porter at

The stationmaster's house, scene of the 1911 murder, showing victim George Wilson (Photograph courtesy John Uren)

Lintz Green station. Atkinson knew of Wilson's routine and the likelihood that he would be carrying significant amounts of money. Several witnesses reported seeing him hanging around the station long after his shift had finished. The suspect's family told officers he was not home but the police nevertheless barged into the house and promptly arrested him before subjecting him to vigorous questioning. Atkinson was arrested on suspicion of murder and brought to Consett police station. He was held for best part of a month and was eventually brought to Durham Crown Court for trial. However, the court room was stunned when the chief constable himself made the admission that the arresting officers had failed to caution Atkinson and that, as all the subsequent evidence against him was inadmissible, the police did not intend proceeding with the case. The judge promptly released Atkinson, although he did reject his claim for compensation. No-one was ever brought to justice for the killing.

ABEL Atherton was not much to look at. He stood just over 5ft 1inch tall and had a noticeably ruddy complexion, partly hidden by his handlebar moustache. At 29 years old, he was stoutly-built, was still single, had developed an unhealthy interest in guns and an even more unhealthy interest in his landlord's teenage daughter.

Atherton, a miner by trade, was originally from Wigan in Lancashire and in the first decade of the 20th Century had done what many an itinerant labourer had done before him and moved to Chopwell to work in the local pit. He worked alongside Jacob Patrick, a mild-mannered and unassuming father of four, who, as a means of bringing in a little extra money, invited Atherton to lodge at the family home in Thames Street. At first things worked out well. Atherton was made welcome and came to look upon Jacob's wife Elizabeth Ann as a second mother. He also seemed to get on well with the children, the boys Joseph and George and the girls, Frances and Maggie. But as the years passed, it became evident he was more interested in young Frances than he should be.

Frances was just 12 when Abel Atherton moved into the family home. Just when his obsession with her developed is anyone's guess, but by the time she had reached 15 she had become the unwilling object of his amorous intentions. On several occasions during the early months of 1909, Atherton put his arms around young Frances' waist and kissed her. The innocent girl would later testify that it meant nothing to her because it was something her father had done regularly since she was a child - but it clearly meant something to Abel Atherton. Jacob could also see what was happening under his roof and, although he said nothing to his lodger, took his daughter to one side and gently warned her not to tolerate such shows of affection in future.

On Easter Monday, Atherton was ill in bed and Frances was the only other person in the house. He asked her to bring him some tea and cakes which she did, laying them on a chair beside the bed before turning to leave. As she did so, Atherton grabbed her by the waist and pulled her to him, kissing her and making an improper suggestion. She struggled free and warned him she would tell if he did such a thing again. But it was not to be the end of it. A month or so later when once more they were alone in the house, he again grabbed her and made crude suggestions. Frances shouted for her mother and Atherton released her from his grip - but once more the teenager did not report the incident to her parents.

The attention was becoming more and more regular. Over the next few weeks, Atherton made several clumsy passes at the young girl although they now became more sinister. He sent her a note which included sickening accusations that Frances had been "carrying on" with her own father. Again, she did not reveal the note to her parents but wrote back to the lodger denying the contents were true. Notes flew back and forth between the pair, each containing ever more lurid allegations of Frances' relationship with her father - all of which the girl destroyed.

On Saturday, July 24th, matters came to a head. In the morning, Atherton cornered Frances in the kitchen, threw his arms around her and tried to kiss her, making his usual suggestive remarks and threatening to report her father to the courts. It was the final straw for Frances. When her father returned from work at lunch-time, Frances told him that either the lodger should leave or she would. That evening, Jacob Patrick told Abel Atherton that - after two years living with the family - he was no longer welcome in the house. Atherton made a great show of packing away his meagre possessions - his box, his gramophone and, ominously, his rifle - but grudgingly went on his way. He did not, however, go far.

Atherton found new lodgings just yards away in Mersey Street with Isabella Forster and her husband.

Immediately, Abel Atherton was telling anyone who would listen to him of the wrong that had been done to him and the unnatural relationship between Jacob Patrick and his daughter Frances. He told his new landlady, Mrs Forster: "Its a good job I left the Patricks' house before I did some mischief. I have carried these about all day," he added, reaching into his pocket and producing three rifle cartridges. "One of these was meant for Frances, one for Patrick and one for myself." The following day he met his former Thames Street neighbours and told them he would "finish the lot next door". Although he had never once had the bravery to make the accusation to Jacob's face, the unfounded gossip spread like wildfire around the small pit village. On August 8, worse for drink, he turned up on the Patricks' doorstep and told Frances: "You have done your worst for me and I will do my worst for you". The following night he was back, repeating his allegations of incest and again on August 10th when he warned Frances the courts would take his allegations seriously.

On the day of the murder, Wednesday August 11th, Abel Atherton walked uninvited into the Thames Street house at 10am to deliver a letter. Frances half-read the note, which was in fact addressed to her mother, crumpled it up and threw it on the open fire. Raging, Atherton repeated his tirade of accusations and walked out of the house. Frances waited a while to let him get back to his lodgings then left the house, going on a series of errands which kept her busy all day. When she returned at 5.45pm, she found Atherton sitting calmly talking to her mother at the kitchen table. The atmosphere changed as she entered, the former lodger repeated the accusations of incest to Mrs Patrick. But Elizabeth Ann was having none of it. She was by all accounts a big woman and not afraid to stand up for herself. She interrupted his flow in mid sentence, saying she was sick of the trouble his lies were causing the family and told him to get out of the house.

Spurned by Frances and chased and humiliated by her mother, Abel Atherton scurried back to his new lodgings in Mersey Street where his landlady Isabella Forster found him checking his gun. When asked what he was doing, Atherton said he was going to have some sport and then, with tears in his eyes, he thanked Isabella for taking him in. He tucked the rifle under his arm and made for the door. Mrs Forster begged her lodger not to leave with the gun, but he told her: "Stand back, or I'll shoot," before exiting by the back door. The landlady rushed to the front to watch him walk away and, with a heavy heart, she waited anxiously for news.

Within half an hour, the door of the Patricks' kitchen was thrown open and there stood Abel Atherton, gun in hand. The entire family were gathered around the kitchen table chatting with neighbour Elizabeth Marlowe over a large pot of tea and a plate of biscuits. All eyes turned to Atherton - and the rifle he carried crooked under his arm. Mrs Patrick leapt to her feet and shouted: "What are you going to do with that? You are not going to use that here!" For a moment the world stood still. No-one moved as Atherton's glare turned to the object of his lust - Frances. Mrs Marlowe - unaware of the build up to this terrifying moment - was too dumbfounded by the presence of the gunman to react. Mr Patrick, wedged between wall and table, was unable to move and young Frances sat paralysed with fear listening to her own pounding heartbeat. Only Elizabeth Patrick had the presence of mind to act. She leapt at Atherton like a wild woman, frantically clutching at the gun to point it away from her loved ones. For what seemed like an eternity the pair wrestled and grappled together, scattering pots and pans from the kitchen. Frances leapt to help her mother but Mrs Marlowe held her back as the battle went on. The gun went off and a bullet whizzed out into the back lane behind the house. Then a second shot went off.

Elizabeth Patrick staggered out into the street crying out: "Oh my leg" then collapsed in a crumpled heap at the back door. Abel Atherton threw the gun out of the door and, in a fit of remorse, knelt down to kiss the woman he always claimed had been his second mother. But it was too late for tears. The bullet had wounded Elizabeth in the thigh and severed her femoral artery. She bled to death in minutes, surrounded by the family she had fought so feverishly to protect. Abel Atherton stood up and produced a penknife from his pocket which he used in a pathetic attempt to cut his own throat. Then, bleeding, he left the Patricks' house one last time.

Police constable John Coulson was on patrol when a member of the public ran up to him to report shooting in Thames Street. The officer hurried to the scene where he found the dishevelled figure of

Chopwell miner Abel Atherton, who was convicted of murder in 1909

Abel Atherton who walked up to him and said: "I am the man you want. She is quite dead. It is a pity I did not finish myself off as well, it's a bad job for me." PC Coulson frisked Atherton on the spot and discovered 12 gun cartridges, a penknife and a letter to his friend Dick Symons, dated July 18 but never posted, which would prove very important in the case. In it, a private letter he apparently expected only to be read after his death, Abel Atherton maintained he still believed Frances and her father were involved in some sort of incestuous relationship.

He wrote: "You are the only friend I have in the world - when you get this letter I will be in a different world. I told her if we got catched I would do the job for her and myself as well and she's turned her back on me. They will think I am daft. But I am tired of living, I have my senses Dick and she is thick with her father as anybody what is married is with their wives. I have written this for fear I do not get catched and as soon as I get catched it must be the finish for both of us. So this is the last letter from your old chum Abel Atherton - Goodbye for ever."

A large crowd had gathered in Thames Street when PC Coulson arrived back with Abel Atherton. Frances was crying and cradling her mother's head. Jacob Patrick was standing useless with shock. The officer could find no pulse but did retrieve the murder weapon then escorted Atherton to Blaydon Police Station where he was charged with attempted suicide and murder. On hearing the charge, Atherton said: "The knife was not sharp enough. The other was a pure accident. She fired one shot in the air and the other she shot herself."

The following day, August 12th, Atherton made his first appearance at court where he vehemently protested his innocence to magistrates during a short hearing at which he was remanded in custody. The inquest into the death of Elizabeth Ann Patrick opened at the Workmen's Institute at Chopwell on Friday, August 13th when the only witness was 14-year-old Joseph. The hearing was adjourned so the family could bury the body. Her cortege left Chopwell at noon on Saturday, August 14th and she was interred at Tow Law Cemetery as the choir sang Lead Kindly Light. The inquest resumed on August 17th when Frances gave evidence of the repeated immoral suggestions put to her by Abel Atherton. Meanwhile, enraged by the evil rumours which had swept the tiny pit village, Jacob Patrick took the remarkable step of asking the village GP Dr Bulkley to attest to his daughter's virginity. Following an examination at his surgery, the doctor gave evidence to coroner John Graham that: "I can give positive evidence to the existence of her virginity. Mr Patrick is very anxious that I should give evidence to this affect at the inquest so as to silence the foul gossip which he says is prevalent in the village." The coroner's jury took just 15 minutes to return the verdict of wilful murder in the case and Mr Graham added: "I think I may take it upon myself to say that the jury are satisfied that the allegations made against Mr Patrick and his daughter are wholly unfounded."

Abel Atherton was eventually committed for trial at Durham Assizes in November 1909 before Justice Walton. Defence lawyer Morgan Griffiths Jones claimed the killing had been manslaughter and that the gun had discharged accidentally. Constable Coulson told the court that Atherton had admitted to him that he had brought the gun to the house with the intention of frightening the family.

Throughout the two-day trial - as at all previous hearings - Abel Atherton denied shooting Elizabeth Ann Patrick. He insisted that the woman had accidentally shot herself, having grabbed the barrel of the gun. She was undoubtedly a powerfully-built woman and Atherton was small in stature and none of the family members were able to say precisely what had happened. But a firearms expert testified that from experiments on her clothing he concluded that the

Elizabeth Patrick, shot dead by her former lodger Abel Atherton

victim was shot from a distance of at least 27 inches - which made it impossible that Elizabeth Patrick's finger was on the trigger.

It took the jury less than 45 minutes to find Abel Atherton guilty of murder. As the judge donned his black cap he asked the prisoner if he had anything to say before sentence was passed. "Yes," said Atherton with a smile. "Can I have a fresh trial?"

For the month before sentence was carried out, he maintained his innocence, convinced a reprieve would come. But it did not. On December 5th he was informed that he had been refused leave to appeal and he wrote a last letter to his father and mother. "You will very likely know the sad news before you get this letter - that there is no more hope for me in this world. But I will have to put my trust in the Lord, he is the One we all have to answer to sooner or later. There is one thing that I will not have to answer for and that is what I am sentenced to death for, of which I am innocent and my life is on the hands of those I told you about. You can believe me what I told you; it is the God's truth. It won't do me any good to tell lies."

Executioner Henry Pierrepoint and his assistant William Willis arrived in Durham on Tuesday, December 7th. A chill, wintry wind was blowing through the city as they checked into the hotel opposite

Abel Atherton being led into court by a policeman

the prison. As the pair ate their lunch, Atherton's father and sister-in-law walked in - already dressed in black - and spoke at length to the landlord about Abel, his innocence and the last letters they had just received from him. The hangman watched them go, finished his lunch and then crossed the street to visit Atherton in his cell - and calculate his weight.

It was clear and frosty when Abel Atherton woke up at 6am on Wednesday, December 8th. For the first time since he was arrested, he was allowed to dress in his own clothes and was visited by the chaplain who arrived at the prison at 7am. He ate a breakfast of bread and butter washed down with a mug of tea then spent his final hour chatting with two warders and the chaplain. With minutes to go before 8am, Pierrepoint walked into the condemned cell. He later said: "Atherton was looking a little terrified. I pinioned his arms and prepared his neck then I gently tapped him on the shoulder and said: 'Keep your pluck up, my lad.' This put life in him. I said I would get it over as quickly as possible and I brought him out into the corridor. The procession started."

Across Durham, the bells rang and the colliery buzzers sounded. In the prison, the witnesses could just about hear the outside din as the chaplain began to recite the first lines of the burial service as the prisoner walked towards his fate. Calm, composed and with firm step, Abel Atherton walked to the gallows. He arrived on the trapdoor and as Willis strapped his ankles together, the cap was pulled from his head and Pierrepoint fastened the noose around his neck. "You are hanging an innocent man," cried Atherton. "Whether I was or not," recalled the hangman later, "I could not flinch." He pulled the lever and Abel Atherton dropped out of sight before the clock has ceased striking. Outside, it started to snow.

BIBLIOGRAPHY

THE Dark Side Of The Dale was never intended to be an academic study and I therefore took the decision not to include references to source material within the body of the book, which somewhat gets in the way of enjoying the story. However, throughout the book I have drawn heavily on a number of previously published works which are outlined below for anyone interested in further reading on any of the subjects covered.

Books - Although by no means an exhaustive list, the following books have proved extremely useful and provide further information on all the major topics covered in this book.

•Maureen Anderson
Foul Deeds And Suspicious Deaths In And Around Durham - Wharncliffe Books 2003
•Maureen Anderson
Foul Deeds And Suspicious Deaths In And Around Newcastle - Wharncliffe Books 2004
•Roy Anderson
The Violent Kingdom - Butler Publishing 1971
•Ralph Arnold
The Unhappy Countess - Constable 1987
•Jo Bath
Dancing With the Devil And Other True Tales Of Northern Witchcraft - Tyne Bridge 2002
•Huw Beynon & Terry Austrin
Masters and Servants - Rivers Oram Press 1994
•David Butler
The Battle of Neville's Cross: An Illustrated History - Durham County Council 1998
•John Bygate
The Hollow Blade - Durham In History 1999
•Consett Lions Club
The Consett Story - Williams 1963
•Robert Colls
The Pitmen Of The Northern Coalfield - Manchester University Press 1987
•David Cranston
Derwentcote Steel Furnace - Lancaster University 1997
•Lilian Dixon
Lanchester In Times Past - Countryside Publication Ltd 1987

•Martin Dufferwell
Durham: A Thousand Years Of History And Legend - Mainstream Publishing 1996
•Durham County Local History Society
Parliamentary Survey of Muggleswick 1649
•John Eddleston
Murderous Tyneside - Breedon Books 1997
•Norman Emery
The Coal Miners Of Durham - Sutton 1994
•JW Fawcett
A History Of The Parish Of Dipton - Fawcett 1911
•Ross Forbes (ed)
Polisses And Candymen: The Complete Works of Tommy Armstrong - Tommy Armstrong Memorial Trust 1987
•W Fordyce
The History and Antiquities Of The County Palatine - Fullerton & Co 1857
•Eric Forster
The Death Pit - Graham 1970
•Leo Gooch
The Desperate Faction - University of Hull Press 1995
•John Hodgson
A History Of Northumberland - Hodgson 1820
•E Hughes
North Country Life In The 18th Century - Oxford University Press 1952
•CJ Hunt
The Lead Mines of the Northern Pennines - Manchester University Press 1970
•W Hutchinson
Antiquities Of The County Palatine - Walker 1823
•Steve Jones
Northumberland And Durham The Sinister Side - Wicked Publications 1999
•Richard Lomas
North-East England In the Middle Ages - Donald 1992
•Richard Lomas
County of Conflict: Northumberland From Conquest To Civil War - Tuckwell 1996
•Mackenzie & Ross
History Of The County Of Durham - publisher and date unknown
•Tommy Moore
The Industrial Past of Shotley Bridge and Consett - Moore 1988
•Tommy Moore
Consett: A Town In The Making - County Durham Books 1992

•Geoffrey Moorhouse
The Pilgrimage Of Grace - Weidenfeld & Nicolson 2002
•Gwenda Morgan and Peter Rushton
Rogues, Thieves and the Rule of Law - UCL 1998
•G Neasham
Views and Portraits Of The Derwent Valley - Neasham 1884
•G Neasham
The History And Biography Of West Durham - Neasham 1890
•AC Newton
Edmundbyers - Deorwenta 1990
•AC Newton
Animal Myths of County Durham - Deorwenta 1993
•WK Pirt & JM Dodds
Lead Mining In The Derwent Valley - Northern Mine Research Society 2002
•A Raistrick and R Jennings
A History of Lead Mining In The Pennines - Longmans 1965
•Guy Ragland Phillips
Brigantia - RKP 1976
•William Seymour
Battles in Britain - Wordsworth 1975
•James Sharpe
Instruments of Darkness: Witchcraft In England 1550-1750 - Penguin 1997
•R Surtees
History And Antiquities Of The County Palatinate of Durham 1840
•John Sykes and others
Local Records or Historical Register Of Remarkable Events - 1866
•Ray Thompson
Historical Notes on Healeyfield Lead Mine - Thompson 1999
•John Uren
Around Burnopfield - Tempus Publishing 2000
•Douglas Vernon
Thread Of Iron - Able Publishing 2003
•Fred Wade
The Story of Annfield Plain and District - Wade 1966
•Fred Wade
The Story of Tanfield and Beamish - Wade 1968
•Fred Wade
The Upper Derwent Valley - Wade 1967-75

•K Warren
Consett Iron - Oxford 1990
•Godfrey Watson
The Border Reivers - Hale 1974
•AS Wilson
Consett Iron Company - University of Durham 1973
•Winlaton and District Local History Society
A History of Blaydon - Gateshead Metropolitan Borough Council 1975

Websites - the research for this book involved visiting countless websites, some of which I have used as a source of information. Chief among these is the exceptional Durham Mining Museum website at www.dmm.org.uk, which goes into fantastic detail on the individual pits in the area.

Other important websites include the Gateshead Local Studies Online website can be accessed at www.**gateshead**.gov.uk/ls for detailed information on the part of the valley now in Gateshead Borough, www.keystothepast.info for detailed information on some of the villages of Northumberland and Durham, www.**roman**-britain.org for detail of the Roman occupation of Britain and the history of the Brigantes, www.**genuki**.org.uk which provides an extensive range of help for local historians and www.northumbrianjacobites.org.uk, the home page of the Northumbrian Jacobite Society.

Illustrations - All photographs, maps and other illustrations are credited on the page.